I0135064

DADDIES OF A DIFFERENT KIND

Daddies of a Different Kind

Sex and Romance Between Older and Younger Adult Gay Men

Tony Silva

NEW YORK UNIVERSITY PRESS
New York

NEW YORK UNIVERSITY PRESS
New York
www.nyupress.org

© 2023 by New York University
All rights reserved

Library of Congress Cataloging-in-Publication Data
Names: Silva, Tony J., author.
Title: Daddies of a different kind : sex and romance between older
and younger adult gay men / Tony Silva.
Description: New York : New York University Press, [2023] |
Includes bibliographical references and index.
Identifiers: LCCN 2022051837 | ISBN 9781479817023 (hardback) |
ISBN 9781479817030 (paperback) | ISBN 9781479817047 (ebook) |
ISBN 9781479817054 (ebook other)
Subjects: LCSH: Older gays—Attitudes. | Older gays—Sexual behavior. |
oung gay men—Attitudes. | Young gay men—Sexual behavior. | Aging.
Classification: LCC HQ76.27.O44 S56 2023 | DDC 306.76/60846—dc23/eng/20230112
LC record available at https://lccn.loc.gov/2022051837

This book is printed on acid-free paper, and its binding materials are chosen for strength and durability. We strive to use environmentally responsible suppliers and materials to the greatest extent possible in publishing our books.

Manufactured in the United States of America

10 9 8 7 6 5 4 3 2 1

Also available as an ebook

CONTENTS

Introduction

Over the past several years the term "daddy" has increased in popularity.[1] Similar terms such as "DILF" ("dad I'd like to fuck") are widespread.[2] There is even a mobile game app called "Dream Daddy" in which "you play as a Dad and your goal is to meet and romance other hot Dads."[3] In 2018, *Saturday Night Live* ran a skit called the "Westminster Daddy Show," in which different men competed for the title. It is also common for people to express attraction to "dad bods," a term that refers to men with "average" body types.[4] Clearly, interest in older men has grown.

The term "daddy" has existed for centuries, but its meaning has changed over time. From the 1600s through the early 1900s, "daddy" often referred to pimps or clients in sex work.[5] Later it morphed into "sugar daddy" among heterosexuals, referring to older men who provide money, expensive gifts, or bill payments in exchange for sex with younger women.[6] Today "daddy" often refers to desirable older men, although not necessarily in a sugar daddy context, among both heterosexuals and gay and bisexual men.[7] LGBTQ (lesbian, gay, bisexual, transgender, and queer) women and nonbinary people may also identify as daddies or "daddis," but there is less press coverage of this phenomenon and little academic research.[8]

Daddies appear to be particularly popular among gay men today—and indeed, in the Western world, man-man couples are far more likely to have large age gaps compared to woman-man and woman-woman partnerships.[9] Older men in these partnerships do not necessarily identify as daddies. Some men may find the term offensive, whereas other men may not mind the term but simply do not identify with it. How to define the term "daddy" is a controversial topic today among gay and bisexual men.[10]

The commonality of age gaps among man-man couples shows that gay and bisexual men think about age, and age differences, differently than heterosexuals and LGBTQ women. Gay and bisexual men may *care less* about age differences between themselves and a potential partner than heterosexuals or LGBTQ women—or, alternatively, they may *desire age differences more*. Other research has similarly found that gay men are more likely than other groups to have partners who are different from them in terms of race and class.[11] Gay men approach dating differently than other groups do.

Existing research has not determined why age gaps are more common among man-man couples than woman-man or woman-woman couples. Talking to gay and bisexual men who partner with adult men much older or younger than themselves helps to solve this puzzle. Talking to daddies, specifically, also shows how masculinity and sexual practices shift over the life course in ways unique to gay and bisexual men.

This project has three main research questions: How do older men who pair with younger adult men understand what it means to be a daddy? How do age-gap pairings between adults relate to the ways in which they understand their masculinity? Why do younger adult men sexually or romantically partner with much older men? ("Age-gap pairing" is an umbrella term I use to indicate a romantic partnership, sexual friendship, or purely sexual relationship with a large age gap. "Age-gap partnership" is a term I use to indicate a *romantic* partnership, specifically, with a large age gap.)[12]

This project is the first to analyze the stories of gay and bisexual daddies, and the first to interview younger adult men about why they are interested in older men.[13] By doing so, it helps to uncover why it is more common for gay and bisexual men to have large age gaps in relationships than heterosexuals or LGBTQ women. Additionally, the stories of the men I talked to provide data on a topic that few others have explored. While many people have heard of "daddy" as a sexual term, little research has explored what this term means to the men who describe themselves in this way. Similarly, little research has focused on younger adult men to understand why they prefer much older men.

I talked to thirty-nine self-described daddies between the ages of forty-three and seventy, as well as twenty-six younger men between the ages of twenty-three and thirty-three who formed sexual or romantic relationships with men much older than themselves. I talked to gay and bisexual men, specifically, given that they have the highest rates of age-gap partnerships in the Western world. I focused on age gaps of ten years or more; differences of fifteen to thirty years were common. Some older men explicitly identified as daddies, whereas others reported that they "felt" like daddies when with younger adult men or explained that they fulfilled a daddy "role," for instance by mentoring younger adult men.

One thing I should make clear: the older men I talked to only discussed relationships with younger *adult* men aged eighteen or older. Most, notably, wanted nothing to do with men under the age of twenty-one because they considered these men *too* young, even though men who are eighteen, nineteen, and twenty years old are adults. Similarly, the youngest man I talked to was twenty-three years old. Men in their twenties and early thirties discussed sexual and romantic encounters they had had as adults aged eighteen or older. Contrary to homophobic stereotypes, none of the men I talked to reported any interest in, or history of, sexual encounters with minors. This book is exclusively about relationships between adults of different ages.

Age-Gap Partnerships

Most research about age-gap partnerships is demographic in nature and focuses on woman-man couples. In most of the Americas, eastern Asia, and Europe, women are typically within four years of their male partners.[14] In contrast, average age gaps are four to eight years in much of southern Africa, south Asia, and the Middle East, and more than eight years in central Africa.[15] The age differences that count as large gaps in the Western world vary by study. Researchers have used cutoffs of five, eight, or ten years, for instance, whereas others use different age-gap lengths in the same project based on whether a partnership is woman-older or man-older.[16]

Regardless of the exact definition, most age-gap partnerships are man-older. Their prevalence has declined in Western nations over time while the prevalence of woman-older age-gap partnerships has increased, even as woman-older pairings remain much less common than man-older pairings.[17] Large age gaps between men and women in the Western world declined in the nineteenth and twentieth centuries in part because people increasingly associated large age gaps with an inappropriate power imbalance.[18] Around this time, ideals of complementary marriages based on love became more popular (even as gender inequalities remained).[19]

Gender and national inequalities shape the formation of woman-man age-gap partnerships, but associations with economic factors are more complex. Age-gap partnerships become more likely as people marry at older ages and remarry.[20] This pattern is driven at least in part by gender inequality.[21] The older a man is when he marries, the larger the age gap between him and his wife, even when both are past their reproductive years.[22] Factors other than child-rearing intentions affect age-gap partnerships, especially society's devaluation of women as they age. Age-gap partnerships are also more common among women who immigrate from low- or middle-income nations to high-income nations.[23]

Individuals in woman-man age-gap partnerships, regardless of gender or whether they are older or younger, typically have lower incomes and educational attainment than their counterparts who are in partnerships with someone around their own age.[24] This pattern likely exists in part because individuals who are less likely to be high earners or to attain higher educational degrees are more likely to enter into age-gap partnerships,[25] perhaps because they spend less time in institutions such as universities that typically have people around the same age who look for partners.[26] Thus, while there are romantic partnerships between wealthy older people and less wealthy younger people, they are uncommon.

Studies have compared heterosexuals in age-gap partnerships to their counterparts in age-similar partnerships. Outcomes vary depending on the study. Mental health and mortality differences emerge in some studies.[27] Men in age-gap partnerships, whether younger or older, have lower average cognitive abilities than their counterparts who are partnered to someone around their own age, and men in man-older partnerships are also rated as less physically attractive by interviewers.[28] There are also some differences in subjective partnership satisfaction and sexual satisfaction, particularly among women partnered to much older men.[29] However, relationship attachment styles are similar in women regardless of whether they are partnered to a man around their age or to a substantially older man.[30]

Despite some differences, most measures of mental health, partnership satisfaction, and sexual well-being do not substantially differ according to whether someone is in an age-similar or an age-gap partnership, and there is extensive variability in outcomes when differences do emerge.[31] Differences that do exist likely stem from a combination of selection effects of who enters these partnerships, dynamics that exist within these partnerships, and social stigma attached to age-gap partnerships (particularly woman-older partnerships).[32]

Little research examines the attitudes of individuals in age-gap pairings, whether sexual or romantic. Survey research of adults in their fifties or older suggests that there are no major differences in attitudes about gender roles between individuals in heterosexual age-gap partnerships (whether man or woman, older or younger) compared to individuals in age-similar partnerships.[33] Other research suggests that women aged thirty-five to forty-four who are five or ten years older than a male sexual partner are more liberal in certain attitudes than their counterparts who sexually partner with men around their own age.[34] This same research also, however, found that women who sexually partner with older men do not have significantly different attitudes than women who sexually partner with men around their own age.[35] Overall, among heterosexuals, there are some but not many differences in attitudes about gender and sexuality based on the age gap between individuals in sexual or romantic pairings.

Although there has been some interview research with individuals in "sugar" arrangements,[36] there is little interview research about individuals in age-gap pairings that are not sugar relationships. Like demographic studies, most interview studies of age-gap romantic partnerships focus on woman-man partnerships. Prior research has found that individuals in age-gap partnerships discuss how the partnership is simultaneously unique (for instance, the younger partner is more mature than others their age) and similar to those of other partnerships (for instance, both partners love one another).[37] While individuals in man-older partnerships discuss inequalities based on intersections of gender and age, they typically frame these inequalities as individual issues that are either unproblematic or able to be resolved through future relationship work.[38] In contrast, some women in woman-older partnerships seek to retain independence in their partnership, in part due to experiences of gender inequality in former age-similar relationships, but simultaneously fear being neglected as they age.[39]

Other researchers have talked to women aged thirty to sixty who dated men at least five years younger than themselves and found that these women felt that sex with younger men, compared to sex with men their age or older, was more sexually satisfying and allowed them to be more sexually assertive.[40] At the same time, gender inequality—in particular social stigma about women's sexuality and the devaluation of women as they age—also shaped how these women described initiating contact and began dating younger men.[41] Outside of global regions in which large age gaps are common, age-gap partnerships are often stigmatized—particularly woman-older partnerships.[42]

Same-Sex Age-Gap Pairings

Little research examines age-gap pairings (romantic or sexual) among LGBTQ people. Only one prior interview study has investigated man-man romantic partnerships with a large age gap. It analyzed seven couples in which there was an eighteen- to twenty-two-year age gap between partners.[43] That study found that both older and younger partners described themselves as working toward shared goals and a future together, although they also reported concerns about differences in life expectancy.[44] Both groups also explained benefits to having a much older or younger partner: for instance, younger men appreciated the mentorship of older men whereas older men felt that a younger partner kept them feeling young.[45] That research did not, however, examine daddy identities or nonromantic age-gap pairings, as this book does.

Demographic research shows that man-man couples throughout the West are more likely to have large age gaps than either woman-man or woman-woman couples.[46] In Belgium, for instance, 24.5 percent of man-man couples have an age difference of six to ten years whereas 16.8 percent have a difference of eleven or more years; comparable figures for woman-woman couples are 21.8 percent and 10.5 percent, compared to 13.3 percent and 3.5 percent for woman-man couples.[47] Similarly, correlations between couple ages are .56 for man-man couples, .66 for woman-woman couples, .68 for woman-man cohabiting couples, and .76 for married woman-man couples in California.[48] These figures show that man-man couples have the least similarity in partner ages, on average.

Gay and bisexual men have a limited dating pool in most areas, given that a small percentage of men identify as gay or bisexual. A limited dating pool is not the only explanation for high rates of age-gap partnerships, however, for two main reasons. First, demographic features of local dating markets are strongly associated with interracial partnership formation among different-sex couples but less so among same-sex couples.[49] In other words, interracial partnerships are more common among same-sex couples than among different-sex couples, and partner availability does not entirely explain these different rates. Higher rates of interracial partnerships among same-sex couples may exist because LGBTQ people are more likely to challenge relational norms than are heterosexuals,[50] and this logic may apply to age-gap partnerships as well.

Second, the greater commonality of age gaps among man-man couples compared to woman-woman couples suggests that unique dynamics related to gay and bisexual men's communities shape their partnering practices. Women and men who form same-sex partnerships both experience limited dating pools, but this pattern does not lead to similar rates of age-gap partnerships. Thus, even when one considers partner availability, there remains a puzzle about why rates of age-gap partnerships are higher among man-man couples than any other couple type. Understanding daddy identities among gay and bisexual men provides insight into why age gaps are common among man-man couples. So does talking to younger adult men who pair with older men.

Daddy identities and age-gap partnerships are not identical topics. Older partners in older-younger pairings may not identify as daddies; individuals in many older-younger pairings are both at or past midlife (for instance, one partner is in his forties and the other is in his sixties); and many self-described daddies sexually, but not romantically, partner with younger adult men. Nonetheless, these topics are related, and understanding more about one topic helps advance understanding about the other, even as they are distinct.

LGBTQ Subcultures

There are a variety of sexual subcultures among gay and bisexual men.[51] Subcultures that have received particular focus in research include leathermen,[52] bears,[53] urban sexual cultures that manifest in circuit parties and pop-up events,[54] and, more recently, puppies.[55] How age relates to sexual partnering among men is less clear. Gay and bisexual men have long eroticized older men, and recently there has been a resurgence of interest in pornography featuring middle-aged men and sexual encounters between older and younger adults.[56]

Although no researchers have interviewed men who describe themselves as daddies, one researcher has analyzed bear terminology, explaining,[57]

> Although the *cub* and *daddy* elements of the code are generally associated with age, they actually refer to a set of characteristics that may be independent of the actual age of the bear in question. In addition to potentially being relatively young among bears, one might identify as a cub because he is new to the bear scene, because he is searching for a nurturing partner, or even because he is a bottom (the receptive partner in anal intercourse). Similarly, a daddy may simply be nurturing, a long-time bear, or a top (the insertive partner in anal intercourse) so that identifying as a daddy does not mean that one is necessarily older than those who identify as cubs.

The meaning of "daddy," at least among bears in the 1990s, typically involves an age gap but is also influenced by other factors.

Relatedly, one interview project conducted in the 1990s found that gay and bisexual men commonly reported preferences for adult men much older or younger than themselves.[58] The author insightfully wrote, "The interviewees' descriptions of preferences for older men, perhaps more than for younger, reveal the vitality of a somewhat subterranean cultural tradition that is now little celebrated."[59] Since the time of that research, older-younger pairings between adults have become more popular and visible.[60]

Gay men's use of the term "daddy" emerged in gay leather communities. As one team of researchers found,[61] "Although all leathermen were described as portraying a 'tough' attitude, some of the characteristics the participants used to differentiate the two roles were physical appearance and age, attitude, and experience. For example, leathermen who were physically larger, older, had more sexual experiences, or sadomasochistic expertise typically would adopt a 'Daddy' role. Conversely, 'Boys' would adopt a submissive sexual role. This role-playing allowed participants to meet other leathermen who shared compatible sexual interests, to discuss these interests and, eventually, to find sexual partners." They went on to explain, "Healthy and functional leather sexuality was thought to be based in leather and leather/masculine symbols and sexual roles, such as Daddy and Boy, could accentuate this masculinity by dramatizing differences in power."[62] "Daddy" has historically had specific meanings within gay leather communities, which are tied to age, consensual power dynamics between adults, and/or body type. (As another chapter will explain, "boy" is a term sometimes applied to adult men. "Boy" does not refer to children, nor does it refer to role play in which someone pretends to be a child. Just as heterosexuals use the term "girl" to refer to adult women, gay men sometimes use "boy" to refer to adult men.) Gay leather communities have shaped contemporary understandings of "daddy" among gay and bisexual men.[63]

Two researchers examined LGBTQ subcultures in which age is a central component, although both did so among communities comprised primarily of nonbinary people and women (transgender or "cisgender," which means not transgender), with some involvement of transgender men but rarely of cisgender men. For instance, one researcher wrote a personal-experience essay in which he focused on his experience with "leatherdyke boys and their leatherdyke daddies,"[64] whereas another interviewed BDSM practitioners.[65] Neither researcher focused on daddy identities specifically, nor did they investigate age gaps between partners. Their work shows that adults who "role play" an age different from their own age are able to explore gender expressions and vulnerable emotions. In contrast, gay and bisexual men are more likely to partner with someone who is much older or younger than themselves and are less likely to role play an age different from their own.

Are Daddies a Subculture?

As I found in this research, daddy-younger relationships between adults do not necessarily constitute a subculture. They can be *part* of a subculture and may take unique forms in particular subcultures (such as leather daddies among leathermen and bear daddies among bears), but daddy-younger relationships do not usually constitute a subculture in and of themselves. Two factors that undergird cultures are collective self-definitions and institutions such as bars.[66] While daddies do for the most part share a collective definition of daddyness,[67] they are not necessarily anchored by institutions that specifically cater to daddies or older-younger pairings between adults. There are bars that cater to gay and bisexual men at or past midlife, but these bars are not necessarily "daddy" bars, since age is not the only factor that defines daddyness. Many men at or past middle age do not perceive themselves as daddies or even want to have sex with younger adult men. Daddy events are also not as common as events for other established subcultures such as leather and bears.

There are three main additional reasons why older-younger pairings between adults do not constitute a subculture among gay and bisexual men. First, older-younger pairings exist among men who have little contact with LGBTQ institutions. For instance, several of the older men I interviewed were partnered to women and were secretive about their sex with men. Second, older-younger pairings cross-cut other established subcultures such as bears and leather. Third, daddies and men interested in daddies have a "rotating" membership because men age into daddyness and out of ages typically associated with a younger man in a daddy-younger pairing (most commonly, early twenties through early thirties). Stated differently, older-younger pairings between adults and daddy identities today appear to be common among gay and bisexual men. They are not limited to a small subculture.

There are, of course, some apps and events that cater to older-younger pairings between adults. For instance, an app called Daddyhunt has over five million users.[68] Several years ago a heartwarming web series called *Daddyhunt: The Serial* was released to promote the app. The series has been viewed over thirty million times and has won several awards.[69] There is a traveling event called the DILF Party that hosts events throughout the United States and Canada,[70] and gay bars in major cities occasionally host daddy-themed events. Both SCRUFF and Grindr have a "daddy" box users can check.[71] Daddyness is becoming more institutionalized, but most men who form older-younger pairings are not involved with apps or events specifically dedicated to these pairings. Instead, today, older-younger pairings between adults exist across subcultures and segments of the gay world.

How I Conducted This Research

Finding Daddies and the Younger Adult Men Who Like Them

I recruited men via the mobile application SCRUFF, which has over twenty million users worldwide.[72] SCRUFF, as the name implies, caters to older and hairier men (and their admirers), and appears to be the most popular mobile application in North America to target this specific population.[73] For one week in early 2020, SCRUFF ran an advertisement that appeared to all men who opened the app within the Chicago metropolitan area. Each user saw the ad once: the first time they opened SCRUFF after the ad campaign was launched. It appeared over the user's entire phone screen. The ad, which was written to conform to guidelines established by SCRUFF and Northwestern University's research ethics board, read, "Are you a daddy? Do a research interview! Do you think of yourself as a daddy? Do you partner with younger adult men? I'm a researcher at Northwestern University hoping to talk to you." Users could select a "learn more" tab that directed them to a website that provided more information about the study. Men were eligible to participate if they were aged thirty-five or older and engaged in consensual sexual or romantic relationships with adults ten or more years younger than they. An age cutoff of thirty-five was selected because one goal of this study is to analyze the relationship between masculinity and age-gap pairings among self-described daddies in midlife or older adulthood. During the second phase of the research project, SCRUFF ran a similar advertisement for one week in early 2020. The advertisement read, "Are you into daddies? Do a research interview! Do you partner with men much older than you? Are you between the ages of 21 and 34? I'm a researcher at Northwestern University hoping to talk to you." Users could select a "learn more" tab, as in the first advertisement.

SCRUFF runs advertisements in specific metropolitan areas. Chicago was selected because the city has a rich history of cultivating gay and bisexual men's sexual subcultures. For instance, Chicago has held the International Mr. Leather (IML) competition, the world's largest, since its inception in 1979; it has similarly held the Mr. International Rubber (MIR) competition, also the largest of its kind, since its founding in 1998; and it has one of the world's largest museums dedicated to leather, kink, and fetish.[74] Chicago is also one of the few major cities in North America that today contains multiple bars with basements or back rooms that allow sex between men.[75] In short, Chicago has a rich history of shaping gay and bisexual men's sexual subcultures.[76]

While older-younger pairings between adults do not constitute a subculture in and of themselves, Chicago's sexual openness makes it an ideal place to recruit men to discuss what some consider a sensitive topic. Chicago is also a rich site for recruitment because despite its important LGBTQ history, it has been underexamined in studies of American LGBTQ life compared to coastal cities such as New York and San Francisco.[77] Several men I talked to did not live in the Chicago metropolitan area, however; they saw the ad when they visited the area or after someone they knew sent the project information to them.

Interview Process

Thirty-nine older men agreed to talk to me, and I assigned them pseudonyms. They answered a variety of questions, including the following: What does it mean to you to be a daddy? What are some daddy traits that you have? What are some things you do that are related to you being a daddy? In what ways is being a daddy related to finances, if at all? When did you first think of yourself as a daddy? What are your favorite and least favorite aspects of being a daddy? Can you describe yourself in terms of masculinity and femininity?

Twenty-six younger men also talked to me. They answered numerous questions, including the following: What are the reasons you sexually or romantically partner with much older men? What do you find most and least attractive about older men? Please describe yourself in terms of masculinity and femininity. Please walk me through your first experience where you sexually or romantically partnered with a much older man. Thinking of your last [or current] romantic relationship, what were your favorite parts of that relationship? What were its main challenges? If you were to describe what it meant to be a daddy to another person who did not know what daddies were, what would you say?

Interviews lasted approximately one hour, and most took place over the phone. Seven interviews with older men took place on the Northwestern University campus. Transcripts were uploaded to the qualitative software NVivo and coded for recurring themes. I first applied broad codes that reflected key concepts of interest, and later applied more specific codes once I refined analytical concepts and new concepts of interest emerged from the data.[78] For instance, one broad code was "meaning of daddy." There were multiple meanings attached to daddyness across and within transcripts, so I created more specific codes under that umbrella concept, including "nurture/mentor" and "protective/caring." I read transcripts multiple times to apply new codes, and to identify overarching themes across transcripts and connections between themes.[79] I then organized codes into main themes of analytical interest. I lightly edited quotations for clarity and to preserve confidentiality.

Readers may understandably wonder how my own characteristics shaped this research. My age helped me build rapport with both younger and older men, in different ways. At the time of this research I was in my late twenties, which meant I was close in age to the young men. I could understand their terminology and pop culture references, and younger men also likely perceived me as similar enough to themselves to understand their stories. Older men, on the other hand, knew that I was in the age group they "daddied." They were used to talking to younger men, which meant that our interview was not too out of the ordinary for them. Additionally, it is possible that many older men viewed participation as a way to professionally help a younger man in a way that paralleled their mentorship of other younger men. Put differently, their participation may have been a platonic manifestation of their daddyness.

Sample

Although thirty-five was the minimum age for older men's eligibility, the range was between forty-three and seventy; the median age was fifty-seven. See table A.1 for a listing of pseudonyms and ages. Thirty-three men identified as gay, three as bisexual, one as queer, and two reported that they were somewhere between gay and bisexual.[80] All older men identified as cisgender.[81] The vast majority of older men were middle-class. In terms of education level, one reported a high school diploma or GED as his highest; five, some college; one, an associate's degree; eleven, a bachelor's; nineteen, a master's; and two, a doctorate or professional degree. Income ranged from zero (a man who was unemployed at the time of the interview) to $600,000 US, with a median of $99,000 and a mean of approximately $124,000. Occupations were mostly but not exclusively white-collar. Of the thirty-nine older men, thirty-one identified as white, one as Middle Eastern, and seven as Latino.

Among younger men, ages ranged between twenty-three and thirty-three. The median age was twenty-seven. Twenty identified as gay, one as bisexual, and five as queer. Twenty-three men identified as cisgender, two identified as transgender men, and one identified as nonbinary and was assigned a male sex at birth. Most had earned a higher education degree: one reported a high school degree as his highest degree, three reported some college, three reported an associate's degree, nine reported a bachelor's, and ten reported a master's. Income was far lower than that of the older men. The median was $37,000 US, whereas the mean was $42,000, with a range between zero (a man who was unemployed at the time) and $90,000. Of the younger men, seventeen identified as white and three each as Latino, Black, and Middle Eastern.

Key Themes

The stories of the men I talked to were not consistent with a sugar daddy/gold digger stereotype.[82] Younger men did not pair with older men because they had few other options. Instead, they desired older men for many reasons: emotional maturity, physical attractiveness, and a wish to learn from older men were among the reasons younger men offered. Both older and younger adult men found age-gap pairings between adults sexually exciting, emotionally fulfilling, and mostly absent sugar daddy dynamics. Complications or frustrations can occur in any type of relationship, and age-gap pairings are no exception. Yet men overwhelmingly described the pairings they formed as positive.

One theme that became clear is that demographic research understates how common age-gap pairings are among gay and bisexual men. Demographic research shows that age gaps are more common among man-man romantic partnerships than other couple types—but romantic partnerships are only a small portion of total age-gap pairings, many of which are sexual but not romantic in nature. Nonromantic relationships are typically not measured in demographic studies.

Instead of age-gap romantic partnerships, most of the men I talked to formed emotionally intimate friends-with-benefits (FWB) arrangements, ongoing sexual relationships, or hookups with adult men much older or younger than themselves. Mentorship was often a key component of these relationships. Romantic partnerships are not the only meaningful relationships individuals can form.[83] FWBs are common among gay men, who often consider them to be similar to other types of friendships, except that they include sex.[84] Most of the men I talked to did not seek age-gap romantic partnerships, but they did form nonromantic age-gap pairings that they found meaningful.

Notably, too, there were not large mismatches between the perceptions of younger and older men. Both sets of men viewed age-gap pairings between adults positively and described them in similar ways. For instance, both older and younger men described the value of the mentorship typically involved with older-younger pairings. Indeed, the main trait men associated with daddyness was mentorship or nurturance of younger adult men. While both older and younger men also described frustrating situations they had experienced, men viewed most of their age-gap pairings positively.

Only a minority of the men I talked to were in a romantic partnership with a man much older or younger than themselves. Many men were, in fact, in an open relationship with a man around their own age. (In "open relationships," partners agree that it is acceptable to have sex with other people.) In total, twenty-two older men were in a romantic partnership, and of them, only seven were partnered to men in their twenties or early thirties. Eleven younger men were in a romantic partnership, and of them seven (the same number as older men) were partnered to men ten or more years older than themselves.

Most age-gap romantic partnerships functioned similarly to partnerships between two men of the same age, even as the age gap added certain complications such as differences in career stage. Notably, a majority of younger men reported attractions to older men but a desire to partner with men around their own age. They wanted an age-similar partnership to prevent what they saw as potential issues, including differences in life expectancy or the possibility of power imbalances. Most of the single older men similarly reported that they were not interested in a romantic partnership with a much younger man. Contrary to stereotypes, I found little evidence of widespread power differentials in age-gap romantic partnerships that harmed either older or younger men. A handful of men described partnerships with a problematic power imbalance, but these types of asymmetrical partnerships were uncommon.

Another major finding is that several older men experienced daddyness as a life course phenomenon: as young adult men, they sexually or romantically paired with much older men, and as older men, they became daddies to younger men in their twenties and early thirties. This finding highlights how many gay and bisexual men experience sexual flexibility over the life course. Additionally, the fact that men aged into daddyness shows that the life cycle for gay and bisexual men has different milestones than for other groups.[85]

Many older men experienced boosts to their masculinity as they aged, related to mentoring or feeling desired by younger adult men. Age-gap pairings can bolster masculinity in midlife or older adulthood when aging can otherwise threaten it. Many gay and bisexual men do not necessarily need to "compensate" for their age through wealth because the aging process actually enhances their sexual desirability to many younger adult men. This enhanced desirability is another reason why sugar daddy dynamics were rare: younger men found older men attractive for reasons beyond finances.

Ageism is unfortunately common within gay and bisexual male communities, and it negatively affects the well-being of older men. Yet the older men I talked to rarely discussed ageism. A substantial portion of gay and bisexual men value men who are in midlife or older adulthood, and specifically men in their forties through their sixties. While ageism affects most people in midlife and older adulthood, to varying degrees, the valuation of daddyness helps to insulate many older men from its effects. Being desired in midlife and older adulthood was invigorating for many older men.

Daddies shape gay and bisexual communities both culturally and sexually. Culturally, daddies mentor younger adult men and transmit knowledge intergenerationally. This knowledge includes information about how to navigate homophobia, about how to access gay communities (particularly for men who are not yet "out" or only recently "out"), and about what life was like for gay and bisexual men in prior decades.

Older-younger pairings between adults help perpetuate gay and bisexual cultural life, which can only exist if new members are integrated into it. Unlike ethnic communities, for instance, people are not born into gay and bisexual communities; individuals must join them after they come out as LGBTQ. This fact necessarily means that men who have recently come out will need to learn what it means to be gay or bisexual, where to meet other gay and bisexual men, and practices associated with gay and bisexual communities (for instance, the greater prevalence of open relationships among gay men compared to other groups).[86] (In contrast to homophobic beliefs about older LGBTQ people "grooming" younger people, the younger men I talked to identified as gay, bisexual, or queer well before their sexual encounters with older men—which, again, happened when the younger men were adults.) Older-younger pairings—whether in romantic partnerships, emotionally intimate sexual friendships, or purely sexual relationships—connected different cohorts of adult gay and bisexual men and helped form a sense of community.

Relatedly, daddies serve important sexual roles in gay and bisexual communities as well. As adults, younger gay and bisexual men must learn how to have sex with other men, given that there is little formal education about male-male sex (for example, in sex education curricula). By teaching younger adult men about life in gay and bisexual communities and by connecting cohorts of adult gay and bisexual men, daddies help to perpetuate both cultural and sexual life in their communities. Older-younger pairings between adults are uniquely important to social life for gay and bisexual men.

1

Becoming a Daddy

Most of the older men I talked to reported that they aged into daddyness, at different times in their lives depending on life circumstances such as relationship status and mobile-app use. Most men reported that it happened between their midthirties and late sixties, with the modal time in their forties. Additionally, although most men explained that daddyness involved many factors, almost all of them also noted that age was a key component of it. As Dustin (70) stated simply, "For me, being a daddy means that I am older." Diego (43) also explained, "As you reach a certain age now in the gay world you start getting referred to as daddy. It's a colloquialism, I guess. So yeah, I view myself as being in that age range now." This finding is in contrast to how many young heterosexuals use "daddy" to refer to particular types of demeanor, style, personality, or power dynamics regardless of age.[1] The older men I talked to could, hypothetically, have perceived themselves as daddies as far back as their twenties or early thirties—yet few did. Among men in midlife or older adulthood who see themselves as daddies, age is a key component of that self-perception.

In various ways and to different extents, men connected daddyness to three similar but distinct age-related matters: their age, the age of the younger adult man, and the age gap between them. "I would say that my age plays a big role in how I perceive myself as a daddy and the age of the person I'm relating to," Greg (50) stated. He continued, "Their age matters, my age matters, the age difference matters a lot." In total, thirty-six of thirty-nine older men connected daddyness to their age, and thirty-three connected it to a substantial age difference between two men, especially but not exclusively between middle-aged men and men aged eighteen through their early thirties. Notably, however, most middle-aged men did not desire adult men under the age of twenty-one (men aged eighteen, nineteen, or twenty).

Interestingly, even as seventeen older men explained that daddyness was a "state of mind" or was not necessarily tied to age, most simultaneously connected daddyness to age to some extent. Similarly, twenty-five of twenty-six younger men also tied daddyness to age and age gaps between two men—even as twelve simultaneously noted that daddyness was an "energy," a "dynamic," or a "state of mind" not necessarily connected to age. Tellingly, few men described situations in which the older partner called the younger partner "daddy," even when the younger partner was more sexually dominant or topped. Although these situations occurred, they were uncommon.

The relationship between daddyness and age was one of the few topics where men contradicted themselves. Some men, especially younger men and men involved in leather, stated that daddyness could transcend age. Most, however, *also* described age or age gaps between men as a major feature of daddyness. In short, despite some inconsistent responses, most of the men I talked to—older and younger—tied daddyness to age and age gaps between partners, at least to some extent. Age is not the only factor that constitutes daddyness, but it is one defining component.

Men I talked to understood that this subject could be controversial. Michael (30), for instance, referred to the topic of daddies as "a hot subject right now in the gay community because there are men that are like early thirties calling themselves daddies." He himself, however, felt that men could be daddies starting "probably somewhere in their early- to midforties and above." Similarly, James (28) acknowledged that it was "controversial" to say that daddyness begins at age forty, but it was nonetheless his opinion. Several men laughed at the idea of younger men being daddies. As Brett (43) noted, "It's so funny to me when you see these guys on Grindr or SCRUFF, and they're like twenty-nine and thirty and thirty-one and they're calling themselves a daddy, and I'm like, 'Come on. You're hardly a daddy.' You've got to be like late thirties, for sure."

Almost all men connected daddyness to age—or age gaps between partners—to at least some extent. As Cody (59) detailed, even though he thinks daddyness "depends on the person," he also reported, "I remember vividly rolling my eyes and doing it almost out loud, 'oh please,' of seeing people in their early thirties that put 'daddy' in their profile." Similarly, Neil (51) explained that age is "the starting point" for a relationship with daddy dynamics. Jordy (57) elaborated, "I feel like forty and above would be a daddy because I see younger men online and they may be in their early thirties and they say they're a daddy. And I think, 'Well, that's not really true, you're not old enough to be a daddy.' I think in my mind, there is a difference. Daddies probably start around forty."

The Daddy Spectrum

Interest from younger adult men encouraged many of the men I communicated with to consider the possibility that they could be daddies. As Cody (59) detailed, "I was in my thirties when my hair started going gray, early midthirties, thirty-four-ish. And I fought that one like you wouldn't believe and dyeing my hair and looking like an idiot." However, Cody continued, "The minute I gave up and let my hair go gray, I had guys literally climbing all over me, like, 'Daddy, daddy, daddy!'" These reactions were often initially surprising. As Caleb (57) explained about being called a daddy, "As time progressed, it became more a term of flattery, more of a something that I was looking for that I liked. But the first time or two was a little shocking."

Most men did not perceive themselves as daddies prior to midlife; instead, a spike in interest from younger adult men as they approached or were in midlife encouraged them to consider this descriptor. Thus, daddyness was initially an ascribed status (something that other people placed on them). Later, however, it became as much achieved as ascribed for most men as they started to engage in daddy practices such as mentorship. Daddyness, in short, involves components that are ascribed as well as components that are achieved. Older men embraced daddyness to different extents and referred to it as an identity, a role, a dynamic, a feeling, or as something younger adult men placed on them.

Several men explained that it took them time to accept the daddy identity or "role" that younger adult men associated with them. "I really just fell into it. It wasn't a situation where I was attracted to younger guys," Seth (65) explained. "It's just that all of a sudden younger guys were attracted to me, and it went from there." As a result, Seth noted, "I see myself more as a daddy now." Jordy (57) agreed: "I didn't expect to be a daddy, it just kind of happened." He elaborated, "It was gradual. They started [calling me daddy] in my early forties and probably when I was around forty-five, forty-six, I accepted the role even though I wouldn't refer to myself as a daddy those early years. Because I didn't go after younger men." Nonetheless, Jordy continued, "But they just kept contacting me and they were hot and young and it just kept happening so much. I gave in probably when I was like forty-five, forty-six, and accepted it and liked it." Jordy came to accept and enjoy his "role" as a daddy. Mateo (55) similarly noted, "I started to get approached by several younger men in their twenty-to-thirty range. And they started to say like, 'Well you're a nice daddy.' It's like, 'Am I? I don't understand.' I didn't know if I should take it as an insult or as a compliment. And lately, I have been embracing it." These responses highlight how daddyness for some men is initially ascribed on the basis of their age, and then later transitions to being a mixture of ascribed and achieved status as men "embrace" the role.

Other men described daddyness in more complex ways: as both ascribed and achieved, but not necessarily as an identity. As Zachary (59) explained, "I probably have never really seen myself that way. It's a term that was probably given to me based on my age, my body type. I've been really accepting of that." Zachary understood that "accepting" daddyness could benefit his social and sexual relationships, as younger men expected him to be a daddy. Relatedly, Santiago (43) explained, "I like the idea, but I am not completely sure that I consider myself to be a daddy, even though I like dating guys way younger than me." Santiago continued, "So I would not call myself a daddy, even though it feels good sometimes when somebody says that. So I don't know. It's intriguing, I will say. It's intriguing, but it's not necessarily something I embrace 100 percent." Santiago accepted the "role" of daddy even as he did not necessarily identify as a daddy. Connor (59), like others, deployed daddyness strategically: although being called "daddy" "is not something I encourage," he navigates it "from a marketing standpoint"—to secure sex. Several men similarly explained that they did not necessarily identify as daddies but were fine with others seeing them that way. As Wyatt (66) noted, "I don't necessarily look at that as the primary identity that I have for myself. . . . I'm comfortable enough with myself that if somebody wants to look at me as a daddy, that's fine, I'll be the daddy." Jorge (47) echoed this feeling: "I see myself as one, but I don't really say that I am one. It's like people put [that] on me and okay, I see myself as that." Some older men adopted a daddy "role" after they experienced interest from younger men as well as expectations that they should be daddies.

As these responses show, older men were on a daddy spectrum. On one end, men actively identified as daddies. On the other end, men did not necessarily identify as daddies, but they consciously fulfilled a daddy "role" and were aware that others saw them as daddies. Men across the daddy spectrum were similar in that they engaged in daddy practices, like mentorship of younger adult men and sex with younger adult men, and they also consciously connected these practices to daddyness. In short, all the older men saw themselves as daddies to various extents, but not all of them identified as daddies. Jorge, above, articulated this dynamic well: he noted that he *sees* himself as a daddy but does not necessarily *identify* as a daddy.

Being a daddy meant (1) fulfilling a daddy role, which involved sex with younger adult men and, often, mentorship of younger men, (2) explicitly connecting these practices to the concept of daddyness, and (3) being aware that others perceived them as daddies. Thus, for some men daddyness was a role and for others it was both an identity and a role. There were few notable differences between these two groups, except that the latter group saw daddyness as more central to who they are as a person.

Emergence of the Daddy Consciousness

Many older men reported that they formed a daddy consciousness in large part because younger adult men contacted them on apps. As Diego (43) explained, "I would say like the past five years, from like thirty-eight I started to think, 'Oh, I'm getting some gray in my beard, I'm looking more daddy-like, and I'm being called daddy more on apps and things of that nature.' And I was out of a relationship. I had a relationship end and I was out on the market again, out on the apps more, etc., and I was definitely noticing now that this time around I'm being approached and referred to as 'daddy' more." At first, Diego did not consider the possibility that he could be a daddy because he was in a relationship and not active on apps. Once that relationship ended and he was back on the dating market, Diego realized that younger men perceived him as a daddy. Brian (61), too, explained that "I found that all the people that I was interested in meeting and being involved with sexually were so much younger than me," and began feeling like a daddy around age forty-five as a result. Logan was sixty (his current age) when he first felt like a daddy, and it was because he downloaded Grindr: "It wasn't until I got on Grindr and [received messages from] these guys from eighteen to twenty-five or thirty. Then all of a sudden it dawned on me that, hey, these guys think I'm a daddy. So it's relatively recent." Other research has similarly found that app use is associated with meeting much older or younger men.[2] In addition to connecting adult men of different cohorts, app use can lead men to adopt a daddy identity or role after they experience interest from younger adult men and realize that younger men expect them to be daddies.

Ryan (48) similarly explained that emergent feelings of daddyness, in his midthirties, preceded daddy identification: "It was before Grindr and all that. It was one of the online apps on your computer and someone called me 'daddy.' I distinctly remember it and thinking, 'Whoa, I never really thought of myself in that way.' I don't remember exactly how old he was. Probably like twenty-one, something like that, if I had to guess. And I remember that very first time vividly and never thinking of myself in that way. And then . . . over that next year or so warmed me up to that idea and getting more into it, I would say." Thinking of himself as a daddy was initially difficult. "Culturally, there's this emphasis on being young. There is. I thought of myself as young. I didn't think of myself as old. But then I'm like, Well, these guys are really cute, and I'm attracted to them, and they're attracted to me, and it's fun, so why be weird about it in my head, or why fight it or whatever.' And then I eventually embraced it. Thinking back, it wasn't a super-drawn-out process. I mean, over less than a year, I would say, it developed." There was a clear progression in how Ryan perceived daddyness: at first, it was "probably more like a feeling and just a fun little thing. And maybe by upper thirties where it was more of an identity, or like late thirties, early forties where it was more of an identity rather than just a fun thing talking to guys on the Internet or whatever."

Interest from younger adult men resulted in a *feeling* of daddyness, which eventually manifested into Ryan's daddy *identity*. As many of these stories demonstrate, app use was critical to men's transformation into daddies: younger and older men could connect more easily, and younger adult men could explore desires for older men that their peer groups might not have understood. (Because I recruited men via SCRUFF, the finding that app use helped transform men into daddies could reflect a selection effect of men who use apps. Men who do not use apps may still turn into daddies in response to interest from younger adult men they meet in person.) Most of the men I talked to did not independently decide to become daddies. Instead, a combination of aging and interest from younger adult men helped create a daddy consciousness.

The fact that men aged into daddyness highlights how sexual practices are dynamic over the life course. Becoming a daddy reflected, for many men, new patterns of sexual involvement with men in their twenties and early thirties, rather than a continuation of preexisting tendencies to have sex with men of this age range. In other words, many men began to have more frequent sex with much younger adult men, and this change went hand in hand with a newfound daddy consciousness. Regardless of exact circumstance—becoming sexually active with men later in life, exiting a relationship near or in middle age, or using mobile apps—men reported that they became daddies after experiencing interest from, and sex with, younger adult men.

Daddyness over the Life Course

Notably, many men became daddies after they themselves engaged in relationships with older men through their thirties. Many men experienced daddyness on both sides of the coin: as the younger man and as the older man, at different times in their lives. Daddyness, in other words, can be a life course phenomenon among gay and bisexual men. Importantly, most of the men I talked to did not call their former, older sexual or romantic partners "daddy" when they were together. Most men noted that widespread usage of the term is recent.

In total twenty older men (51 percent) reported a history of sex or romance with substantially older men in their young adulthood, either by preference or by happenstance. Turning into daddies themselves reflected how they aged into the daddy category and experienced interest from younger adult men. Greg (50), for instance, reflected on past relationships with older men, explaining that they were "very constructive and edifying relationships" that were "lovely role models on what it can [mean] to be a daddy." Greg and several other men used their past experiences with older men as a blueprint for what it means to be daddies themselves.

When I asked Tomas (44) about his sexual history, he noted, "I'm thinking of when I was in my twenties and I was looking for daddy, that type of thing." Yet he began feeling like a daddy around age forty himself, in part because he experienced a "midlife crisis": "It was like, 'Okay, I can no longer pretend that I'm twenty-nine plus one anymore. I'm almost halfway through my life and what am I going to do and how am I going to go through it?' It was a certain amount of midlife crisis but it's like, 'Okay, is this really how I need to be or where I am at?' And I really stopped and took a look at my life and where I was and who I was." After much reflection, Tomas explained, "It all kind of fell into place about the same time where my looking at it and then the way people would treat me and respond back to me." Having experienced what it was like being the younger man, Tomas eventually became a daddy. He did so after he evaluated his life at midlife and saw that younger adult men expected him to be a daddy, two events that happened simultaneously. He considered daddyness a new and important role for him later in life.

Caleb (57), too, explained that he became a daddy after he had previously sought older men. At the time of the interview, he noted, "My preference is somebody in that twenty to early thirties range." This preference was a marked change from earlier in life: "My preference when I was younger was to sleep with older men. And my first partner that I had was about fifteen years older than I was. And so I think when he and I broke up, I was in my midforties when our relationship ended." Entering the dating market as a single, middle-aged man changed how he saw himself as well as his sex life. "It was very obvious when I was out in the world and starting to date again that I had become the daddy [laughs]. And I hadn't really realized it before then. But at that age when I was online and in clubs, or bathhouses, or whatever, that I had become, that this role was now me." Caleb did not perceive this change negatively; in fact, as he noted, "It fit me. It actually was what I needed at the time." Caleb's shift was profound and also satisfying. Like Tomas, Caleb considered daddyness to be an important role for him at midlife.

Some men described initial reluctance at becoming a daddy, but later acceptance of that role. As Luis (54) explained, "My tendency when I was younger was to have relationships mostly with older men." This pattern later changed when younger men began looking at him as a daddy. "It's interesting to be on the other side," Luis noted. "And it's hard to explain because it's odd to be on the other side without my choosing to. They're the ones who see me as the daddy, rather than my internalizing and presenting myself as a daddy. So that's a curious experience." He continued, "I never really thought of myself as a daddy, until others started seeing me as a daddy. It was not a role I had thought about except as having the other person being older than me. And so it was curious when I was old enough that people were young enough that started seeing me as a daddy. And so it was not a decision that I made. It was almost a role I discovered by others identifying me as one." While this shift was initially confusing, Luis eventually came to accept his new role as a daddy. Luis, like many others, began to think of himself as a daddy only after younger men expected him to be a daddy.

Similarly, although Edgar (46) expressed mixed feelings at becoming a daddy due to his perception that many young men have a unidimensional idea of what a daddy is (i.e., assertive and inclined to top), he also noted that his preferences for men had changed. "I used to really gravitate towards guys who were ten years older," he explained. "And now the idea of somebody ten years older than me is typically not appealing." He attributed this change to his belief that older men are "overly set in their ways." Edgar's transition to daddyness was fairly recent. "I used to only like older guys, and then I became an older guy. And then I was like, 'What are all these younger people bothering me for?' I'm like, 'Oh, okay.' And so it's only been in the last couple years when I'm trying to lean into daddyhood I suppose." While still hesitant about embracing "daddyhood," Edgar nonetheless began to "lean into" it and, just as profoundly, began to prefer sex with men younger than himself up to around his own age.

While Mateo (55) did not report an extensive history of older men, as others did, he perfectly articulated the transformation from being the younger man to being the daddy: "You stop seeking a daddy when you become a daddy yourself." He continued, "In my opinion, when you are looking for a daddy it's because you're seeking that comfort, that refuge, that mentorship, that safety. When you start providing that for somebody else, you realize that now you have the responsibility. So it's almost like, I would say that you're acknowledging that you can also provide, what you have been given previously."

For several men, daddyness was something they experienced throughout their adult life course: having relationships with daddies and later becoming a daddy. This finding highlights two main themes. First, it shows that older-younger pairings between adults, whether sexual or romantic, are so deeply ingrained in communities of gay and bisexual men that some men adopt "roles" as the younger partner *and* the daddy over the course of their lives. Although many older men noted that the term "daddy" became widespread only recently, many also explained that relationships between older and younger adult men did exist in their youth. These relationships were not necessarily as widespread or popular as they are today, but they did exist. Second, the finding that many older men transformed from *having* relationships with daddies to *becoming* daddies shows that sexual practices for many gay and bisexual men are dynamic across the life course.

Given these stories, it is likely that many younger adult men today who are involved with older men will themselves transform into daddies during midlife. Of course, not all men will become daddies. Today some men in midlife and older adulthood only have sex with men around their own age, whereas others are sexually involved with younger adult men but avoid a daddy identity or role. At least some young men today will transition into one of those two categories over the coming decades instead of becoming a daddy. Many younger men will transition into daddyness, but not all men will do so. Factors such as personal preferences and external expectations also shape who becomes a daddy.

Why Did Daddies Become Popular?

Older-younger pairings between adults have existed for some time,[3] but the older men I talked to made it clear that older-younger pairings have become more popular over the past several years. "I think it truly is a phenomenon of the last decade," Neil (51) explained. Overall, "Daddies are really in right now," and are "considered sexy and sought after." As Ethan (60) similarly noted, "Within the last probably eight to ten years it seems like daddy was not an undesirable thing. I always felt like," he began, "back when I was younger it seemed like you had to be young, good-looking, with a good body, and nicely endowed to be a sexually attractive candidate in the gay world." Fortunately for Ethan, however, this pattern changed: "Now as I aged, I aged into this idea that being older wasn't a component that was a negative quantifier, and that when I got into that age in the late forties, fifties, that that component was actually desirable to men a generation younger than I am."

Seth (65) explained that the mainstream gay community adopted the daddy archetype from leather communities. "Someone my age now, when I was in my twenties, would be called a troll because the daddy thing wasn't a thing. The only part of the gay community where an older person had any level of dignity was in the leather community, and then you were referred to as old guard." Current meanings of "daddy" are rooted in gay leather communities.[4] Increased interest and visibility of older-younger pairings between adults, however, likely has as much to do with technological changes (such as apps) as the dissemination of daddy identities and desire for older men from leather communities. Regardless of the exact reasons behind this change, it is notable that older men went from being perceived as "trolls" to being perceived as highly desirable among a large segment of the gay world.

Older-younger pairings between adults may be more popular and visible today than they were in prior decades because the Internet and mobile applications allow men with desires for much older or younger adult men to connect more easily. "I've identified this way for over ten years," Ryan (48) began, "but I feel like in the last five it feels like to me the daddy culture has really come out more and is a bigger thing, and more common." He speculated, "The apps play into it. I mean, everything is so accessible. Whatever niche you like you can, you don't have to go to a bar and search all around or go to a cruising place or whatever, you can just go right on the apps and target whatever your niche is." Ryan may be onto something: perhaps the acceptability of desire for older men has increased hand in hand with the newfound ease of meeting much older or younger adult partners through apps. Zachary (59) agreed that the popularity of daddies had increased over the previous several years. "To me it seems like it's a newer term. I mean, maybe it was used in certain communities. I'm not sure. But when I was growing up I don't ever remember hearing that term. I mean, when I was a young gay man in my twenties and even thirties." Apps were a major reason why daddies became more popular, in his opinion. "When I was younger I never experienced talking with younger guys about daddies. I mean, you knew that there were a handful of guys, older guys that liked younger guys and vice versa, but it was a different, I don't know, it had a different feel to it. It was more like yeah, there wasn't this whole—because now there's even more hookups, I think, than there were back in the '70s and '80s in terms of—I mean, you can go online and get a hookup at any time, right?" It is not simply the newfound ease of meeting other men that drives the recent interest in daddies, according to Zachary. The interactional norms on the apps also affect the formation of older-younger pairings between adults. "Because you're kind of hiding behind your profile, I think people banter around these sexual terms or these terms that are related to sexual things more than you would even at a bar," he noted, including the term "daddy."

Importantly, the AIDS crisis also shaped the availability of men who were, or would have become, daddies. In the 1980s and 1990s, hundreds of thousands of gay and bisexual men in the United States died, particularly those aged thirty-five to forty-four.[5] Many men who were in or approaching midlife died. When Cody (59) was younger, "There really weren't many mentors or people even ten or fifteen years older at the time" due to the devastation wrought by AIDS. Mateo (55) similarly noted, "They're more common [today] because there are daddies. I mean I didn't have a daddy because our generation . . . I'm fifty-five. Fifty-five to seventy-five, that segment of the gay population was decimated. One of the reasons we couldn't find a role model is because there were none living. And it presents a very stark realiz[ation] that we lost a generation, we lost [a] wealth of knowledge right there." This loss profoundly affected some men. Greg (50) explained that his least favorite thing about being a daddy "is sometimes feeling insecure about what I have to offer or being aware of the fact that as gay men of a certain age—as a result of the AIDS crisis—there's not a whole lot of gay men alive who are older than me, at all. So there's sometimes I feel a sense of gap of like, "Whoa, how do I do this? Who are my daddies?'" This mass death severed existing older-younger pairings between adults and prevented other ties from forming. Additionally, older men who did survive may have experienced a loss in social status because younger gay men associated them with the AIDS crisis. Both reasons reduced the likelihood that older-younger pairings would form.

Recently, medical advances have greatly changed how HIV/AIDS is managed. Ryan (48) shared, "The whole PrEP thing and HIV being manageable and all that to me has revolutionized a lot of things. Like when I was a teenager and in my twenties, AIDS was a death sentence, and scary, and everyone was terrified, and condoms, condoms, condoms, condoms. And a lot of what would have been the daddies to me, part of that generation died out," Ryan explained, "whereas the daddies now, like forties, fifties now is a huge community, and [today] we're not scared of AIDS like we were. So it's just there's more daddies around, and we've gone through a lot since our twenties." Generation X has reached daddy age due to reduced rates of HIV transmission and medical technologies that allow people with HIV to live healthy lives. Similarly, preexposure prophylaxis (PrEP) allows men who are currently HIV negative to stay that way. All of these factors have increased older-younger pairings between adults today compared to the past several decades—and some older men are figuring out what "daddy" means as they go.

Other historical developments also likely affected the increase in desire for older men, including greater support for LGBTQ rights and greater tolerance for niche sexual interests.[6] Zachary (59) explained, "And then also being gay being more acceptable, even culture in general has been more sexual, so it's a little easier to, like more fetish type things and sexual things are more socially acceptable. I think all of that plays into it, why it's more common or acceptable or however you'd want to say it. I think it's always probably been there, younger guys into older guys and vice versa and all that. And now we kind of fetishize a lot of things, too, so it's become its own thing." Greater openness toward a variety of niche sexual interests, combined with support for LGBTQ rights, may have also facilitated greater interest in daddies. Reduced stigma toward nonnormative sexual desires, in other words, may have encouraged men to explore desires for adults much older or younger than themselves.

Other men suggested that the interest in daddies is due to younger men wanting a masculine role model, in addition to other historical factors. "The psychosexual phenomenon that's going on is like the most, probably the largest thing that's happened in the gay movement since—a few things have happened," Jake (52) noted. "Stonewall, the '70s, the AIDS epidemic, the very liberal coming out of the 2000s and '90s, the pride of it, the actual liberation, and then the absolute movement of young men being drawn to a father figure." A variety of social changes have led to greater visibility, acceptance, and interest in older-younger pairings between adults. Whether young men today are in fact more drawn to a gay or bisexual "father figure" than in prior decades is speculation that requires empirical support. Although this topic requires further research, the stories of the men I talked to provide important insights into why older-younger pairings between adults have become more popular over the past ten to fifteen years. Mobile apps that connect adult men of different cohorts, medical advances that treat or prevent HIV/AIDS, and greater social acceptance of sexual diversity have all likely increased the popularity of daddies.

2

What It Means to Be a Daddy

Apart from age and certain body traits, like looking older or having gray hair, the men I talked to described several aspects of daddyness. Their collective responses show that "daddy" is imbued with complex meanings and is not simply a sexual or physical archetype. Older and younger men described similar characteristics associated with daddyness. There were three main categories of these traits. First were age-related traits such as experience and stability. Second were personality traits, particularly dominance and leadership abilities. Third were characteristics that involved connections between older and younger adult men, including mentorship and nurturance. Each of these broad categories overlapped to form a common set of traits associated with daddyness. Although most older and younger men associated daddyness with age to at least some degree, most men also agreed that age alone was not sufficient to make one a daddy.

Notably, "daddy" did not mean "sugar daddy." Both older and younger men tied daddyness to financial stability, but few shared stories about sugar daddy arrangements such as paying for sex or purchasing expensive gifts. Older men did more often pay for dates and typically paid a higher proportion of household expenses (if they lived with a younger man), but did so because they had much higher incomes. Most men, both older and younger, explicitly stated that they did not seek sugar daddy dynamics in their pairings.

Daddyness is also racialized. The older men I interviewed identified as white, Latino, and Middle Eastern, rather than Black or Asian American, despite large populations of both groups in the Chicago metro area. Racist stereotypes of Black men as hypermasculine and Asian men as submissive likely constrain their ability to adopt secondary sexual identities such as daddy. Additionally, the meanings men associated with daddyness are racialized: leadership, for instance, is a characteristic associated with white masculinity. Although men of all racial/ethnic identities can embody daddy characteristics, racist stereotypes none-theless shape people's perceptions of these traits, either consciously or subconsciously.

Two other important themes arose when men told me their stories. First, older Latinos discussed the difference between "daddy" and "*papi*." The meanings of "*papi*" differ depending on the cultural context and situation. However, the meanings and practices Latinos associated with daddyness were similar to those of white men. Thus, "daddy" and "*papi*" have different meanings; they are not simply different words for the same concept.

Second, stories of the younger men show that the term "boy" is not simply the reverse of "daddy." (As a later section will explain, "boy" is sometimes applied to adult men aged eighteen and older.) Few younger men identified as boys, and there were fewer practices and meanings associated with "boy" than with "daddy." Thus, whereas daddy was a fairly well-developed identity with a rich set of meanings and practices associated with it, the same was not true for boy among most of the men I talked to.

Age-Related Traits

Experience

Eighteen of the older men tied daddyness to nonsexual experience, and eleven tied it to sexual experience. As Todd (57) explained, daddies are "a little bit more experienced and settled in general life issues." The term "daddy" "connotes more experience, [a] more experienced older gay guy" (Ryan, 48). This kind of life experience only comes with age, most explained. Brett (43), for instance, noted, "Somebody could be really successful and really far along in their career at the age of twenty-nine, but I don't feel like they have the same life experience. I'm a completely different person now than I was at twenty-nine. I'm a completely different person now than I was at thirty-five. And for the better, I think. So in terms of age, I guess it's not necessarily the number, it's how long you've been around and how much you've experienced." Life experience affected how older men interacted with younger adult men, and vice versa. "People realize that being older, that you have more experiences in the world and that they can learn from that," Neil (51) explained.

Younger men often intentionally sought to learn from the experiences of older men, and older men appreciated this dynamic.

Older men's experience did not simply fade into the background; it was a foundation on which older and younger adult men could connect. Charlie (49), for instance, reflected on a dynamic he had with a man about half his age: "I'm twice your age, I've lived a much longer life, I've got a much more full history of experiences. And we're at different places in our lives. At certain levels we meet and we can connect." Several men noted that daddies were marked by "emotional stability," Steven (60) described, due to the fact that "they've been through the whole emotional roller coaster of their twenties." This stability put men in a position to mentor younger men and help them through issues they were experiencing. Although meanings of daddy that originated from leather communities typically refer to sexual experience,[1] responses of the men I talked to indicate that, among the wider population of gay and bisexual men, nonsexual experience is also a basis for connections between older and younger adult men.

At the same time, other men specified that sexual experience, specifically, allowed them to make older-younger pairings fulfilling for the younger adult man. "I would say having been involved in active sexual relations for a couple of decades," Todd (57) began, "[I have] a lot of different experiences to pull from. And that definitely helps for younger guys that are trying to figure things out and have lots of questions." Sexual experience came with a sense of responsibility for some men. "I guess there's a responsibility, because you're older, of watching out for younger guys and making sure that what I do with them is exciting to them and fun, more so than if they were older and I wouldn't have to worry about it so much," Logan (60) explained. Having sex with younger adult men was, in part, an intergenerational transfer of knowledge: "We all can certainly recognize when we make love with someone who is experienced and what that's like," Graham (51) noted. "And so there's a lot of information in that. And then there's also the cultural information." Indeed, "lovemaking," he said, is itself "a piece of information." Older men enjoyed the sex they had with younger adult men, and they also used these encounters as an opportunity to teach younger adult men how to have good sex.

Older men's sexual experience was particularly important for some young adult men, who had little to no prior experience with other men.

"In some instances, some of the guys would like to have their very first sexual experience and I'm happy to assist with that, realizing that it may be a little clumsy or a little more brief than I would prefer, but I'm okay with that," Jay (58) explained. "I let them choose what we do and when we do it and how fast we go or don't go," to ensure that the experience is "nonthreatening" and "positive" for the younger man. One reason why Jay is okay with "clumsy" sexual encounters is that Jay "didn't come out of the closet until very, very late in life. And," he said, "I think had I had someone to mentor me or someone to help me, I'd [have] had a very, very different life than I ended up having." Sexual experience and the informal mentorship associated with it could help younger adult men learn how to have fulfilling sex with other men. Because there is little formal education that teaches men how to have male-male sex, most such knowledge is gained through discussions and sexual encounters with other men. Older men's greater sexual experience, and their desire to use it to teach younger adult men how to have fulfilling sex, constitute an intergenerational transfer of knowledge specific to gay and bisexual men.

Different levels of experience between older and younger adult men could result in a power dynamic, but not necessarily a manipulative one. "I guess there's a bit of a power dynamic, too, where the older guy [has] power over the younger ones, but not in any kind of coercive or evil sense," Logan (60) explained. "It's just like, 'Hey, I've been around the block, I know more than you, so just sit back and enjoy that and let me take you for a good ride.'" Relatedly, "I'm better at sex than younger people because of my experience," Jordy (57) began. "I expect more and I want to do more and if they don't kiss well or something, I'm more proactive in making things more fun and with my experience and not making it just so emotionless and just sex and leave." He continued, "So when I'm feeling like that kind of daddy role . . . it's not just sex and feeling more kind of something more emotional, I guess, during sex." While all types of power dynamics can be abused, few men—older or younger—reported dynamics that seemed coercive or manipulative. Instead, older men used their greater experience to make sexual encounters more enjoyable for younger adult men.

Younger adult men, too, connected experience to daddyness. Like older men, younger men referred to both nonsexual and sexual experience. Tyler (33) reported that older men "tend to have a lot of patience to deal with life issues because they've lived longer." Experience did not lead only to greater knowledge. According to Tyler, experience also made older men more patient and willing to help younger men. Terry (24) similarly explained, "The more life experience you gain, the more naturally you assume the mentorship role in the first place. And so people who are older can tend to adapt daddy-like conduct and qualities over time as a result of their personal maturation and development." Cyrus (25) explained this dynamic slightly differently, noting that older men have "a mature perspective" and "that's important to me, perspective." Jamal (23) provided a more detailed description: "It also entails a certain psychology of a person who's been around the block and has ideas on how things should go, and has a confidence to their walk, like they've got a mature man's swagger, for lack of better words. I feel like men walk and boys trot, but men who are daddies have a swagger to their step where they're confident in who they are and where they want to be in the world, and even when they're unsure of things they still pursue that unsureness with confidence." The confidence associated with experience distinguishes daddies from younger men. Daddies are not simply older men; they are experienced, patient, and confident older men who use their knowledge to mentor younger adult men.

Several older men also explained that daddies are confident because of their life experience. This confidence exists because, as Ryan (48) explained, "You're older, you're more confident than when you're in your twenties." Ryan elaborated, "Being established in my career, and having the extra income" is also related to "the confidence thing." Confidence emerged from both sexual and nonsexual experience. Wyatt (66) described that a daddy is "a guy who's confident and in charge and willing to take control in whatever situation you may find yourself in." Being confident, for Wyatt, means "a lot of things. For me first would probably be personal security in terms of sense of self—that I know who I am, I'm comfortable with that, I see other people in relationship to where, [I know] who I am, not trying to fit myself into who they are. I think it also goes with some sense of financial security—that I think probably people associate daddy with somebody who has some things figured out. I wouldn't expect somebody to be identifying as a daddy who didn't have some sense of security in various ways." The contrast between the level of experience—and confidence—of older and younger adult men appealed to several men. Caleb (57) explained, "I'm confident in myself, I'm confident in my sexuality, I'm confident in who I am in a sexual relationship. And I think that that's maybe why I like to sleep with younger men because maybe they're not so much. Maybe they are kind of learning that or maybe they're really into it or whatever, but they don't have a lot of experience. . . . There's an eagerness that they bring to it that it's nice to be able to mix with some experience and with a different take on it." Caleb and other middle-aged men enjoyed sex with less experienced younger adult men. The reason for this preference was twofold: sex with younger adult men was an opportunity to sexually mentor them, and the large age gap added a unique dynamic to sexual relationships. Older men's experience also gave them the confidence to make encounters with younger adult men enjoyable for both parties.

Stability

Several older men noted that stability, whether emotional or financial, is a component of daddyness. Men did not describe this characteristic as often as other traits, but it was important for those who did describe it. Stability is tightly connected to experience, given that men's life experience provided a solid foundation from which to mentor younger adult men. As Todd (57) described, daddyness involves "providing that sounding board and voice of guidance on some things and that general feel of stability . . . I guess whether they're looking for it in their own lives or it's something that's currently lacking, perhaps. Or they didn't feel that they got enough of that and so they're still looking for a little bit more of that guidance and stability as they're getting a little bit older, but venturing out into new things, and they're a little unsure about what's going on." Younger men may be attracted to older men's stability, as they may desire a role model who can show them how to navigate life. Steven (60), relatedly, defined a daddy as "an older man that I think younger men look up to as far as stability. I would just say someone that's older and grounded and mature."

Graham (51) specified that emotional stability is central to daddyness. "Going a little deeper, I have emotional stability and I think that also reverberates in my household between me and my husband. We have emotional stability so therefore our household has emotional stability."

This stability comforted the younger adult men in their lives. "I'm really proud of our whole network of boys, brothers, that we call brothers. Everyone here enjoys that emotional stability and they tell us that, and they tell me that." Graham took pride in this emotional stability and the effects it had on the younger men in his life. "So that's the thing I'm the most proud of, I think, from a daddy [trait]. I've got my emotional shit together. And I'm happy to share in that or not. I can live in it and be in it, and a lot of guys enjoy that. There doesn't need to be discussion or I'm not a therapist. . . . I'm leading by example, and I think that's a good daddy trait. There you go. Lead by example. That is definitely my best daddy trait." As with the theme of life experience, older men associated their own stability with the ability to mentor younger men or to provide a blueprint for how to navigate life. Tomas (44), relatedly, reported that for some men, "I'm perfectly okay with being the solid rock in their life right now." He elaborated, "To me, daddy is somebody who you can come back to and feel comfortable with. And I'm glad that they felt comfortable to come back to me and to curl up against me and talk about it and work through something together and experience something together and then when we were both ready, move on." Older men used their emotional stability to emotionally support younger adult men.

Greg (50) provided a helpful contrast between "daddy" as a casual descriptor versus "daddy" as a set of characteristics that facilitate meaningful relationships with younger adult men. On one hand, "Different people use the term differently of course, and in some situations it's used more loosely, like if a guy at a bar or online is like, 'Hey, daddy'—to me, that's a fetish, fetishistic thing. He wants to fuck around with an older guy who he can call 'daddy,' that's cool." In terms of daddy-younger relationships, however, a different dynamic is present. "But, fathering or daddy in one of our relationships—like with the younger men who I mentioned earlier—it's more, it's a little more substantive. I think my husband [Graham] may have mentioned this to you, but we frequently hear from other guys that our marriage and our presence in their lives creates a sense of emotional stability. And that to me is a parenting thing that bleeds over into daddy, I guess." A key component of daddyness is the ability to use personal stability to create meaningful connections between older and younger adult men. Older-younger connections are not exclusively sexual; they are often emotional too.

Personality Traits

Dominance, Control, or Leadership

Apart from age and mentorship, dominance or control was one of the primary themes older and younger men described as central to daddyness. Put simply, being a daddy could mean that a man likes to "take charge" (Zachary, 59) or "gives the lead role" (Steven, 60). This tendency was often tied to an imperative to care for younger adult men. Steven (60) phrased it simply: a daddy is "more of a caregiver, like more the one that leads." Similarly, as Diego (43) explained, "I would describe it generally as a dynamic between two people where one is taking on a more perhaps dominant or taking care of, or . . . I think it can be multiple things, right, depending on the people and whatever. But taking on some sort of role that could be associated to age or fatherly or whatever in the dynamic to somebody who is on the other end of a spectrum." As Diego's response indicates, dominance is not always sexual. Although being dominant *could* signal problematic power imbalances, few younger men discussed this issue. Sexual dominance (which did not necessarily mean topping) was tied to consensual power dynamics that both older and younger adult men found arousing. Nonsexual dominance was more limited in scope and referred to specific situations in which younger and older men preferred the older man to be assertive.

Several older men reported that daddies were dominant in both nonsexual and sexual contexts. As Wyatt (66) pointed out about daddyness, "Partly it's a matter of control. And there I don't even mean control in a traditional sexual way of calling all the shots, although I'm very capable of doing that and very comfortable doing that." Instead, Wyatt explained, "It's a sense of control of I feel like I'm always in control, even if I'm not being the more assertive in a given situation. It's always like I can step back and I'm able to look at whatever situation it is and continue to make decisions for myself that I'm comfortable with and I know what's going on." In other words, for several men, including Wyatt, *control* was not necessarily being *controlling*; control could simply mean being assertive. It could also mean, as Charlie (49) mentioned, being "dependable," "reliable," and making sure "that everything will be taken care of."

Younger men agreed that daddyness was tied to dominance in some sense, albeit within a consensual dynamic. The younger men I talked to sometimes found this dynamic difficult to explain. "I don't want to say authoritarian, that's the wrong word," Joshua (23) noted. "And not paternal, either, because that gets messy." Instead, "An element of age-based authority to it, I guess is the easiest way that I could put it." This "authority" was welcome. As Tyler (33) described, "A daddy needs to take on part of that to where there's just a little bit more dominance exuded." He continued, "With some of the older people I've been with, the ones I do find least attractive are probably the ones that are the most even-keeled or just even energy, they're neither submissive nor dominant. And I think the ones that I have enjoyed the most are probably the ones that are a little bit more on the hyper-dominant side. And those would be the ones I guess I consider daddies." Tyler, like several other younger men, preferred older men to be dominant in some way. Putting this differently, Jacob (27) noted that daddies have "a general sort of assertiveness, or being daddy in the sense of like daddy calls the shots kind of thing." Younger men did not simply tolerate older men's assertiveness; many preferred it.

As James (28) detailed, a daddy is "someone who exudes gentle dominance and who at least carries an air of experience that you don't have, and someone who is very nurturing." He elaborated, "A daddy is someone who is more probably dominant or someone who is, I guess, the one who sets the pace. He has his idea of how things are going to go and he is telling you as the older figure, the father figure, the daddy, leading you along the way."

Why do many younger men prefer older men to take control, particularly when men are taught to be assertive? David (27) offered an answer: "It's just nice sometimes to follow somebody else's lead and take a more submissive role." Daddies allow younger men to experience a break from the pressures of masculinity. "I feel like the confidence that comes with being a daddy helps them take that lead and make decisions and stuff in the bedroom and outside of it, and that's really nice and feels good when somebody first expresses an interest [in] you and also then kind of determines the course of the experience. It's nice to just roll with it," David elaborated. Austin (27) explained a similar dynamic. "Most attractive is I think the confidence and the domineeringness because [in my job] . . . I'm always having to be in control of my environment." Consequently, "When I am partnered with someone who can take control, I feel I can trust to take control, then that makes me feel a lot better. And usually it's easier to trust someone else to take control, and I feel that they are more experienced and they have that confident air about them, that is usually correlated with older men for me." Sex with older men gave Austin the opportunity to enjoy sexual pleasure but without feeling pressure to be in control, which he may feel with someone his own age.

Allowing daddies to be dominant in certain situations fulfilled three main functions for younger adult men. First, older men's leadership allowed younger men to learn how to handle particular situations. For instance, in sexual encounters, seeing how older men proceeded from one step to the next gave younger adult men knowledge about how to navigate similar situations in the future. Second, as the next section explains, older men's sexual dominance fulfilled a sexual kink for many younger adult men. Many found it arousing to have sex with someone in a different life stage.

Third, and relatedly, older men's dominance provided younger men a reprieve from the pressures of masculinity. These pressures are particularly stressful during emerging adulthood, between the ages of eighteen and twenty-nine, a time during which individuals establish their career, determine what they want out of life, consider how they can achieve their life goals, explore their identities, and experience continual change in relationships, work, education, and residential location.[2] Put simply, being a young person is stressful. Some younger men want a more experienced older man to take control. Handing over control in certain situations, especially sexual ones, affords young adult men sexual pleasure without pressures or expectations they experience in other parts of their lives.

Sexual Dominance

The majority of both older and younger men tied dominance to a consensual sexual power dynamic between adults, or what Ryan (48) referred to as a "submissive-dominant relationship" and Graham (51) described as a "power exchange." Finn (64) explained that being a daddy means that he is sexually "somewhat alpha I guess. And I'm not like [into] domination or anything, or S&M, but I kind of take charge. I'm not passive sexually." Tomas (44) was on the same page, saying older-younger play "tends to be a lot more dominant type of position, energy, and behavior." Robert (69) similarly mentioned, "Sometimes it's a little discipline, sometimes taking the dominant role, sometimes encouraging a boy to think outside the box and explore a little bit." This "encouragement" was tied to mentorship: "Spanking, bondage, I have some experience in BDSM. And sometimes like to help someone explore that side that they have an interest in but haven't found someone that they either trust or that they're comfortable with." Older men who were interested in BDSM enjoyed teaching these practices to younger adult men, whereas younger men who were interested in BDSM appreciated older men's greater experience.

Todd (57) explained the dynamic of dominance clearly, and like several others, tied daddyness to topping: "Typically with the daddy scenario it's really more of taking the lead and being the more dominant one in the sexual experience." He continued,

> Well, generally, for most of these kinds of situations, I'm pretty much the more dominant and aggressor, or shall I say initiator of any contact, so it's like I'll be the first one to engage in touching and kissing and be the one to guide from one step to the next. Kind of leading when the clothes come off and moving from one position to the next. So it's definitely a lead kind of a position. Ninety-nine percent of the time I'm the top, so if there's ultimately going to be anal intercourse, I'll be the top for that sort of a thing. It doesn't happen in all cases. Sometimes the sexual contact might just be oral. So it just depends from one guy to the next.

Jake (52), similarly, explained, "Generally they'll want me to be the top. They will definitely want to be bred," which means having sex without a condom, resulting in the top ejaculating inside the bottom.[3] Ethan (60) agreed and shared that younger adult men "want their daddy to breed them." Similarly, Seth (65) noted, "Being a top is a big part of it because I think daddies who are tops are much more common than daddies that are bottoms. And if you look at the apps or you look at the sites, the daddies that are bottoms identify and they make a point of saying that, where tops don't. I think the daddy role, the assumption is—well, at least from what I've noticed over the years—is that I think daddies in general are thought of more as tops, so they're thought more of as a dominant individual." Not all older men are tops, but the association between age and topping encouraged bottom daddies to explicitly state their preferences for bottoming in their online profiles. Daddies who topped did not necessarily have to state their preference, since younger adult men may simply assume it. Several (although not all) men who enjoyed topping younger adult men tied this practice to dominance as a manifestation of daddyness.

Greg (50) provided a more nuanced account of dominance and topping. Although Greg described himself as versatile, he also noted that he typically tops. Unlike many other men, however, he clarified, "I can be very directive sexually, saying what I want or asking for what I want, but I don't see that as being authoritative or dominating. It's like a form of leadership, I guess, or initiative." This leadership was not necessarily dominance. Nonetheless, he noted that a lot of younger adult men "want to please daddy and that's fun sexually." Greg also implicitly tied topping to daddyness, particularly on apps. "If I'm on the app—whether I'm in town or out of town and I'm looking for sex now and I see a younger guy's profile, who specifies that he's open to daddies, it's my opening line, like. 'Big dick daddy here.' Boom. Or, 'Want some daddy dick?' So yeah, I'm very, pretty direct and pretty straightforward about it." Dominance and leadership are distinct, and topping is not necessarily related to either, although some older men described these three concepts as overlapping.

Many younger men echoed these themes of dominance and, often, topping. Chris (33) explained that a daddy is "someone who tends to be more dominant, someone who tops more often. But also is respectful." Tyler (33) too explained that a daddy is "an older guy that is verse or top verse in the bedroom, that likes to take control." ("Verse," which stands for "versatile," refers to interest in both topping and bottoming. "Top verse" or "verse top" signal an openness to bottoming, but a preference for topping.) Justin (26) agreed. "I'd say I guess a daddy is typically a top, typically more—I don't want to say caring, but like takes care of the relationship or the sexual relationship, is more in charge, kind of is the one who calls the shots or says what it is, and a daddy is someone who is obviously older." For some men, including Benjamin (26), verbalizing these dynamics was also tied to daddyness. "It plays out in a lot of verbal ways. I think, just to throw some terminology out there, but 'breeding their boy' is used, and 'taking care of daddy,' 'obeying daddy.' I think it really does take on kind of a verbal manner, the relationship." Daddies could demonstrate dominance in a variety of ways: by topping, "calling the shots," leading the sexual encounter, or verbalizing power differentials in the context of role play.

Even as there was a common association between topping and daddyness, this association was not universal. Many men *did* tie penetration practices to daddyness: nineteen older men noted that topping younger adult men was part of daddyness. Others were versatile with younger men, preferred to bottom, or were tops but simply did not consider topping to be a daddy trait. Relatedly, twenty-five older men tied daddyness to consensual power dynamics, but several noted that control was not necessarily the same thing as topping. As Zachary (59) explained, "Even though I'm lately advertising myself as more of a bottom I still have younger guys approach me, so they'll approach me as a daddy, but knowing that I'm going to play more of the submissive role. But I think even with that said, except for a few circumstances, at the end of the day I'll be telling them what to do. So I'm that daddy role. I'm more of the boss role. Even though I may be sexually subservient." Sexual control or dominance was not necessarily tied to penetration for Zachary or others. Instead, being assertive or leading a sexual encounter were how some older men established dominance, particularly those who bottomed. Steven (60) echoed this thought: "Currently I would say the daddy role plays itself out into I direct what we're doing and let's try this position, now let's move here. I would say that's more of a daddy role, taking charge of it." Daddies could "take charge" regardless of whether they topped, bottomed, both topped and bottomed, or strictly engaged in oral sex.

Indeed, bottoming could *enhance* daddy dynamics because some older men were more verbal about daddy language when they bottomed to reinforce their sense of control. As Diego (43) mentioned, "Sexual position definitely plays a part in it. If they're more of a top and I'm looking to get pounded or something, then I'm definitely going to be like talking daddy, yeah." This type of "talking," he said, "I would tie it to dominance and submission." Even Todd (57), who described himself as a top "99 percent" of the time, noted that daddies could bottom. Reflecting on a recent sexual encounter, he noted, "Well, even though he was topping, I was still the more dominant in that scenario and still even led where that scene was going, even though I was bottoming in that particular case. So how it's similar is I'm still in the lead position, being the more dominant." He continued, "I don't necessarily see the daddy position as necessarily having to be top versus bottom."

Older men engaged in a variety of sexual practices and had many preferences, which did not necessarily reflect a "dom top daddy" archetype. Even some top daddies explained that topping was not the only ingredient necessary for a dominant-submissive sexual dynamic. Neil (51), for instance, explained, "That's the expectation sexually, not just topping, but there's dominance within that sexual play." Although older men often tied topping to daddyness, they more often tied *dominance* to daddyness—and dominance could be established regardless of penetration practices. Younger men agreed. As Kyle (25) mentioned, "Some daddies can be considered like a bottom guy, but they tend to still be more masculine about it and everything, such as like being a power bottom or something along those lines." Overall, although there is an association between topping and daddyness, as well as between dominance and topping, enough men distinguished these three concepts that it is important to not conflate them. Daddies can be dominant or assertive without topping.

Interestingly, seven younger men typically topped, including with older men. Their topping preferences highlight how penetration practices, while often associated with age gaps, are not universal. Some men simply prefer to top or bottom regardless of the age of their sexual partner. Other younger men I talked to were versatile regardless of the age of their sexual partner. At the same time, seven other younger men indicated that they bottomed more frequently with older men than with younger men.[4] Several explained that this pattern was intentional: they enjoyed bottoming with older men more than topping. As Chris (33) detailed, "I bottom much more often with older men than guys around my age. I'm much more often a top with guys around my age. I let them take control more than I do with guys around my age." What was the reasoning behind this dynamic? "Maybe it's what I seek out with older guys, like the types of older guys that I seek out. I get that experience, I guess, of having someone else be in control." Several younger adult men enjoyed situations in which older men took control, thus giving them a momentary break from the pressures of their lives.

WHAT IT MEANS TO BE A DADDY | 47

Not all younger adult men bottomed for older men solely because they wanted older men to take control, however. Two younger men explained that they bottomed for older men in part because they believed that older men are used to experienced sexual partners and they are not sure they can meet their expectations. As Tyler (33) explained,

> I usually feel comfortable topping people my own age group. I don't know why that is or if just it's easier for me to be dominant closer to someone my own age because I feel like we're in a relatable moment in time for life experience. Whereas when I'm with older guys I would always be a bottom first, and then if they're like, "No, I actually prefer to bottom," then I'd be like, "Okay, gosh, well I can top, that's fine." I mean, or if they said they're a complete bottom, then gosh, I would try to top, but for me it would be slightly embarrassing because I know it probably wouldn't live up to what they were expecting. I think that's the biggest difference.

Tyler enjoyed topping but was self-conscious about his lack of topping experience compared to older men and did not want to disappoint them. David (27) noted a similar dynamic.

> I think with older guys I am much—not much more—but I'm more likely to just bottom 100 percent of the time than with younger guys who I feel a little bit more comfortable with younger guys being casual about it, in a way. So because it's more casual, there's less stress, and less pressure, and then I feel like we can just fuck around and I don't need to be good at it. So I tend to top more with younger guys because I feel less pressure. But that's really variable. I would say I bottom 80 percent of the time across the board.

The stories of Tyler and David suggest that they may become more open to topping older men in the future, if they gain enough experience to be confident about their topping skills.

Overall, younger adult men had a variety of preferences for topping, bottoming, or both, which sometimes varied with the age of their partner but not always. Additionally, younger adult men who bottomed often tied this practice to a desire to be dominated, particularly by older men, but there were also other reasons they bottomed, including a lack of confidence in their topping abilities. In short, men's reasons for topping, bottoming, or both are multifaceted.

What about Sugar Daddies?

In contrast to stereotypes, no older men reported a "sugar daddy" arrangement with younger men. Most older men explicitly stated that they kept finances separate from their sexual or romantic relationships with younger adult men. Many reported that they "blocked" men online who asked them if they were "generous," a coded term that indicates a willingness to pay for sex. The older men I talked to rarely heard these types of requests, however.[5] "Sugar daddy" arrangements appear to be more common among heterosexuals: there are numerous apps/websites for older men and younger women to connect in such a way that a monetary exchange is a central component, compared to fairly few similar types of apps/websites for gay and bisexual men.[6] The stories of the men I talked to echo survey research that shows that older men are much more likely to offer emotional support to younger men than financial support.[7]

In total, twenty-one older men tied finances to daddyness, but all related it to one of three themes distinct from a "sugar daddy" arrangement: their belief that financial stability and career success is part of what it means to be a daddy; their willingness to pay a proportionately higher amount for bills than a romantic partner who earned less than they did; and their choice to treat dates to dinner, drinks, or gifts. Financial stability, for several men, was part of being a role model, but not a sugar daddy. Similarly, several older men found it acceptable to pay more for dates than the younger person, which makes sense given differences in average earning power between older and younger men. (Recall that the median income for the older men I talked to was $99,000, compared to $37,000 for the younger men—a massive gap.) Thus, "daddy" was tied to socioeconomic class, even as "daddy" did not mean "sugar daddy."

Many older men linked financial and career stability to being a daddy, even though they did not spend their money on younger men. When he noted daddy traits of his, Diego (43) said simply, "I am successful" and "I've got a salary that I think makes me financially stable." Caleb (57), relatedly, viewed his financial stability as an example of what younger men could have someday. "I think that just because I am financially stable and I have a nice house and I have a nice car and I've got a job and I'm stable," he began, younger men can see that "stability is certainly available to them too at one point." Financial stability, for several men, was part of being a role model. Jordy (57) relatedly noted, "I have a good job and good home and make decent money and I'm very responsible," and continued, "Part of the daddy experience is that they are meeting somebody that is established and not struggling like they are." Daddyness, according to Robert (69), meant being "financially successful, professionally successful, socially successful. Wore the daddy suit to work every day and went to daddy business dinners and could play the part pretty well because it wasn't even playing. It was who I was." Daddyness, to several men, meant being financially self-sufficient, but it did not mean spending that money on younger men.

Other men connected daddyness to treating dates to dinner, drinks, or gifts such as tickets to theaters or sports stadiums, similar to gendered dynamics among heterosexuals.[8] Santiago (43) explained, "If we go out on a date or out somewhere it gives me a lot of satisfaction to pay for whatever we are doing, using, or consuming," such as drinks. Similarly, Logan (60) noted that with his FWBs, "I'll take them out to dinner, I'll take them to lunch, and the expectation, I mean, I don't know if it's expectation, but I always [end] up paying." He added, "It's not really buying affection, but it's like just helping out somebody who couldn't necessarily afford something." Charlie (49), who made over half a million US dollars annually, also explained that when he and younger male FWBs spend time together in an evening he always pays. "I'm much further in my earnings arc than these people, and it's only natural I would pay and I want to pay. I would never, I don't feel right they pay." Mateo (55) also described this dynamic in pragmatic terms. "If I go with somebody that's under thirty, I'll pay for it. . . . It's simple things, or like if it's just coffee, you don't have to worry, I'll take care of it." This dynamic depended upon the age of the man. "So between thirty and forty, I wait for what the other person does, because I don't want to assume anything about what they do for a living. And at forty I assume that you're more stable. So that's why I assume that we're going to split it." Unlike sex work or sugar daddy relationships, in which money or gifts are explicitly exchanged for sex, several older men explained that they paid for date nights. They felt that this practice was reasonable given that they made more money than the younger adult man.

Most men in romantic partnerships with younger men, past or present, did not describe many asymmetrical financial dynamics. A handful of men noted that they paid more for certain bills, often because their younger partner made less. For example, Brett (43) explained that in a past relationship he paid for vacations he took with his former partner, and also paid two-thirds of their shared rent, for practical reasons: his partner "couldn't afford to pay as much as I could." Daddies are "settled in their career, in their personal, financial life," according to Brett. He further explained, "I liked to be able to be a provider for him." The desire to be a provider is likely linked to masculine ideals and may also reflect an interest in behaving in ways opposite the stereotypes of gay men as frivolous or irresponsible. Cody (59), the only older man in a cohabiting polyamorous relationship with a husband around his age and a much younger man, explained that their younger partner was only able to live in the type of house he did, and drive the car he did, because he lived with his two older partners. Nonetheless, Cody noted that this younger partner "works a full-time job" and that "a substantial amount of his check goes into the household and living expenses and living where and how we do and so on." A handful of men paid proportionally more for expenses than their younger romantic partners, typically because doing so made more financial sense, but even this arrangement was uncommon.

In sum, no older men described a "sugar daddy" relationship. Many did not describe any financial differences in who paid for dates or other expenses, regardless of age or income. Of unequal financial dynamics that did exist, most were such that older men paid more often for dates given that they made more money. Occasionally this asymmetry trickled over into partnerships as well, such that older men sometimes paid proportionally more for certain expenses given their higher incomes. Not all of the older men I talked to paid more for dates with younger men, but those who did typically explained this choice in pragmatic terms: making more money than the younger man. Thus, imbalances in who paid for certain items were not usually a problematic dynamic, but rather a choice that reflected huge income differences.

Younger Men and Financial Dynamics

Younger men described similar dynamics as the older men. Only one respondent, Justin (26), reported a sugar daddy scenario in which two older men on separate occasions paid him several hundred dollars to have sex. This situation happened a handful of times, "but it's not something that I actively seek out," he clarified. Otherwise, however, younger men echoed what the older men did: daddies are "financially established" (James, 28), have "a good job" (Jeffrey, 23), and perhaps pay more for dates or bills in line with their higher incomes. No one other than Justin reported anything similar to a sugar daddy arrangement. Indeed, the majority of younger men stated that there were no substantial unequal financial dynamics that existed between themselves and their older sexual or romantic partners. The connections they drew between daddies and finances were similar to those drawn by the older men, in that daddies were, as Chris (33) noted, "successful in their career, financially stable, all that." Alejandro (26) relatedly noted that a daddy is "someone who is, I guess, financially independent, they're not living with their family or anything, they live alone or are self-sufficient." This advantage cannot be overstated: daddies who live alone can offer a private, comfortable space. Younger men, who are more likely to live with roommates or family, may find this arrangement particularly appealing.

Large income gaps between older and younger men were obvious. "It's impossible to ignore the fact that 99 percent of the time they make more money than I do, they are far more financially stable, they've gotten most of their financial life taken care of, they have a home, they've bought a home or they are comfortable with where they are in their life, their career is mostly completely stable," Anthony (25) explained. Cyrus (25) echoed this sentiment: "To some point you have to accept the fact that somebody who's older by twenty or thirty years is going to be hopefully financially better off than me. And that's something that I'm not ashamed of. In fact they're kind of like a mentor to me in that way, where I could see myself where they're at in whatever, twenty, thirty years." Austin (27) similarly noted, "It's just advice. So it's more so like, 'Hey, I don't really know how to buy a house, what has your experience been?' Or 'I don't know how to go about improving credit score stuff, what's your experience been?' Stuff like that."

Older men's financial stability could improve the relationship they had with younger adult men and provide a blueprint for how younger men could someday have similar financial security. Much like the older men, younger men perceived older men's financial stability as something from which younger men could learn—but not directly benefit from monetarily. In other words, financially stable older men could be a role model for them. Younger men acknowledged that not all older men were financially stable. In their experience, however, middle-aged men were more stable, on average, than men in their twenties and early thirties, and this financial stability meant that younger men could learn from them.

Most younger men described a strong sense of personal autonomy that carried over into financial dynamics. "It's always been equal footing in that sense," explained William (29). Michael (30) added, "I've never been one to ask for money or to gain benefit from it. I'm financially stable. I'm my own man." Like others, Michael explained that there were rare circumstances in which the older man paid more. "Usually, when I was in my relationship, we would go on a date and each night I'd pay or he would pay and vice versa. There were instances, if he wanted to go on a trip and I couldn't afford it, he would subsidize me to go with him, but I would also pay as much as I could, be it hotel, or fees, or when I was going out to eat." Nonetheless, he noted, "I've always maintained my own budget and managed my own finances." Similarly, Joshua (23) mentioned, "I'm not really into the sugar daddy thing. I don't want anybody to pay my way or I don't want anyone to feel like they need to pay for me in any way, shape, or form, so I never ask for it." He will, however, "always take it up if somebody's offering," such as one time when an older man "just decided to buy me an eighty-dollar steak." Nonetheless, he clarified, "That's the farthest extent it goes." Jacob (27), similarly, noted that "I don't have any sugar daddies or anything. I've never really had an older man provide for me financially in that way." He continued, "I really think that financially it really does come down to the smaller things. It's like who buys the drinks if we go to a bar, or who's paying for the movie ticket if we go to the movies or whatever. It sort of defaults to this masculine/feminine role, almost. Or they'll pay for my Uber home or something. But that's sort of the extent of it." Jacob was one of the few younger men who drew parallels to gendered dynamics among heterosexuals.

Most younger men, in contrast, explained asymmetries in who pays for what in terms of income rather than masculinity or femininity. Anthony (25), for instance, explained, "I know that they realize that—because oftentimes we're talking over coffee or over dinner about what I do for work, stuff like that, just in general things that they could pick up on that would make sense to realize that I probably don't make that much money, so they offer to pay for everything." This dynamic was similar to a past partnership in which "I paid for groceries, I paid for some of the small things, Internet, but the big stuff, because he is ultimately the established one and the breadwinner, he paid for the mortgage and the large finances." Anthony was one of the few men who reported this type of asymmetrical financial contribution in a romantic partnership.

A desire for financial self-sufficiency often carried over into romantic relationships. Juan (25) and his partner in his early forties did not live together because "I've always been taught to be self-sufficient. I want to make sure that I can prove—and it's mostly for myself, prove to myself that I can provide for myself, not to depend on anybody else." He elaborated, "We had this conversation about living together, but . . . it brings me to this idea of like I don't have control over where I live because he already has this house, and he already has property that he owns. And so for me it's just like I'm coming into this household where nothing is mine, and so it's hard for me to feel comfortable in that space. Whereas in my space, I pay for my rent, I pay for my utilities, I pay for everything. I never ask him for money." Juan felt most comfortable living alone since he could be independent and have his own space. Amir (24), similarly, did not live with his two older partners (both around the age of sixty) and tried to make sure that finances did not affect their relationship.

> I would say, pretty equitable in terms of, when we go out to eat I try to make sure I'm paying my fair share of the check. Or if we're ordering food we alternate on who is doing the ordering, that kind of thing. There isn't a strong financial dynamic there and I explicitly try to avoid that because I feel like it's a power imbalance that I don't particularly like and I don't think it's a healthy pattern in a relationship. It lends itself to a sort of either a moocher and resentment thing or an exploitive and controlling thing, and either way I'm not a huge fan of that kind of power dynamic.

Amir, as with most of the other men I talked to, preferred egalitarian financial arrangements to avoid power imbalances.

The main financial asymmetries were, as older men also noted, on date nights. Tyrone (32) separately dates two older men (one in his early fifties and the other in his early sixties) and "they can tell I'm not really exactly rolling in it" because he has "a shitty office job." As a result, they were more likely to pay for dinners when they ate out together. Relatedly, Tyler (33) detailed, "Outside of someone being more well off than me there's a mutual understanding that it's less of a burden for them to pay for a dinner, it's never gone past that, just a dinner on a first date kind of thing. There's no financial gifts or shared finances beyond that." Noting a parallel dynamic, Benjamin (26) said, "It's never pay to play. It's never that sort of arrangement. But that being said, there are times when I have an arrangement or an encounter where an older male will take me to dinner, he will pay the bill, and then we have sex after that, so it almost takes on, not a financial situation, but it's, he pays for dinner type of thing." David (27), like others, explained, "I try to keep that [finances] to a minimum just because I like being independent," but he also found it acceptable for older men to pay for dates. "But there are some cases where, I don't know, there's been guys who really want to take me out for dinner as a treat because they're further along in their careers than I am, they have a lot more expendable income. It's like I can't go to a really nice restaurant, I'm living paycheck to paycheck, but they have that ability. . . . There have been a few guys who wanted to do something nice for me, and that is really nice and appreciated." Overwhelmingly, the most common type of asymmetrical financial arrangement was older men paying for a date night. While technically unequal, this dynamic did reflect financial realities: younger men typically made much less than their older sexual or romantic partners and therefore would have had trouble splitting the bill for their night out together.

A minority of young men did not even allow older men to pay for dates, despite their much lower earnings. "I'm a very prideful person, and so I think I go out of my way to ensure that that kind of line is drawn," Aydin (28) explained. "If it's someone that maybe I'm just starting to see or that I haven't seen or known for a while then I'll say, 'Let's go ahead and split the bill.' If it's someone that I've seen regularly, then either I'll offer to pay the bill if I have not yet, and they'll pay it the next time, and we'll take on that role of alternating." Similarly, "I have kept finances out of things. Every so often an older man would want to get me something, but I would always say no," James (28) noted. "If we go out anywhere I make sure the bills are fifty-fifty or I pay for my own things, and I don't accept a gift." This pattern reflected "a desire to remain independent." John (31), relatedly, explained, "There is no financial nothing. At the end of the day I don't necessarily want to be a kept boy because I want a partner, someone to actually walk hand in hand with." Choices to not allow older men to pay even for dates stem from younger men's knowledge that finances can potentially create power imbalances in relationships.

Maintaining financial independence was one way younger adult men sought to preserve their autonomy. It also likely reinforced their masculinity. Younger men described daddies as dominant and masculine, so doubling down on financial autonomy allowed some younger men to feel independent and thus more masculine despite pairing with men who were older, wealthier, and possibly more sexually dominant.

At the same time, the age gap between older and younger men also naturalized differences in income that may have been uncomfortable had the two men been closer in age. Because the higher-earning man was substantially older than the lower-earning man, the earnings difference made sense to both parties. Nonetheless, younger men were mindful of the potential for finances to negatively affect their relationships with older men and tried to prevent this dynamic from happening.

In sum, the men I talked to did not describe sugar daddy dynamics. Younger men were not gold diggers, and older men did not find the thought of being a sugar daddy appealing. Although many men tied financial stability to daddyness, most of the men preferred to keep their sexual and romantic pairings free from substantial asymmetrical financial dynamics. Many older men, though not all, were open to paying for date nights with younger men, and most younger men found this dynamic acceptable as well. Because of the vast earnings differential between younger and older men, most younger men did not consider it inegalitarian to allow older men to pay for dates. By paying a proportionately higher amount for bills and by treating dates to dinner and drinks, some older men "sweetened" their pairings with younger men in ways that are distinct from a sugar daddy arrangement. Both groups attributed this pattern to the reality that older men are typically more financially secure than men decades younger than themselves.

Daddyness and Race

The Chicago metropolitan area is racially/ethnically diverse, and SCRUFF caters to men of a variety of racial/ethnic identities,[9] which means that the lack of Black and Asian representation among the older men I talked to deserves analysis. The fact that no Asian or Black men responded to the research advertisement indicates that daddyness is racialized.

"Daddy" must be examined alongside racist patterns of stereotyping: Asian men are often portrayed as unmasculine,[10] whereas Black men are often framed as hypermasculine.[11] In both cases, racial stereotyping may constrain the secondary sexual identities Black and Asian men are able to adopt, such as "daddy." Black and Asian men experience racial stereotyping that follow them regardless of age. White men do not, and although Latinos also experience racial stereotyping, the type of racial stereotyping they experience evidently does not constrain a daddy identity. Thus, larger patterns of institutional racism, particularly those related to Black and Asian marginalization, shape likelihoods of daddy identification—just as institutional racism affects most aspects of social life.

Additionally, many of the characteristics men associated with daddyness are implicitly racialized. Men of all racial/ethnic identities can demonstrate leadership, for instance, but in the United States people more often associate leadership abilities with white men than with Asian American men or Black men.[12] Many of the daddy traits men described are gendered aspects of what one scholar described as a "normative" model of whiteness that includes "the most popular and idealized ideologies and expected ways of being white in the US context."[13] In other words, even though men of all racial/ethnic identities can display daddy characteristics and engage in daddy practices, many of these characteristics and practices are perceived in racialized ways and therefore perceptions of daddyness are also racialized.

Similarly, the perceived link between daddyness and financial stability likely affects who adopts a daddy identity. On average, Black households have lower incomes than white households, which means that many

WHAT IT MEANS TO BE A DADDY | 57

Black men may be excluded from daddyness due to socioeconomic class.[14] The effects of institutional racism—such as social processes that have denied Black Americans equal opportunity in education, occupations, and the criminal justice system—affect Black Americans' socioeconomic class standing and therefore also Black men's ability to adopt a daddy identity. Although Asian American households have higher average income than white households,[15] Asian American men are often considered less desirable than white men and therefore have more difficulty on the dating market.[16] Overall, racist stereotypes and racialized social processes implicitly racialize daddyness as white.

"*Papi*" and "Daddy"

Three older Latinos I talked to discussed "*papi*" in relation to "daddy." Their stories show that the extent to which "*papi*" and "daddy" share similar meanings for Latinos differs according to cultural and geographic context. Luis (54), who grew up in Puerto Rico, explained that he enjoys the term "*papi*" and that its use is widespread in Puerto Rico—but not necessarily in a sexual context. "Because I'm from Puerto Rico, everybody calls me '*papi*.' I actually like '*papi*.' It to me is very endearing. In Puerto Rico, this is an interesting phenomenon, in Puerto Rico today, straight men call each other '*papi*.' And so it's very, very common in Puerto Rico to use that term as a term of endearment to another man." The trend of straight men using "*papi*" is a recent historical development, however. "*Papi*" used to be limited to gay men. "But that was not the case all the time. I grew up [and] straight men would address each other as 'papa.' And then '*papi*' would be a gay thing, like somebody calls you '*papi*' to your face, it's because they're gay. That has changed. Today every single man, straight or gay, will call another man '*papi*.' And [it] has no sexual connotation at all." The way "*papi*" was used in Luis's young adulthood shaped the way he perceives the term today. "Because I grew up in an era where '*papi*' was a way that gay men would address other men, I have this fondness for it. And when in the United States people call me '*papi*,' I really like it. I really like it. It feels really nice [laughs]. 'Daddy,' remember that at the beginning of our interview, we talked about my first time hearing 'daddy' and sort of giggling because it sounded funny? '*Papi*' has never sounded funny. '*Papi*' has felt very natural. Inside and outside of bed." Luis enjoys the term *"papi"* in part because of meanings it had in Puerto Rico when he was younger. Although today *"papi"* can be a term of endearment between men regardless of sexual identity, it meant something different in his formative years: a term of affection between gay men.

Mateo (55), who was raised in Mexico, provided a different description of *"papi."* He explained that the term is more closely tied to age in Mexico than in the United States. "When I go out with somebody in Mexico, they call me *'papi.'* *'Papi'* in Spanish has a different connotation as *'papi'* in the United States, because literally in Mexico it could be the translation *'daddy.'* But here in the United States *'papi'* means like *'papi chulo,'* which could be somebody younger but dominant [in] the relationship or wants to be considered dominant in the relationship, regardless of age." Mateo described differences in usage "between Latin America and the United States": "The Latino culture in the United States uses the term *'papi'* to single out somebody from Latin descent that is very alluring, attractive—either because he is physically attractive or because he has that characteristic of being very attractive. But that's in the United States. If you go to Los Angeles, you'll see that they're calling someone, 'Oh he's a really nice *papi'* and he's like twenty-five years old. Or New York. Whereas in Mexico, it truly is more like a paternal, daddy, paternal thing." *"Papi"* in Mexico is associated with age, according to Mateo, whereas in the United States it is connected to dominance or attractiveness and not necessarily age. These meanings are quite different from those of *"papi"* in Puerto Rico, which, according to Luis, are tied to affection between men (platonic or otherwise) regardless of age. Clearly, meanings of *"papi"* differ across contexts.

Santiago (43), who grew up in a small central American country (which I will not name to protect his confidentiality), described a different definition of *"papi,"* one that is more negative. "I hate *'papi'* [laughs]. At least from my background, *'papi'* is not a daddy." Santiago elaborated on his disdain for the term. "[A] very spoiled child will call his dad *'papi'* instead of *'papa,'* *'papi.'* And that will be in a lot of circles. But *'papi'* in a more adult sexual way will be a stud. But not a daddy. It could be, but that's not the way you look at it, at least in my background." In parts of central America, *"papi"* may be a term that children use or, alternatively, a description for a desirable man regardless of age. This latter description is closer to the meaning Mateo described for *"papi"* in the United States. These varying explanations of the term *"papi"* suggest that its meaning differs across contexts, as does its relationship to age and sexuality.

"Papi" also takes on different meanings based on whether Latino or non-Latino men use it. Luis explained,

> In the US, I think daddy is racialized by using the word *"papi."* Because it's very clear that when non-Latinos use that word on me, it feels like part of what they're doing is exoticizing my Latinoness in the sexual relation. When other Latinos do it to me, then it becomes sort of a bonding of our Latino experience in the United States. But when white men or Black men or Asian men call me *"papi,"* they're using that word because they're not only excited about this older man, they're also excited about this Latino older man. So there is an element about the exotic when it is not used by Latinos.

Luis does not necessarily mind that non-Latino men called him *"papi,"* however, so long as they do so respectfully.

> As long as they recognize my complexity as a human being, I don't mind very much. I think the trouble is when they start making assumptions about who I am simply because I am Latino. That to me is problematic. But the thing about the fetish is that we are always going to be attracted to things that are different from us. And I don't think there's anything wrong with that as long as that doesn't in a way warp what this person actually is. And so I don't mind it when I am fetishized because that's part of the fantasy work.

Luis clarified, "I'm not having sex to find the father of my children, I'm having sex because I like having sex. And so part of that relationship, there's something very freeing about very open sexuality, because it is very much about fulfilling fantasies." Luis was happy to fulfill that fantasy so long as it did not cross over into how his sexual partners perceived and treated him: "For some people, fulfilling a fantasy is having sex with a Latino, that's fine. I have no problem with that as long as that doesn't turn into, they're making assumptions about who I am and what I'm going to do."

While Luis did not mind that some white, Black, and Asian men fe-tishized him for being Latino—and called him "*papi*" as part of that fetishization—Santiago disagreed. Reflecting on past experiences in which he was called "*papi*," he explained, "I didn't like it. I didn't like the '*papi*' part. Because I felt that if somebody was calling me '*papi*,' especially if it is a white guy, I feel that I was being profiled as a Latino already, and I'd say don't call me that." Like Luis, however, Santiago was comfortable when Latino men called him "*papi*": "There's a friend, an acquaintance who I am really attracted to, even though we haven't had sex. He calls me '*papi*' jokingly, or refers to me, 'Hey, *papi*, how are you? Hey, *papi*, ¿*Cómo estás?*' Like chatting or online or when we meet for drinks, whatever, and for me that's totally cool, and it's totally fine. He's Latino. So I'm totally cool with that. I think the problem with '*papi*' is when a white guy calls me that." Luis and Santiago both reported that non-Latino men used "*papi*" to fetishize them for being older and La-tino, although their reactions to this usage varied. Luis did not mind so long as his sexual partners respected him as a person and did not reduce him to a stereotype, whereas Santiago preferred that only Latinos called him "*papi*."

"*Papi*" and "daddy" are not necessarily interchangeable. The mean-ing of "*papi*" differs across national contexts and depends on who uses the term and in what situation. Interestingly, Luis, Mateo, and Santiago described daddyness in similar ways as the white men I talked to, which suggests that "daddy," unlike "*papi*," takes on meanings in the United States that are similar for Latino and white men. Whereas Latino daddies must navigate possible racial fetishization when non-Latinos call them "*papi*," however, white men do not. Thus, even though daddyness has similar meanings for both Latino and white men, Latinos may deal with racialized encounters that white men do not experience.

What about the Meaning of "Boy"?

The men I talked to occasionally referred to "boys," and some readers may wonder what this term means and whether it parallels "daddy." First, a clarification: "boy" refers to adult men aged eighteen through their early thirties. Just as heterosexuals often use the term "girl" to refer to adult young women, some gay and bisexual men use "boy" to refer to adult young men. The term "boy" can strengthen the playful sexual dynamic that relates to the age difference between two adult men. The term "boy" does not invoke fantasies about children. Furthermore, people who engage in daddy-boy role play do not pretend that the younger adult man is a child, and also do not pretend that the older and younger adult man are related. None of the men I talked to reported any fantasies about child-adult role play—in fact, many explicitly denied them—and as stated in the introduction, all of the men I talked to exclusively discussed sexual encounters with adults aged eighteen and older. Additionally, the youngest man I talked to was twenty-three years old.

"Boy" is not usually an identity or descriptor like "daddy." "Boy" has particular meanings in leather and kink communities, but identification as a boy does not appear to be typical outside of those settings, at least according to the stories of the younger men I talked to. When "boy" is used outside of leather/kink settings, it is often a playful descriptor or a purely sexual term used during flirtation or sexual encounters. In these cases, "boy" refers to a young adult man, often but not always sexually submissive to an older man. Of the twenty-six younger men I interviewed, nine explicitly denied that they perceived themselves as boys, eleven reported that they did not see themselves as boys but sometimes enjoyed the term's use in flirtation or sex, and just six stated that they did see themselves as boys.

Most of the younger men who did not perceive themselves as boys did not elaborate on their reasoning, although a handful did. Nicholas (30) reported that he did not identify as a boy because "daddy-son play in general isn't something that really appeals to me," whereas Alejandro (26) explained, "I don't really identify myself like that, but I've been called that and I don't have a problem with it." He continued, "I don't encourage it. I don't put a halt on it immediately either, but I'd rather them not do that." Amir (24), in contrast, stated, "I would say that's absolutely not how I would identify myself." His reasons relate to the fact that he is "pretty involved in the leather and kink community" and therefore associates "boy" with particular meanings in those settings. "I would say further using the term 'boy' as just for someone who's attracted to older men, it's a little bit disingenuous to use that term with that definition because it's more generally used in the kink community as someone who's submissive to a daddy." Additionally, as he noted, "I'm more dominant and I don't consider myself a quote, unquote, 'boy,' at least not in the leather community sense." Given that "boy" connoted submissiveness within leather/kink settings and was not necessarily tied to age in those settings, Amir did not think the term described him. DaShawn (27) disidentified with "boy" because of its racialized history. "I've never been called that. I haven't even heard it in that sense." He elaborated, "Without really going too deep into it, I think 'boy' is something that I think people in my racial background kind of find derogatory, in a sense, especially if you're an adult, because of [its] history." "Boy" was historically used to demean Black men, and for that reason DaShawn did not find the term appealing.

Eleven young men did not identify as boys, but sometimes found the term's use appealing when they flirted or had sex with older men. As Tyler (33) said, "I don't like being considered a boy." Instead, "It's fun to play that game for a few text messages back and forth," because "it's just nice for someone else to take control, but not in an aggressive sexual play way, just someone take the lead." Tyler had never been called a boy in a sexual situation, nor had he asked anyone to do so. "It's just a temporary flirtatious thing for me." Austin (27) agreed. "I like it when flirting. I don't like it when actually having sex. It's a fun flirty thing to say." Jeffrey (23), similarly, noted that the term "does turn me on a little bit," but at the same time, "it does feel a little weird." For that reason, he does not ask men to call him "boy" and does not give the term too much thought. "'Boy' generally is an okay word, I guess, to be called, for me, at least. I don't really think too much of it."

Other young men did enjoy "boy" in sexual situations, even as they disidentified with the term. "Boy" strengthened the unique dynamics that existed when there was a large age gap between two adult men. Aydin (28) noted, "If it's one of the more prominent identities that I label myself with I would say no. But in the role play sense or the playful sense, yeah." He enjoyed it in sexual encounters. "I think it just highlights the older-younger dynamic and I think that's what makes it exciting and intriguing, is the fact that it plays very much and emphasizes the already existing dynamic." "Boy," in other words, helped make the age gap part of the exciting sexual energy of the encounter. Similarly, "I don't use that word for myself, but I enjoy it when other people do," Jacob (27) explained. "It's predictable, it's stable. Not in a boring way, but like I know my role, and I know my expectations, and I know how to succeed at that. And maybe in some ways it's a way to disarm intimacy." To Jacob, "boy" established a framework for a fulfilling older-younger sexual encounter between adults, with guidelines for interaction. At the same time, "boy" felt objectifying in a way he found arousing.

> It's almost a similar thing of being called a slut, it's almost degrading. Obviously in a different way, like "boy" carries something different than "slut" or "whore" or whatever. But it's similar, belittling, but not in a bad way. I think it's objectifying, which I think is a good thing. It's like "boy," the sense of "boy" in a larger sense is diminutive, and when you think of that smaller thing, it's like you have less agency, maybe, but in this context it's all contextualized by these agreements that these consenting parties have bought into. And so yeah, I think it feels objectifying, which feels good.

"Boy" connoted submissiveness and objectification within consensual boundaries. Overall, the term created a distinct dynamic within older-younger encounters between adults that made them more exciting for younger men like Jacob.

Men who noted that they enjoyed the term "boy" in specific circumstances clarified that "it's almost always sexual. It's almost always during sex," as William (29) noted. "It is not a lifestyle that I have taken on, but it has been a role that I have played with." "Boy" could be fun inside the bedroom or while flirting, but not in most other aspects of life. Indeed, as Anthony (25) explained, "During sex being called 'boy' might be a turn-on. It just has that, not necessarily power dynamic to it, but sometimes the paternal aspect is very appealing." Anthony was not typically called "boy," however, nor did he ask men to call him "boy," since "the dad-son thing has never really worked all that well for me just because I'm independent." While Anthony was attracted to older men and found the use of "boy" during sex intriguing, he also felt that it may create a power dynamic that could infringe upon his autonomy. Joshua (23) agreed. "On the one hand I kind of fantasize about it sometimes, and a few times I've tested it out with someone, that dynamic, and seeing if it's something I like. And it's attractive in the moment. But I don't think I would call myself a boy. And the reason being is I have some, early on after my coming out I had experiences with very manipulative and abusive men, which was a bad experience, but also taught me to be very independent and assertive and knowledgeable of my own worth." Because of negative early experiences with emotionally abusive men, Joshua is wary of how "boy" may make younger adult men feel objectified or diminutive (to borrow a word from Jacob)—even if it is within a playful, consensual sexual dynamic. "So even though in theory I like the dynamic, the boy-daddy dynamic kind of thing, I also don't like it because I don't like someone going out of their way to make me feel small or make me feel subservient. So it's this weird tension between what I find attractive in bed, but also specific boundaries around my self-worth and my self-conception that keeps me from fully diving into that dynamic." In short: "boy" is complicated. Several younger men found the term arousing because it highlighted the age gap in older-younger encounters between adults and created a framework for playful sexual interaction. "Boy" contains elements of objectification and, at times, minimization, which many people find arousing within respectful, consensual sexual frameworks. Yet men who had experienced emotionally abusive partners, or who were particularly concerned about maintaining their autonomy, were wary of the term.

Men Who Identified as Boys

Unsurprisingly, the six men who described themselves as boys were able to articulate more fully what the term means to them and why they enjoy it. Notably, however, only six of twenty-six younger men (23 percent) described themselves as boys, a finding that suggests that active identification with the term is uncommon outside of leather/kink contexts. Five of the six described "boy" as involving sexual submissiveness. Justin (26) was the only man who did not do so; he related the term exclusively to age and appearance. "I think personally a 'boy' refers to someone who's a lot younger, who maybe is a lot more attractive looking." "Boy" is not a term that describes his day-to-day life, however. "I wouldn't say that I walk around every day saying, 'Oh yeah, I'm a boy.' But definitely in that context of the relationship or sexual relationship with an older man, definitely yes."

In contrast, other men tied "boy" to sexual submissiveness. Chris (33) explained, "Boy" means "that I can be more submissive with older men.

It's just an understanding about, I guess, mutual respect and care when it comes to sexual relationships. I like that it frames the relationship as one with someone with more experience, more confidence, more control, but still a respectful and caring relationship." Sexual submissiveness occurred within consensual and respectful boundaries.

A handful of men described submissiveness within both sexual and nonsexual settings. Benjamin (26) explained, "I think in the dynamic of a relationship or a partnership it means being more submissive, whereas the father figure would be more dominant." This submissiveness involved "anal and oral sex," but also, "I think for a partnership it could play out in decision making, so things as simple as what we're going to do tonight, or where we're going to go on vacation, or what's for dinner, like letting them take the lead." Overall, he noted, "I think it could take on almost a more feminine role to be submissive, in my mind. Kind of letting the older, masculine authority take the lead." Benjamin was one of the few younger men to tie femininity to submissiveness, and he did so within a hypothetical framework in which he was a full-time boy to a masculine daddy. David (27), like Benjamin, enjoyed the term. He noted, "I don't know what it is about I am attracted to the whole daddy-boy role-playing thing, but that can be really, really fun. So I'd say when it's good that's my favorite aspect of it. Like when I am just being called 'boy,' being more submissive, more service oriented, that's really fun." Indeed, he elaborated, "It's one of my favorite things to be called in a sexual context, so pretty much any time I go on a date or hook up with an older guy that tends to be what they call me." Unlike Benjamin, however, David preferred to hear the term mostly in sexual contexts.

Two men, James (28) and Jamal (23), identified as boys within leather/kink contexts, in which "boy" involves a more specific set of meanings than other men described. James explained, "It's a little bit kinky for me because I am pretty involved in the BDSM and leather scenes, so I've had a bit of formal training as a boy in that sense. The daddies and sirs just do tend to be older men. It started there and now I just keep that identity regardless of who I'm hooking up with." The type of submissiveness James enacted involved service training over the course of two years. "Service. [Laughs.] A bit of sexual service, a bit of caring for gear and for the household. Knowing how to stand, knowing how to sit, the type of etiquette in bars to display. [Laughs.] Hard to get into all of it. It's pretty involved."

Jamal also used the word "service" to describe boyness. Jamal identifies as a puppy and as a boy; "puppy" refers to pup-handler play, which is a type of BDSM that emerged from the leather community and that involves role playing as dogs or handlers in sexual and nonsexual settings.[17] He noted, "I primarily identify as a puppy, but I do identify as a boy as well. It's like a sixty-forty split kind of thing." "Boy" was imbued with consensual power dynamics. "To me the term 'boy' means somebody who is looking to be of service, but also to learn at the same time." He elaborated, "The idea of being of service to one another in a mutually beneficial kind of way where there's a power exchange involved, but its ultimate goal is that each of us is improving each other. That's what being a boy means to me, is that nurturing relationship with power exchange." Jamal articulated the distinction between "pup" and boy. On one hand, "I feel like being a boy, the sense of security I get is that sense of validation," he noted. "But the security I get of experiencing puppyhood space is more along the idea of my body and my mind are valuable things and I'm able to be loved for who I am as I stand. So it's more of like a primal sense of security. If I was to put it in a Maslow's hierarchy of needs kind of thing, I think that being a puppy satisfies the lower rungs of the ladder, but being a boy satisfies the higher achievement levels of it, like actualization stuff." Being a boy was a core part of Jamal's identity; involvement in a nurturing and consensual submissive-dominant relationship with an older man was deeply fulfilling to him. Notably, no other young man described "boy" as a central aspect of identity like Jamal did.

Overall, according to the stories of the men I talked to, it appears that "boy" as a self-descriptor is not as common as "daddy" is. Not all younger men enjoyed being called "boy," and of those who did, most enjoyed it only within specific circumstances, such as when flirting or having sex. Even in those circumstances, however, most of the younger men heard the term infrequently and did not usually ask older men to call them "boy." The term, for them, typically connoted consensual sexual submissiveness and highlighted the age gap between the two men in ways that made the encounter more exciting. Only six of twenty-six younger men described themselves as boys, and for only a handful of those six was the term a core identity of theirs.

Men articulated a more defined set of characteristics and practices associated with "daddy" than with "boy." Younger adult men who pair with older men are often more sexually submissive and are usually interested in mentorship. Yet these patterns do not lead to widespread adoption of boy identities, nor do they create a boy role that is as well defined as a daddy role. This finding makes sense: by definition, daddies are more experienced and knowledgeable than younger men. Daddies have had more time to figure out who they are and how to achieve their goals. Younger adult men are less experienced than daddies and are still figuring out their lives and identities. It stands to reason that daddyness would be more well defined and involve a more commonly understood set of characteristics than boyness.

Additionally, the age range associated with boys is much shorter than the age range associated with daddies. Daddy dynamics exist between men aged eighteen through their early thirties (about fifteen years maximum), for younger adult men, and their late thirties through their sixties (approximately three decades), for daddies. There is not as much time for younger adult men to figure out a boy identity or role as there is for older men to figure out a daddy identity or role. Men age out of boyness fairly quickly (unless they are in a leather/kink scene, in which case the term is applied more flexibly), whereas daddyness can be a more stable identity or role once adopted later in life. The greater length of time that men can be daddies compared to the time that young adult men can be boys, and the additional life experience involved before men transform into daddies, make it logical for daddy identities and roles to be more widespread and well defined than boy identities and roles.

3

Connections between Older and Younger Adult Men

Nurturance and mentorship of younger adult men were the most common practices older men tied to daddyness; thirty-four of thirty-nine older men made this connection. Fourteen younger adult men also described these practices as part of daddyness. Historically, mentorship was important to help younger adult men learn about male-male sex and navigate a heteronormative and often homophobic world. Today, mentorship is similar: older men can teach younger adult men about topics specific to gay and bisexual men, such as how to have sex, disclose one's sexual identity to others, or navigate homophobia, as well as other matters, such as how to form meaningful relationships and advance in one's career. Gay mentors can serve as role models, "sounding boards" for ideas, or sources of advice. Because older and younger men are "at different stages in our life," explained Logan (60), "I can offer advice and guidance." Being a daddy meant "nurturing, caring, loving, watching out for them, and giving advice," Brian (61) explained, as well as "showing how to get through life." Gay and bisexual men can transmit knowledge intergenerationally and create fulfilling relationships through mentorship of younger adult men. Older men can also offer younger adult men emotional support, and in so doing nurture them during the stressful years of emerging adulthood.[1]

Most of the older men I talked to described mentorship as a way to help younger adult men grow emotionally, intellectually, sexually, or professionally. Older men found it fulfilling, not burdensome. Older-younger pairings between adults fostered unique connections between gay and bisexual men in ways that transmitted knowledge intergenerationally. Daddy mentorship was one of the few ways older men could transfer knowledge to younger cohorts and help young adults grow—albeit in ways obviously distinct from other types of mentorship, given the sex involved. As Mateo (55) reported, "You want to leave somebody in better shape after you're not with them. So as a daddy you want the best for that person throughout the relationship and even afterwards." Doing so "should be the prime directive." Similarly, as Matthew (55) described, daddy relationships are "a connection that is made between an older guy and a younger guy that goes beyond just the age difference. It has to take that into account, but it goes beyond that into more of an emotional connection. Caring and dependency kind of thing in a good way."

Mentorship or Nurturance of Younger Men

Older men described mentorship and nurturance in remarkably similar ways. As Seth (65) explained, a daddy is "an older guy who has relations or gets involved with younger men and is more of a nurturing, basically a little bit more of a nurturing role. Not financially, but emotionally, physically is in more of a nurturing role. And like a teaching role, instructional role." Graham (51) stated that daddyness involves "passing forward information. So life skills, sexual skills." Brad (64) similarly mentioned that "I love advising," which he described as "offering experience in a slightly moderated, protected way." Mateo (55) noted that a daddy is "somebody older within the gay community that has a nurturing feeling or is open to nurture younger gay men," somebody who "can provide insight or advice to somebody that is new or willing to learn." Tomas (44) echoed these sentiments: a "daddy is typically somebody who is an older man who feels comfortable being with a younger person and is there to help and support them and work through things with them. And provides a resource for them to be able to go back to and to work through things." Reflecting on a past partnership with a younger man, Santiago (43) noted, "I felt good taking care of him and providing to him, and advising him, and talking to him about life in general." Mentorship helped adult gay and bisexual men of different cohorts form fulfilling relationships with one another. These responses emphasize the importance of teaching younger adult men or offering advice, as well as providing emotional support. Older men can do so because of their life experience, which allows them to pass on their knowledge to others.

Neil (51) explained that daddy relationships involve "a warmth that's special and different than other friendships." He continued,

There's a level of mentorship, a level of people looking for guidance and wanting to learn something and have a teacherly role, a mentorship type role. Not always formally, but that there is looking at someone who has experience like, "Oh, I can learn something from this person." And not that it doesn't go the other way, because I certainly can learn things from younger folks. I do all the time. But yeah, that aspect of it. And with that there's a certain warmth you have for people in that role that goes beyond what you would have for your peers.

Neil elaborated, "I want to see them do well, and move forward, and learn how to make the most and get the most out of their life and their path in a safe way that leaves them able to explore more." This mentorship could take many forms. "I think just one, being there to listen, to answer questions, to give guidance when sought, and sometimes stepping back when it appears they need to learn through their own experience. And sometimes those lessons are more profound. . . . It's always like, regardless of what the situation is, whether it's investigating a certain type of play, or sometimes it's life questions, or relationship questions, navigating the gay world, the leather world, etc." Along with that "advisor role" came "a sexual aspect." Neil clarified that there "doesn't have to be" sex involved, although there typically is. Mentorship gives younger adult men "a perspective that they don't have yet and that they can't have yet." Mentorship from older gay and bisexual men is similar to mentorship in other types of relationships. "I think [it] is similar to other mentor or other relationships in community similar to like a teacher or something. They have a certain experience of the world—or a coach—that you don't have yet and they're giving you some level of guidance. Whether it's just 'Hey, can I ask you some questions about X, Y, Z?' or getting more concrete and specific about their own situation." Unlike other types of mentor-mentee relationships, however, gay and bisexual men's mentorship often involves matters specific to gay and bisexual men.

Neil's story highlights how emotional intimacy is a defining component of older-younger pairings. Older men can teach younger adult men various life skills, both sexual and nonsexual, many of which are related to being gay or bisexual. Sometimes the mentorship dynamic requires that older men step back and allow younger men to learn from mistakes.

At the heart of this relationship is emotional intimacy and a desire to help the younger adult man grow.

Todd (57) detailed similar themes as Neil but provided further detail on how daddies can help younger adult men learn about male-male sexuality when they have little experience. "Basically it's like a guide and sounding board to allow somebody to help explore different areas of themselves and work on areas of growth, whatever the area for them might be. In this case it happens to be focused a lot around individual sexuality and questions of what it is that they're looking for, especially in the cases with some of the guys that have either little or no experience in relations with other men." He noted, "They pay a little bit more deference to the age difference between us, so there's like this greater respect level for wanting to hear my opinion on certain topics and such." Ultimately, Todd explained, "We're talking about the experience difference and the position of guidance and mentoring to help someone through with their growth and learning processes." This mentorship differed depending on the person. "Well, depending on the individual, sometimes they may be on the young side and may be very new to sexual and romantic relationships, and sometimes they have lots of questions. So sometimes I may take on just a Q&A and mentoring kind of a relationship at first, or the entire thing might just be entirely about conversation and letting them ask questions and explore. Sometimes might just be an entirely sexual type of a relationship. It just depends on the individual." Todd clarified, "The mentor position gives me a little bit of an opportunity to help guide or answer questions," and it goes "at their own pace." This dynamic had been present in a past romantic partnership with a man about twenty years his junior. "We were together for quite a long time, and it was a very noticeable feel in the relationship between the two of us that I was the daddy," Todd explained, "and he was very young and inexperienced, and he was very free in openly admitting this and needing and wanting information and guidance."

Daddyness involves mentoring younger adult men on many topics, sexual and nonsexual. The older men I talked to, including Todd, clarified that they did not condescend to younger adult men for their lack of experience nor pressure them to make certain decisions or try new sexual practices. Instead, they gently offered advice when asked, as well as perspective, and helped younger adult men sexually explore at the pace the younger man found comfortable—if indeed the younger man wanted to explore.

Being Gay or Bisexual

At times older men mentored younger adult men on issues related to being gay or bisexual. Caleb (57) described this practice as "a nurturing kind of thing" related to a feeling of "I've been there, I've done it, I've been where the younger guys are and I've had those experiences in my life and I've lived through them and to be able to help people get through or talk through some of those things if they need to." Specifically, as Caleb recounted,

> I do have a guy that I play with relatively often. And he's going through a tough time in his life where he's come out as gay to his family, they want him to move out, he doesn't really have a place to go. He's just twenty-three years old and trying to figure out what his life is going to be. And I mean so just to let him talk through some of that and offer opinions and help him to, places to look for things and for some support and things. And he's really troubled about the next steps of his life and how he's going to make it through and everything. And it's nice to be able to help support him through some of that.

Caleb found it fulfilling to mentor younger adult men, particularly in situations that involved complicated dynamics related to sexual-identity disclosure. As Brendan (56) similarly described, "Part of it is that I didn't have anybody there to protect me or watch over me when I was younger and coming out. So I think part of it is the need to take care of somebody and guide them and show them and protect them through life when I didn't have [that support]."

On issues related to being gay or bisexual, in particular, older men can offer support. Although public opinion on LGBTQ rights has improved rapidly over the past two decades, 20 percent of Americans still oppose nondiscrimination protections and 30 percent oppose same-sex marriage.[2] Further, many Americans support equal legal rights yet believe that homosexuality is immoral.[3] Youth whose parents dislike LGBTQ people will experience difficulties when they disclose their sexual identity. Daddies can help younger adult men through this process, drawing on their own experiences of coming out during years hostile to LGBTQ people.

Mentoring younger adult men meant providing advice and support based on one's own experiences with sexual-identity disclosure. Logan (60) helped younger men understand "that I could be a source of somebody to rely on," and specifically, "somebody who's been around the block, who's experienced a lot of stuff, and that if they've got issues they can come to me and talk to me about them. Sort of a parent, a father figure." Logan provided mentorship in one situation with a younger man who was not "out" to his family.

> He's not out to his family and he's petrified that if he does, his father is going to kick him out of the house. He's twenty. He's not a young kid. And I basically told him, "Hey, it probably wouldn't be safe for you to come out." But I also told him, "Listen, I'm not inviting you to live with us, but just in case something horrible happens and you get thrown out of the house, think of us as an emergency way station if you need somewhere to stay so that you're not out on the street." But I think the advice I gave him is, "You need to come out and you need to in the situation that you find yourself in."

Logan provided advice and even offered to be a safety net in case the younger man was kicked out of his house. It is unfortunately common for youth to experience housing instability after coming out as LGBTQ,[4] so the kind of willingness to help that Logan expressed could be important for many young men. Brett (43) explained a similar mentorship dynamic as Logan: "Sometimes when I chat with these guys online, they're young, they're in their early twenties, and they're scared to come out, they're scared to tell their parents." He elaborated, "I love being able to tell them that story and say, 'Look, I was terrified too when I was your age. I know what it's like. My coming out experience was great. I can't guarantee that, but,'" he continued, "that's one of the things I like about talking to younger guys." Mentorship is particularly important in delicate situations like sexual-identity disclosure to loved ones.

Steven (60), similarly, explained, "The caregiving aspect is listening to them, maybe they'll ask for advice. I have one gentleman who almost every time we get together is asking me for advice about his wife or his relationships or just, he feels open and safe with me." As Steven's response indicates, caring for younger adult men was particularly important when they were in difficult situations like not being out as gay or bisexual to anyone in their lives. Steven clarified, "I'm definitely not a sugar daddy. I don't have very much money. But I have that sense of caring for people." Numerous older men listened to younger men who were married to a woman but needed to confidentially talk about their same-sex desires.

Sometimes older men helped younger men come out to women with whom they were in a romantic relationship. Finn (64), for instance, began a sexual relationship with a man in his late twenties when Finn was in his early forties. "He needed advice because he was engaged to a woman and he had no intention of disclosing to her that he was bisexual," Finn explained. "And so as our sexual relationship unfolded, I very much advised him that he needed to tell his fiancée that he was bisexual and that he maybe still wanted to be married to her but he also is going to have men on the side. He did disclose that to her, she immediately left him." Happily, however, he "very quickly met" a woman who "had no problem with him being bisexual." Finn's friend was able to form an ethically nonmonogamous relationship in which he was open about his same-sex desires to his woman partner. "I don't think that would have been the case had he not disclosed that to the woman he was engaged to initially," Finn stated. "So that's an example of not just being a daddy sexually, but using my life experience to have an impact on people's living." Daddies provided concrete advice, often based on their own life experiences, that could benefit younger adult men.

Mentorship sometimes involved teaching younger adult men new sexual practices. Wyatt (66) explained that his favorite part of being a daddy "would be how much you still can show them, how much you can contribute in a positive way to what they may have thought they knew, but you can show them that there's much, much more. I really like revealing life and male sexuality to younger men." As Jay (58) also detailed, "Sexually, I've had younger men approach me who are either not out of the closet or thinking about coming out of the closet or whatever and they want somebody that's patient in that, helping them have their initial sexual experience." These situations perfectly matched his definition of a daddy: "somebody who serves as a mentor—either emotionally, intellectually, or physically, meaning sex. For someone who's significantly their junior in years." Daddies could teach younger adult men how to have fulfilling sex, whether younger adult men had nonexistent or limited sexual experience with other men.

Often, sexual and nonsexual mentorship happened alongside one another. As Greg (50) noted, "I feel like my experience of this in gay culture is a blend of mentor slash teacher. But then, we're gay, so there's the fetishistic sexual part of it, too. So I think it's partly about accepting a role in our culture, but also accepting a certain sexual dynamic at times." Mentorship, for Greg, meant offering a "safe place" to his younger friends: "I think part of it, I guess baseline, is a sense of emotional safety, that no one's going to be judged here, and no one's going to be hurt, or made fun of in any way. But also safe in that we've had more than a couple of friends over the last few years who have been struggling with some sort of substance abuse. And the safety means it's a place to be honest about that and get support in getting well." Daddies like Greg sexually and nonsexually mentored younger adult men and provided emotional support. Sometimes emotional support was directed toward younger men in crisis situations like substance abuse, whereas at other times emotional support helped younger men during life stressors typical during emerging adulthood.

Mentorship took place in romantic partnerships with large age gaps in addition to nonromantic pairings. When reminiscing about a past relationship, Brett (43) noted, "I liked being there for him when he was scared about certain things, or wanted advice about certain things, or didn't know what to do about certain things. I loved being there and just giving him advice, and he did it, and it worked out, and he was happier because of that. I loved all that." Mentorship took place in a variety of relationship types that involved younger adult men.

Several men explained that mentorship was one of their favorite aspects of being a daddy or the main trait associated with daddyness. Steven (60) noted that "my favorite is having younger guys look up to me in the sense of like advice or knowing that my home is a safe place for them, or I'm a safe person for them." Luke (68) also mentioned that he enjoys "helping other people's lives improve" and noted, "I would say that a daddy relationship is one that makes you feel secure and somebody that is there for you intellectually, sexually, or emotionally, or all three." This dynamic may involve "trying to protect them from making the mistakes that I've made, or at least learn from the mistakes that I've made." Echoing this thought, Charlie (49) reflected, "I view myself as someone who is a provider, takes care of somebody." He continued, "That's what brings me comfort and joy. I enjoy taking care of someone, which doesn't mean economically, it just means emotionally. It can be physically, it can be whatever the case may be. If you need help, you need someone to talk to, someone with, someone older who's got more wisdom, more life experiences, more whatever they have, because they've lived a more full life, that can be a daddy role." Most men, including Charlie, considered daddyness to be fulfilling because it involved mentorship of younger adult men. Mentorship was not a burden; it was something most older men found fulfilling.

Several men described mentorship as a way to pass on knowledge that they themselves had received earlier in life. Diego (43) explained, "I believe that as gays, we were always helped by somebody older than us at some point in our lives, or most of us are, and that we should have a pay-it-forward mentality because we don't usually have kids and that nature." Diego experienced substance abuse and other concerns when he was younger, and several older men helped him begin a new life trajectory. "The youngest of the three was probably ten years older than me and then it probably went up almost to like sixteen. It ranged from ten years to sixteen years older than me. There was a sexual relationship there, too, but I moved out of the city to the suburbs. They took me in. I lived with them, occasionally had sex with them, got my life cleaned up, quit drugs, etc. And so yeah, I would consider that a very mentorship, fatherly role that they all served for me." This situation "had its whole set of problems," but it nonetheless greatly helped Diego. As a result, "I do think that I've met people that are younger than me, people that are in their twenties, people that I try to either mentor, or," he continued, "I have definitely a want-to-pay-it-forward sort of mentality." In Diego's case, "paying it forward" meant mentoring younger adult men. As Cody (59) also explained, when he mentors younger adult men he tries to focus on "everything that I didn't get from my dad. And there have been a few different aspects of my life where I work very hard to try to correct things that I had missed out on and other people that seem like they have too." Several older men explained that mentorship helped others avoid the mistakes they made or helped younger adult men gain knowledge that the older men did not have when they were younger. Mentorship allowed older men to transmit knowledge intergenerationally.

Daddyness and Fathering

Several men connected mentorship to fathering instincts. "Not in an incestuous way," Jordy (57) clarified, but rather, "I felt like I wanted to help them, I wanted to teach them, I wanted them to learn from my experiences. Which was really strange to me because I had never had any parental longings at all. So it was weird for me to see that side of myself. Because it feels like a parental responsibility, or my intentions, of course besides the sex, is just to help them and if you have questions or they're talking about something, I give them my advice or things with my experience." This dynamic arose several different times, including with a recent sexual partner. "There was a young man that I met online and came over and [we had] great sex. And he was funny, and we seemed to talk easily." Jordy continued, "And he was just at that young age where he was graduated from college and couldn't find a decent job and was depressed about that. And had things like that going on [in] his life, just kind of where I was many years ago and I felt the same way. So I just talked to him a lot about that. I tried slightly to help him find another job, things like that." This dynamic continued in Jordy's current romantic partnership with a man in his late twenties; Jordy said that he feels like a daddy "whenever I'm talking to him" given that Jordy gives him advice. Other men also clearly specified that daddyness did not fulfill an incestuous fantasy, but rather involved a special mentorship unique to gay men.

Several older men described their mentorship as paternal, given the mentorship and support involved with older-younger pairings between adults. "I'd say I'm paternal," said Logan (60). "I'm always there to give you a hug or to give advice to younger guys." Luis (54) noted that a daddy-younger pairing "would be a relationship based on a father figure and . . . it would include notions of protection and leadership in a relationship." This dynamic involved "a nurturing side of my personality," which "comes through in sexual relationships and relationships with other younger men." Sexually, what this referred to is "trying to instill this whole idea that it is a reciprocal relationship rather than a one-way relationship," and that sex is not just about focusing on one's own pleasure. Steven elaborated on this idea: "What I see in the experiences that I've had is a younger man wants somebody to a little bit care for them as a dad, as a father figure that's going to be loving toward them and listening and accepting. So that's the sense of the caregiving." Phrasing these sentiments slightly differently, Tomas (44) explained that a daddy is "an older male that younger men look to for support and guidance and comfort and looking for a male energy in their life."

Men who were biological fathers drew upon their parenting instincts to explain their sense of protection for younger adult men, even as their relationships with their children were obviously much different from their relationships with younger adult gay and bisexual men. "First of all, I'm a father," Aram (60) explained. "So in the sense of being a parent, I have a very strong paternal instinct. I love my children and I think I have a good relationship with both of them. They both turned out to be wonderful." He continued, "Some of that caring, and I would say that I'm very empathetic and nurturing by nature, carries over into intimate relationships with younger men. And so I think that definition of 'daddy' is more about being a mentor but also being appreciated as an older partner." Putting this differently, Aram explained that mentoring younger men "clicks into the nurturing gene." Similarly, Robert (69) explained, "First of all, I'm a real-life daddy, so a nurturing, very stable, encouraging, nonjudgmental person who finds an opportunity to really be a sounding board and perhaps help people accept themselves a little better, having been on that path myself." Overall, daddyness involved being "a father figure, mentor, elder of the tribe, if you will, to younger men." Daddyness could involve many things, including "talking about careers, talking about where they are in their lives, talking about sex, being a steadfast person who may be able to serve as a point of resource and information, and maybe a steadying role." Greg (50) echoed these sentiments. "I'm also a father; I have a grown [child] from my first marriage," Greg explained. "So I think people pick up on that vibe of—to me, part of being a father and being a daddy involves a sense of providing and a sense of protection. I consider myself to be pretty nurturing and pretty loving." He continued, "My protective instincts are like through the roof, so I think daddy characteristics to me are very similar to parenting characteristics."

Why would daddies describe their relationships with younger adult men as paternal, given that older-younger pairings between adults—which often involve sex—are clearly different from father-son relationships? Part of the answer is that there are few other words to describe older-younger relationships between adults. It is common for people to describe platonic intimate relationships between older and younger adults as parental, maternal, or paternal, even when they are not family. Similarly, the men I talked to described some of their relationships as paternal or fatherly even though this description did not exactly match the relationships they formed, given the sex involved. Daddies did not replace fathers or exactly parallel them, but in the absence of other common cultural frameworks to describe older-younger pairings between adults, men drew on archetypes of father-son relationships to describe nonsexual daddy dynamics between older and younger adult men.

Daddy relationships with younger adult men, like parental relationships, involved mentorship and an understanding that younger men were still maturing as adults. This understanding meant that older men were sometimes protective of younger adult men and treated them with care—a dynamic younger men described as well. Of course, daddy-younger relationships are distinct because they are between adults who are not related and involve sex. These relationships did not fulfill an incestuous fantasy, nor did most young men describe them as a substitute for relationships with their own fathers. These ideas are misconceptions that describe few people.

It is hypothetically possible that some of the men I talked to secretly had an interest in what is called fantasy "family play," a type of fetish in which two adults who are not family members pretend to be. This fetish is popular on pornography websites, and producers target both heterosexuals and gay men. Analysis that uses psychoanalytic theory may suggest that family play fantasies could be responsible for some older-younger pairings between adults. None of the men I talked to, however, either older or younger, reported that they had this fantasy. While it is possible that some men did secretly have this fantasy and did not say so because they feared stigma, the fact that no men discussed it means I cannot say anything else about the topic. However, given that men described other intimate details of their lives, even parts that they found difficult to discuss, the fact that not a single man described family play fantasies makes it reasonable to conclude that many of them likely did not have those fantasies.

Younger Men's Appreciation of Mentorship

The majority of younger men explicitly defined mentorship or nurturance as part of daddyness or stated that mentorship was one reason they paired with older men. Putting it simply, Jamal (23) explained that a daddy is "committed to being a role model." Tyrone (32) explained, "I would say if you can possibly divorce the idea of what the ideal father is, the familial aspect of it from the relation aspect of it, so think about someone who's nurturing, someone who provides for you, someone who just makes you feel safe, but also they're really hot, I think that would be my outline for it." Phrasing similar sentiments differently, Michael (30) described a daddy as "mentally someone who has a lot of wisdom, who's someone you can look to for advice, someone you can look up to from a psychological standpoint." Indeed, "There is a strong sense of mentorship and there's a strong sense of gentleness," according to Terry (24), and the term "daddy" is "tied to a sense of paternalistic warmth."

The fact that younger men agreed with older men that mentorship is a defining component of daddyness indicates two main things. First, older men did not misunderstand the relationship they had with younger adult men; both parties did indeed see mentorship and nurturance as defining features of older-younger pairings between adults. Second, older men did not condescendingly impose ideas or expectations onto younger men. Although undoubtedly condescension does occur in some situations, younger men overwhelmingly described mentorship as positive, and this perception is one reason they pair with older men.

As these responses also suggest, age is not the sole criterion necessary to be a daddy. Other characteristics are necessary as well. David (27) explained, "It's more than just age, though. I think it's a, not necessarily a personality, but a behavioral thing. You have to embody the personality of a daddy to be one, I think, embody the actions and you've got to be nurturing, you have to like [to] take control. It's not just like, 'You're thirty years older than me.'" These qualities were what defined a daddy, even though "if I just saw somebody on the street who was thirty years older than me I would call him daddy if I found him attractive."

"Daddy" could thus be used as a casual descriptor for attractive older men, but older men needed to have other characteristics to be "true" daddies. David continued, "I do have a lot of nerves when it comes to meeting up with guys, dating, sex, all that." He enjoyed being with older men because "it's a lot more emotional and I feel like it's a mentoring thing, and they can help me get more confident in myself." Additionally, "I find that men who are older and embody a more daddy role, they're really good at helping me break out of my nervousness." With older men, "It becomes a lot less just about getting off and it's a lot more about a physical connection between two people." In contrast, with younger men, "It's just an exercise in getting off sometimes." Men with anxiety, such as David, found it comforting to pair with older men. Daddies made sexual encounters emotionally intimate and physically pleasurable, and older-younger pairings between adults did not create as many pressures as age-similar pairings did.

Other younger men also saw nurturance as a defining feature of older-younger pairings between adults. James (28) explained, "Most have been nurturing. Most of the older men I pursue, I pursue because I like the guidance aspect and the caring aspect to it." He elaborated, "I appreciate men who have time to walk me through things and explain things to me and who assert a very genuine care in my progress as a person and sexually." This care was more typical of daddies than men around James's own age. Similarly, Austin (27) noted both sexual and nonsexual mentorship with daddies. Things he learned included "skills of what makes something pleasurable for someone else" but also how to "manage emotions, how to even manage finances, I would say. And how to manage your space, your body, your emotions, how you go about communicating." Indeed, Austin mentioned, "When there's a daddy-boy relationship, one person is in control and one person is learning from them." He continued, "There's more of an equal give and take with other relationships, whereas with daddy-boy the boy is taking a lot and the daddy is giving a lot." "Giving" and "taking," in this case, involved younger men learning from daddies. Nurturance and intergenerational transmissions of knowledge were features central to older-younger pairings between adults.

Mentorship could occur naturally, such that younger adult men learned sexual techniques over time that positively affected their sexual knowledge and confidence. Tyler (33) detailed this scenario with one sexual relationship with an older man: "A lot of older guys, what I want from them is for them to take control. But the contrary of what's been happening is like after the first encounter of control where they lead, they're dominant, I'm usually a bottom, something to that effect, the relationship does grow a little bit to where I don't know if they see my weaknesses or they see things that I want, because it's usually not something I have to verbalize, but it's almost been like a training course." He elaborated on one "training course" an older man provided to him without Tyler having to ask: "I was with one older guy and he really was persistent about wanting me to top him, and it led to this whole thing where we would flip fuck every time we were together, up until the point where he—it was kind of cute—he goes, 'Wow, you've earned your horns.' In terms of being a top. Which I thought was really cute, but it's been almost like a fostering program lately." Even though Tyler enjoyed bottoming with older men, he also appreciated that older men taught him how to top effectively.

A handful of older and younger men alike understood that mentorship could be complicated, given that younger men sometimes need to learn from experience—and mistakes. Dustin (70) explained that the main challenges with one of the men he mentored were "knowing when to step in and when not to. Knowing when to give advice and knowing when to keep my mouth shut and let him learn on his own." Tyler, relatedly, explained, "It's just a bit frustrating when they try to teach you things that you don't have the experience yet to truly understand and it needs to be like a more natural learning process." In any type of mentor relationship, there is a tension between the older person's desire to help the younger person, and the younger person's desire for autonomy and the freedom to learn through experience. Some men I talked to described this dynamic as well, although surprisingly few younger (or older) men raised this issue when they discussed mentorship.

Leather

Most of the men I talked to were not involved in leather communities, although a handful were. Mentorship was just as important to them, although it took somewhat different forms. "It took me a long time to come to the daddy stage," Dustin (70) explained. "I've always been a master. But mentoring has gotten more important to me, so from a daddy standpoint it's passing on basically my old-guard values to a new set of players." These values included "consent, mental fitness, communication." His favorite part about being a daddy is "the joy of seeing boys grow." Dustin was tightly integrated into leather communities.

Cody (59), relatedly, explained that he began thinking of himself as a daddy after involvement in the leather community, which gave him perspective on the dynamics he enjoyed with younger adult men. Reflecting back several decades, he explained, "I realized that most of why I was really involved with the leather community was at the time it was like the only outlet for my dominant mentoring side. You couldn't go date somebody younger and be dominant and mentoring. Obviously not that it couldn't happen, but it was very difficult to find, and needle in the haystack kind of thing. But in the leather community, there were people that were immediately looking for dominant mentoring people and people like me who were looking for the opposite." This realization encouraged Cody to reflect on what he was seeking in the leather community, and who he connected with the most. "I realized when I started looking at all of the different aspects of what comprised the leather community, every single aspect to me came back to boy, not to slave, not to sub, not to doms. It was the guys who want somebody to be a dominant aspect in their life, the nurturing, mentoring, [and] so on." Nonetheless, there was one particular situation that reinforced to Cody that he was a daddy when he was between forty-eight and fifty. "I also specifically remember [one] guy," Cody began. "I will never forget one time after sex, both still naked, I was leaning up against the wall in his bed and he literally climbed up, curled up in my lap, and said, 'Oh my God daddy, you're so comfortable.' And that situation and that phrase stuck in my head." He continued, "That was the first time that it actually clicked to me I don't have to be a dom, I don't have to be in the leather community because this is what I am."

This situation showed Cody that he was a daddy—and that he could be a daddy both inside and outside the leather community. As a result of this realization, Cody is no longer very involved in leather communities. He is a daddy in most situations with younger adult men, not just those that take place in leather spaces.

Terry (24) offered perspective as a younger person involved in leather and described an appreciation for learning about history within leather and kink communities.

> I think a lot of the things that I enjoy about playing with older guys is that it allows me to connect my current personal sexual practices to the sense of shared history and of shared community by doing things like flagging [signaling sexual interest with colored handkerchiefs] . . . whatever I'm able to tap into, this decades-old history of what being gay has meant, what being gay and kinky has meant, what being a person of leather has meant, and I find that very personally fulfilling. I find that very affirming of masculinity and I find that very fulfilling in a, like a relationship way or obviously in an erotic way.

Pairing with older men allowed Terry to learn leather practices that are rooted in decades of history.

Leather daddies are crucial to the functioning and well-being of leather communities given their mentorship practices, which are particularly important to leather communities for two primary reasons. First, like all subcultures, leather communities have complex norms, values, and practices that new members must learn. Second, because leathermen often engage in consensual relations of dominance and submission, some of which involve the consensual infliction of pain (for instance, flogging), it is critically important that more experienced leathermen teach new members how to safely engage with other men. Experience is strongly associated with age. The importance of daddies to leather communities, both historically and today, cannot be overstated.

Protecting or Caring for Younger Men

The majority of older men connected daddyness to nurturance: that is, protecting or caring for younger adult men. While similar to mentorship, nurturance/care does not necessarily involve teaching younger men new skills or modeling certain behaviors, as is common with mentorship. Instead, this theme refers more to how daddies emotionally support younger adult men. As Matthew (55) explained, "It puts on—and I mean this in a positive way—it puts a burden on me for caring." Daddies are "more like a protective type," Brett (43) stated, and Brendan (56) noted that the main thing that comes to mind when he thinks about himself as a daddy is that "I like to take care of people," in ways that are "kind of like a parent or a daddy or whatever." Indeed, "I like feeling like I'm a protector," Brett added. Logan (60) expressed similar thoughts slightly differently. "I like the fact that I can be somebody that a younger friend, even if they're a sex partner, can rely on. [I like] that they take comfort in knowing that I'm their friend."

Protection and care typically did not involve material support, although for some men it did. Charlie (49), for example, allowed a young adult man who had been (illegally) kicked out of his apartment for being gay to stay with him for a time. That situation happened only once, but "someone who's down on their luck or just needed someone, struggling a little bit here and there, that's happened a few times," noted Charlie. The types of relationships Charlie has with men "are more paternalistic," given that younger men he knows often need help.

> But people who are looking for someone, because they've had, they're at a hard time in their life. And that's how I've met a bunch of people who are younger than me. Or they need, they're lost in a way, or they're temporarily down on their luck or something like that. It seems like I've met a few people who I have relationships with in that way. And it's oftentimes me helping them out, not necessarily money, but just like, "Oh, do you need some advice? Do you need somewhere to stay for a week? Do you need some food? Do you need some support or just someone to talk to?" And stuff like that.

Importantly, this assistance "runs the range of things," and it is not always sexual. "People always jump to a conclusion like it's sexual. And it's not. I'd say half of my relationships, it's not sexual at all. It's just a relationship, and I feel like I can relate to younger guys better, oftentimes, than people my own age. I just feel more comfortable."

Although Charlie's relationships sometimes involved material support to struggling young adult men, protection and care were typically more emotional. "I guess they're looking to be cared for, not necessarily in a financial way," Enrique (62) explained, "but in more of an emotional setting." For Tomas (44) this care involved "a lot of checking up on people randomly" to make sure they have "a solid rock in your life at the moment," particularly for younger friends who experienced mental health issues such as depression. As Graham (51) explained, "The small things, like hearing someone relate to you 'I'm proud of you' is mind-blowing for people who don't ever get that. It's so powerful to hear, especially someone who is older and he considers that we have our shit together, which I think is wonderful." Nurturing younger adult men meant emotionally supporting them.

Several of the younger men I talked to also described care and protection as nurturing daddy traits. Michael (30) explained, "There's also the daddy that wants to look after someone, not necessarily in a financial standpoint, but be a caregiver and be someone who's going to provide them shelter and provide them security and things of that nature." Anthony (25) similarly noted, "I would describe a daddy as an older guy that is, if you're taking on the role of daddy, an older guy that is paternal, takes on those caring aspects . . . Your relationship is very, not revolved around, but very closely tied to that paternal dynamic." Often this care was both sexual and nonsexual. According to Tyrone (32), daddies are willing to "take care of you both inside and outside of the bedroom." Similarly, William (29) described, "There's definitely an aspect of control and an aspect of power, but it definitely comes with caring for the other person, and that then translates inside and outside of sexual scenarios." Daddies protected and took care of younger adult men in both sexual and nonsexual contexts.

Connections between Cohorts

Apart from nurturance and mentorship, several men explicitly tied daddyness to connecting different cohorts of adult gay men. While similar to the theme of mentorship, this theme reflects how many men perceived older-younger relationships as not just connecting *individuals* who are different ages but connecting *cohorts*—and building communities. Luis

(54) noted that "daddyness is about a relationship, a generational relationship." For Greg (50) this relationship involved "maybe a sense of providing guidance to some of our boys or younger gay friends, also a sense of responsibility to community. What does it mean to set a good example," and to provide "responsibility in terms of leadership." Greg reflected, "This is a way for mature men and younger guys to stay connected to each other and I see that as being a very positive thing." Indeed, he elaborated, "That unity in the queer community is vitally important, especially in today's political climate."

Graham (51) provided a particularly thoughtful explanation of how being a daddy connects him to other men. "I feel like I am creating a connection with previous generations of queer people. I feel like that's part of being a daddy for me." He continued,

> There's information to be shared between these generations. It's like we all have dads or moms and we all have grandparents. Some of us are lucky enough to have great-grandparents alive when we're alive. And there's a lot of us in the gay community that are aware of the gap of people who died in the '80s and '90s, mostly, and for people my age—I'm fifty-one— there wasn't a connection with that generation because [many of them] died, so for me being a daddy means a lot of different things with respect to that. And then of course there's also the play, fetish component, which, I like a little bit of that, but to me it's more about being a cultural daddy and sexual daddy, too. It's making possible filling information that's shared between queer generations.

Graham explained that connecting with younger adult men is "very edifying and it feels good. It feels healthy." These relationships, which he noted involve a "bonding experience," which are "brother-to-brother," are also potentially ongoing: "Our sexual relationships are so powerful because they can be ongoing as we age, right? And the bonds can happen at any point in our life and then continue throughout the rest of our life if we choose." Graham noted, "I want that community or that sense of belonging, and I do want that kind of social protection as I grow older."

As Graham's response highlights, new medications allow people with HIV to live healthy lives. In prior decades, in contrast, hundreds of thousands of men in the United States died after contracting HIV,[5] which devastated older cohorts of gay and bisexual men and as a result prevented many intergenerational ties that may have otherwise formed. Intergenerational transmissions of knowledge are particularly meaningful for daddies whose relationships with older men were cut short in prior decades due to AIDS.

Caleb (57) similarly viewed daddy relationships as forming a "bridge" between older and younger adult men. Specifically, he noted, "My favorite aspect is just it's that contact with this younger person with a different background and a different place in his life and different things are important to him, but yet there's an attraction of him to me and me to him. And that moment that you're first together and that first kiss and embrace and just like a jolt of energy and it's just, it's very life-giving, it fuels you." Caleb continued, "There's a protective care and nurturing kind of thing that I like about it that the younger guys totally get into." Older men often felt fulfillment and connection when they mentored younger adult men. The "bridge" Caleb noted is both a point of connection and a way that older men can transmit knowledge intergenerationally.

Older-younger pairings between adults are a two-way street: the older and younger adult men form mutually beneficial, emotionally intimate connections. Indeed, Greg (50) noted that he and his husband around his age give and receive "affection and affirmation." He continued, "We give that, I give that to our boys for sure. And we receive that back from a lot of our boys. So that affirmation and affection and love is a huge uptick for me." Charlie (49) phrased this sentiment differently: "They have a much different outlook. They're young, grew up in a different generation, have different views, and I think it's a fresh way of looking at things. And I'm never, it never ceases to amaze me some of the things they think about or things that go on in their lives, just being from a completely different generation." Mateo (55) also noted that "I see being a daddy more of a nurturing relationship. And I want to say nurturing is both ways. Because a daddy also gets a lot from the younger person." He also learned much about what it means to be a young gay man today.

> I like the perspective. I like their life experiences from their age group, their point of view. Younger guys nowadays, I'm going to sound like an old fogey, have it easier coming out of the closet, because the trail has been blazed. There's a lot more support. You have the Internet as a source

of information. Not all of it good, but you have a source of information. I struggled because I didn't have that information, I didn't have the support. So I love learning about their coming-out experience and their acceptance within society, because it gives me a lot of joy to hear that it's much easier now. And it's a different perspective.

Overall, daddy-younger relationships between adults are characterized by "what kind of knowledge is being passed from one to the other," according to Mateo. Brad (64) also detailed, "I would say there are lovely advantages to this fashion of daddy, where I meet more younger, more active people. That's an entirely other generation or two generations from me. That's fascinating. I know a whole lot more about what's going on in the world than most of my friends who are my age. That's an enormous advantage." Daddyness is fulfilling in part because it allows older men to connect with younger cohorts of adult gay and bisexual men who have had different experiences than they.

Several older men also explained that they found it fulfilling to connect with younger adult men who have a different energy than men around their own age. As Jorge (47) explained, "Being able to still connect with people younger than you, I think that's the biggest thing." He continued, "The ability to connect to that and still tap into that and still have a certain sense of self and excitement and interest and finding that creativity and that uniqueness that still is imbued with youth probably is a wonderful dynamic. So there's that sense of connection. Being connected, still connected to something young and free and vibrant." Additionally, as Ryan (48) explained, "I like the youthfulness. Kind of feel like sometimes it helps me stay younger, feel younger and in touch with younger people." Tomas (44) relatedly described, "It gives me a certain satisfaction to work with people or to talk with people or to be in relationships with folks that are younger than me, but that I can share my experiences with and be close with."

Aram (60) echoed this sentiment: "When you get older you feel like you're on the decline," he noted, and it is nice to "feel that someone who is decades younger has the same virility or sexual drive." Older-younger pairings between adults were especially fulfilling for Aram because they helped him feel as though he was reclaiming opportunities he did not have earlier in life, when he was married to a woman and did not have sex with men. With younger adult men, "I have no problem maintaining an erection for a very long time. And so that correlates more to the sexual energy of a younger man." He continued, "It's sort of putting me back in that time in my life when that would have happened naturally. And so I'm sort of self-conscious, but not necessarily down on myself about having given up that time. And feel that I can reclaim it in a way so that I can age without regret."

Older-younger relationships between adults occur between people of any gender or sexual identity. They do, however, take unique forms among gay and bisexual men, for whom connections involve intergenerational transmissions of knowledge unique to gay and bisexual men, both sexual and nonsexual. Older-younger pairings also strengthen social ties between cohorts of adult gay and bisexual men. More generally, too, they give older and younger men the opportunity to learn the perspectives of adults who are in different stages in life.

Several younger men also described older-younger pairings as special intergenerational connections, even as fourteen also noted that generational disconnects could be challenging due to differences in attitudes, knowledge about popular culture, hobbies, and tastes. "You look to your father as someone you look up to, someone that can provide you wisdom, someone that you can look to for advice," explained Michael (30). "I've used that thinking talking to some older men at times and give my due diligence of gay history and what they've gone through and things of that nature." It was fulfilling to talk to older men because they had both more experience generally and experience with gay history specifically. Similarly, "I also like learning from older men about parts of the gay experience that I wasn't a part of," David (27) explained.

At other times generational connections were not necessarily related to gay history, but younger men still valued them. As Jacob (27) explained, "There's something very sweet about an intergenerational experience to me. It's comforting to be with and see someone who's maybe been through or done what I'm going through or doing and is still kicking." Additionally, the disconnect in generational experiences could lead to better communication.

> When I'm speaking with somebody of my own generation there's a lot more that can go unsaid because there tends to be more of a complex

shared vernacular, whether that's in the way we talk, or what we're talking about. But when it's with older guys it feels more intentional because it's an intergenerational experience. It feels more like, "Ah, you are distinctly different than I." And of course everybody is, but it feels maybe in a more sizable or noticeable way when it's like, "I can't just reference something and expect you to laugh or expect you to know what I'm referencing." I guess the conversation is more intentionally inquisitive or intentionally careful towards each other.

Even as differences in knowledge of popular culture could make it difficult for older and younger men to find common interests, these disconnects could also lead to more intentional communication that could form stronger connections. Jamal (23) agreed with Jacob. "I'd say that being with younger men is easier since we have more things to bond over, because we grew up in similar time periods. But I think that that's not as big of an attractor because I can find somebody who's older who is into those same things, and I think that being able to bond over something new together for the first time is really important to me." Although generational differences could pose challenges, older and younger adult men nonetheless appreciated these differences because they could learn from one another and form stronger connections.

4

Daddy Desirability

I asked younger adult men why they chose older men for sexual or romantic relationships. Many of their reasons overlapped with definitions they gave about what it means to be a daddy. This chapter, however, specifically focuses on why younger men pair with older men, not just their thoughts on what it means to be a daddy. Overwhelmingly, younger men reported that they connect with older men better than with men around their own age.

There were three main reasons younger men enjoyed pairing with older men. The first reason involves desirable characteristics of older men: emotional maturity, stability, and nonsexual experience. The second reason involves feeling better connection or compatibility with older men compared to men their own age. Younger men discussed sharing similar life goals and perspectives; feeling comforted, cared for, or protected around older men; enjoyment of mentorship and nurturance; and distinct interpersonal dynamics that were difficult to explain.[1] The third theme involves physicality and sex. Younger adult men, unsurprisingly, reported physical attraction to older men. Many also reported that they had better sex with older men and noticed unique and enjoyable sexual dynamics not present when they had sex with men around their own age. Some younger adult men also wanted to be sexually dominated by older men as part of a consensual sexual dynamic. Many themes overlap and are interconnected.

It is not merely happenstance that younger adult men paired with older men, nor were these pairings driven primarily by older men. Most younger men actively sought older-younger pairings. In contrast to stereotypes, most younger men did not report issues with their biological fathers that made older men more appealing. Instead, they desired older men for a variety of reasons that had little to do with younger men's personal backgrounds.

Desirable Characteristics of Older Men
Emotional Maturity

Fifteen younger men explained that they partner with older men in part due to older men's emotional maturity, which they believe younger men often lack. "I've noticed that I'm drawn to older guys mostly because there's an emotional maturity there," Joshua (23) noted, "that I sometimes don't see among people my own age, and that appeals to me." Similarly, "I find that maturity level with people my age or around my age can be very hit or miss," Terry (24) noted. "And so I like that I can consistently expect a higher standard of behavior and a more mature handling of things that come up. Of course that's not universally the case, but certainly is more commonly the case." Amir (24) agreed. "I generally also find them a little bit more mature emotionally. A lot of times people my age seem to be a little bit less emotionally well balanced than older men." On a related note, DaShawn (27) explained, "I believe that also I'm attracted to older men because it's a sense of safety. I think maybe emotional security, almost. Sometimes I feel like people my own age are immature." Older men, according to Anthony (25), "have their lives together, have most of their life figured out, got everything together pretty much." This trait is in contrast "to guys around my age, who I find not to be mature or just aren't experienced," Jeffrey (23) noted. Phrasing this sentiment humorously, Jamal (23) stated, "That's a thing I think is especially pushing me towards dating older men, is that feeling of a person who is a more adequate human, for lack of better words, like better at communicating and being a healthy adult."

Younger men found older men's emotional maturity attractive and considered the lack of emotional maturity in men around their own age irritating. Younger men did not pair with older men out of happenstance or because younger men gave in after older men relentlessly pursued them. Instead, younger men actively sought older men for sexual or romantic relationships.

Older men's emotional maturity meant that younger men connected with them more strongly than with men around their own age. "I've always been an old soul," Benjamin (26) began, "so I think that just the dynamic, there's more of a chemistry for me in terms of the maturity level, a closer match. I guess I just identify more with their mindset." William (29) echoed these sentiments. "There's also this, I don't know, enjoyable thing of the potential wisdom that might come with age. I've always felt potentially a little bit old for my own age, so I like that there's a potential wiser or more adult conversation." Juan (25) too explained that he connected better with older men because of their emotional maturity. "I started dating guys that were similar to my age, but I've always had a difficulty connecting with them in the intellectual level. Not just having intellectual conversations," he clarified, "but emotionally intellectual conversations and emotional connection was really hard for me to build with younger men around my age. And again, it was that sense of not having your own identity." Tyrone (32) also appreciated that "as far as older guys, I feel like there's less expectation for me to be performing." Men around Tyrone's age were concerned about appearances: "What are you doing in your thirties, what's your career, how much are you out on the town, what's your gay clout, basically," he explained. "And I feel like with older guys they don't care as much about the gay clout thing." Older men "have been through it." Older men are often less concerned about appearances than younger men and have a self-image less affected by other people's opinions.

Younger men's perception that older men are more emotionally mature than men in their twenties or early thirties, on average, was central to their choice to pair with older men. They knew that not all older men are emotionally mature, but they did notice that older men are more likely to be mature than younger men. This theme also demonstrates that younger adult men did not pair with older men simply because they have a sexual fetish. Most were indeed physically attracted to older men, but their choice to pair with older men was not just sexual. Instead, younger men felt as though they emotionally connected with older men more easily than men around their own age due to older men's emotional maturity.

Stability

Nine younger men stated that they enjoy being with older men because they are stable or more established than younger men. This theme is similar to the theme of emotional maturity, except that it involves the likely outcome of emotional security: stable lives or a stable personality. As Nicholas (30) explained, "In general, through my twenties . . . I think a large part of what has drawn me towards older men is a sense of stability, and oftentimes a level of maturity that a lot of gay guys in their twenties don't really get to." DaShawn (27) shared a similar sentiment: "What I find most attractive, I think, is the sense, it might not always be true, but the sense that they are established and they have a little bit more understanding on life." Similarly, "My favorite aspect would be having a little bit more stability," Amir (24) noted, "a little bit less of emotional turmoil you experience with some younger guys. Again, not all, but some. They can be a little less emotionally established and have more shit to unpack, so to speak." Younger men acknowledged that not all older men were stable or mature. Still, younger men felt that older men were typically more stable than men around their own age. This perception makes sense given that older men have had several more decades to establish their lives.

Older men's stability—whether emotional or financial—made connections between older and younger adult men more enjoyable. "I think that it's partly, like one, they are more established, they know what they want. It's a little less of a hassle trying to figure out what we're doing," Justin (26) explained. "They've had more experience, for the most part. They know what they want. They're established not necessarily in their personal life, like not necessarily in their goals, but just in who they are. They know who they are and they're not wishy-washy about anything." Even though older men continue to change as people and to pursue goals, they are often stable and know who they are and what they want. Anthony (25) echoed these sentiments. "Generally it's the maturity. They have their lives together, have most of their life figured out, got everything together pretty much." Kyle (25) agreed. "I guess it's the maturity behind it. And the knowledge of what you want to do in your life. You're kind of set at that point, maybe." This stability shapes older men's personalities, too. "On a personality note, they know where they're going in their life and everything like that, not still fumbling around trying to find out what they want to do," Kyle elaborated.

Older men are often more emotionally stable than younger men, and this stability means that older men are capable of creating fulfilling connections with other people to a degree unlike most men in their twenties and early thirties. Although there are, of course, many emotionally mature young men, it is true that most younger people experience tumultuous years of emerging adulthood that can affect their relationships with other people. The younger men I talked to preferred to pair with older men who had moved past those tumultuous years.

Nonsexual Experience

Twelve younger men noted that older men's experience outside of the bedroom is attractive. "Emotionally I like that older men tend to be more experienced," David (27) explained. Several younger men stated that this experience resulted in older men having greater confidence or assertiveness. The trait Chris (33) liked most about older men "would be experience. Tend to be more confident, know more what they like, what they don't like." Similarly, as Jacob (27) said, "The most attractive is a certain assertiveness or a knowing what's good and what they want from experience." This trait could, "on the other side of the coin," mean that older men are "sort of stuck in their way." Despite the risk that older men could be rigid in their beliefs or routines, younger men nonetheless enjoyed older men's experience and the ways in which this experience affected how older men interact with others.

Sometimes older men's experience was simply interesting. For instance, "Just for casual dating I like hearing their stories. They usually have a lot of good stories to tell," James (28) noted. Similarly, Cyrus (25) referred to a specific older man when he explained, "I had never met somebody in their twenties or thirties who would talk about life the way he talks about life. He's lived one. He's had several lives. And it's like a different perspective on everything. It's very interesting." Cyrus continued, "Hearing about how many lovers he's had, and how many relationships he's had, and how many places he's been to, and career changes, and tragedies, and successes. It's such a turn-on to me to be with someone who's lived it. As opposed to somebody who's tweeting at night." By virtue of having lived decades longer than men in their twenties or early thirties, older men have more stories to share. Younger men found older men's experience both exciting and arousing.

These stories could also help younger men understand more about the world outside of their own experience. William (29) enjoyed being able to "engage in a different way" with older men. "I appreciate the type of conversation I do get to have with men that are older, hearing more—I feel like there's a lot more experiences to draw upon for conversation." This dynamic could be difficult to put into words, but the effect was nonetheless noticeable. "I really enjoy conversation that is stimulating and that draws me outside of my small, like the world that I know, and so I like hearing about different experiences. And I think that dating older men gets to that at certain times." Older men's greater experience helped establish a connection with younger adult men and taught younger men how other generations of gay men have experienced the world.

Older men's greater experience also made connections with them easier. As James (28) put it, "It really does just narrow down to experience. I guess it would be experience and the energy. Older guys tend to know what they want. They've lived long enough where they're pretty certain that this is what works for them. So I like that. I like a little bit of direction." Anthony (25) shared a similar feeling. "I like the experience that older guys have," he said. "When I'm first meeting somebody it tends to feel like I can get over that hurdle a little bit quicker with older guys. A lot of them have that air of, what's the word I'm looking for? Like because they have experience it's a little bit easier for me to relax around them." Older men's experience and sense of direction established a comfortable dynamic in older-younger pairings in ways that younger men sometimes struggled to describe.

Experience could also mean that older men were more confident and assertive. In particular, "Sometimes there's an attitude of authority that I personally find attractive," as well as "a greater degree of confidence," Joshua (23) began. "Like older men, it seems to me, know more who they are and are more assertive in their attitude and in their identity." Further, he continued, "That assertiveness is something that, I don't know, gets something going in me." Older men's confidence was also helpful for Cyrus (25). "They're usually, the ones I have dated, have almost always been successful or passionate about what they do, which is important to me because I'm figuring out my career. I've found it very helpful to be with someone who was confident in what they do. And I feed off of that confidence." Older men's greater experience—and their confidence as a result of that experience—shaped their personality and how they interacted with younger men. The younger men I talked to found this dynamic attractive.

It is usually difficult for people to describe why they connect well with other people. "Chemistry" is the word many people use. Younger men overwhelmingly felt as though they had better chemistry and formed stronger connections with older men. Their personalities "clicked" better. It is possible that the younger men I talked to were more emotionally mature than others around their own age and therefore connected with older men more easily. (It is also possible that men who become daddies are more easily able to connect with younger adult men than older men who do not become daddies.) Regardless of the reasons why, younger men appreciated older men's emotional maturity, stability, and experience, and these three factors were central to why younger men chose to pair with men much older than themselves.

Better Connection or Compatibility with Older Men
Similar Goals and Outlook

In line with older men's emotional maturity, stability, and experience, eight younger men reported that they connected with older men better than men around their own age because they shared similar goals and values. "I do feel like I match well with older guys," Aydin (28) explained. "I think my thought process, the way that I view the world is aligned with maybe the way that some older men view it." He stated succinctly, "Overall our views of the world may be similar." Michael (30) provided specific reasons for this belief. "I think part of the reason that I've always been attracted to older guys is I tend to relate to them better on a mental and emotional standpoint. And partnering with them allowed me to mature a little bit quicker, I feel like. They have different expectations dealing with a younger person, but when I came into the scene they kind of understood who I was and what I stood for, and that I was a little bit farther along in the emotional development than most boys/men my age." Michael sought a similar lifestyle as older men, too. "Part of the reason I'm not really attracted to younger men," he began, is that "they were living the typical college lifestyle of going out and partying, and getting drunk, and were living out that typical kind of frat-y lifestyle, where that was not my scene. It never really has been." Notably, he also explained that he would be open to dating men around his age now that he is thirty. "But as I've gotten older, obviously some of the younger men have matured and I'd be open to dating them now that they're reaching a sense of maturity around my age, where I'm thirty, and they're thirty, and they're looking to partner for something longer-term." Even as Michael expressed openness to dating men around his own age, he also explained that he has not had sex with someone around his age for approximately a decade. Most of his sexual and romantic partners have been between twenty and thirty years older than he.

Juan (25) shared Michael's belief that older men are a better match for him. "I have this idea that older men are more mature and are more willing to settle down. I consider myself a very homebody introverted person, and I don't like going out partying or going out to bars as much as people my age normally would do or engage in those behaviors." He continued, saying, "I want a peaceful relationship," and "my perspective was older guys have that mentality more because they most likely have been through all these experiences already." He acknowledged, "I may be generalizing, but for me that seems to be more of a probability than dating a younger guy." Similarity in values was particularly evident when it came to dating. "My experiences with younger men were always very similar in terms of they didn't really know what they wanted, and there was always this conversation of like, 'I don't know what you want, what I want.' And I started to see kind of the similarity of them having this perspective of the grass is always greener on the other side." This pattern of experiences with men around his own age was frustrating. "I feel like they were always looking for the next best. And for me it was frustrating because I've always been willing, if I have what I have right now, I want to grow it here, water it here. I don't want to look for something else out there because there will probably be something else better out there, but it was so exhausting for me. So being with younger men, that seemed to be a similar trait that they portrayed." Older men were completely different, in his experience. "Whereas with older men, I think they have a better idea, or from my experiences with older men, they had a better idea and sense of 'this is what I have right now and I want to cultivate it and I want to just water it here and not spend so much time dwelling on, it could be better if I was with somebody else,' or 'you don't have this, and therefore I'm going to look for it in somebody else somewhere else.'"

Juan appreciated the fact that older men were more willing to commit to a relationship rather than wait for a hypothetical perfect person.

Cyrus (25) shared these sentiments. "Older guys tend to stick around longer is the bottom line." In contrast, "I have dated and been in a relationship and had hookups with men my age, but they tend to lose interest, which I do, too. I understand, I get it. There's so many hot twenty-five-year-olds, like sure, let's move on to the next one." Older men provided a more stable relationship experience. "The more mature guys age-wise will stick around. They'll stay with you. While maintaining their own circle of friends and daily life." Not all the younger men I interviewed sought romantic relationships with much older men. Those who did, however, felt that older men were more serious about committing to a relationship than younger men were. Whereas many younger men party, date around, or remain unsure about what they want, older men may be more interested in a stable partnership.

Even outside of dating or a partnership, young men appreciated that older men were more willing to form lasting connections. With younger guys, "It tends to be that you hook up and you never hear from them again," James (28) explained. Older men were different, in his experience.

> Whereas older men, I mean, when I was twenty-four, I hooked up with somebody who was forty-eight, which I thought was pretty fun at the time because that was double my age. We still talk pretty frequently. Our dynamic is platonic now and has been for years, but it's become a very nice friendship. I like that I have a friendship with this man now. Whereas a lot of the men that I hook up with who are around my age, it's just a one and done—sometimes two. But usually it's one time and then I never see them again.

Even absent romantic ties, it was nice to form lasting relationships with people, and older men were more likely to do so, according to James. Whether these connections turned into sexual or platonic friendships, many younger men enjoyed older men's lasting involvement.

Other younger men described their similar values with older men in terms of not being interested in drinking and partying. "In general there's a level of maturity," Nicholas (30) explained. "For example, going out drinking being a priority for a lot of people when they're younger.

A lot of people don't age out of that, but as people get older sometimes they strike a balance and have various priorities in their lives and have their priorities a little bit more settled, whereas guys closer to my age sometimes tend to be a little bit more of a mess or just not have clarity as to what their priorities are." Alejandro (26) described similar thoughts. "I guess I myself am not big on going out to bars, or parties, or drinking, or drugs or such, so with older guys they're usually not either, so I feel more comfortable just staying indoors or just a simple dinner. And maybe I'm weird, but the topics of conversation are usually more in-depth with older guys. With younger people it's more superficial, like TV shows or entertainment news, stuff like that that I don't really care about." For a multitude of reasons, including less emphasis on partying, more interest in dating or relationships, more clarity on life goals, and less emphasis on vapid popular culture, younger men felt that they could connect with older men more easily than men around their own age. This feeling encouraged them to pair with much older men.

Feeling Comforted

For reasons that were sometimes difficult to articulate, four younger men described a feeling of comfort being around older men, whereas five felt validated in the presence of an older man. When I asked Tyler (33) to explain why he paired with older men, he noted that it was "primarily comfort." He continued, "I guess it goes way back, right? So there's more comfort. I've never really been a person that relates well to my own peer group, so it's almost just not in my mental process to be attracted, hang out around or I guess fraternize with people my own age. I tend to stick to an older group." Comfort had much to do with Tyler's anxieties. "When I say 'comfort,' I suppose not being concerned with my own anxieties. There's something about being with older men for me where I just don't feel anxious. So I guess my own fears, maybe, are something that I don't think I have to worry about when I'm not with people my own age." Putting it differently, he noted, "Usually I'm the younger person going after an older guy, wanting to be emotionally affirmed because of my own anxieties." Tyler's decision to pair with older men was practical: he felt less anxious around older men, and connected with them more strongly, compared to men his own age.

Kyle (25) agreed that the company of older men was more comforting than that of younger men, albeit for reasons related to emotional intimacy: "It was more of a comforting type of feeling I got from older men to be around." He continued, "Older guys tend to be a little more sensual rather than just a heated, horny desire type of thing that you get out of younger guys. The younger guys I've been with, like before my relationship, when I'd hook up, it was more of get it done and leave type thing. But with the older guys, they wanted you to stay and to cuddle, and just be around, and just talk and whatnot. So I don't know, that's always been a driving factor of my attraction." Kyle, like older men, enjoyed cuddling and emotional intimacy more than many men around his age. Even in hookups, many younger adult men enjoyed emotional intimacy. Their sexual relationships with older men were not emotionless. Even purely sexual pairings with older men often contained more emotional intimacy than pairings with men around their own age.

Other men described a sense of validation when they were with older men. "I still feel nervous a lot when it comes to sex and I feel nervous when it comes to relationships, and when somebody calls me a boy it's like them just saying I accept you and I like you," David (27) explained. "I guess I feel flattered that somebody with so much more experience and so much more history would want to be with me, so that feels good." DaShawn (27) shared a similar sentiment about being with older men. "It felt like I was accepted," he noted, "somebody liked me, and they were older. I had something to give." Amir (24) described this dynamic with one of his older romantic partners. "I've also had some mentorship from him in terms of accepting myself as part of a community and feeling, I guess, validated and like I'm, I suppose, good enough or attractive, or likeable, or all these things." He clarified, "Part of it is validation that you get from a partner regardless of their age, but part of it is the 'I've been through this already and I know it's going to get better for you' sort of mentorship, which is important to me." Interest from older men increased several younger men's sense of self-worth.

Two men described a feeling of validation that was narcissistic. Justin (26) noted, "It's nice to feel young, comparatively, and that dynamic"—with older men—"is nice and does that." Similarly, Cyrus (25) explained that when he was nineteen, he "started noticing a trend," which was "wanting the attention from guys who were older than me." Cyrus spent quite a bit of time reflecting on this dynamic. "I've thought about this and I've had therapy and whatever, so I have uncovered it as much as I can. And I really like—this is going to sound so bad—but I really like being treated like a prize. I find that guys who are older will usually, for some reason, feel kind of like grateful that someone much younger is interested in them. And I know that sounds so bad, but I think that's one of the reasons." As Cyrus elaborated, one attractive trait of older men is "that they find me attractive. I like that." This dynamic clearly differed by age. "I tend to stay away from thirty-year-olds because I feel like that's too close to my age. See, there's a difference between dating an older guy and dating an older, older guy. Like as a twenty-five-year-old a thirty-five-year-old is older. And it's not old enough. I feel like they're established, they're confident in what they do, but I feel like they're going to be judgmental about the choices that I make in my life, and I don't like that in a man." He continued, "I feel like then they feel like they're the prize. So I stay away from guys in their early to mid-thirties. I tend to seek for forties, like midforties, fifties. There's a difference. There's a distinct difference between somebody in their midthirties and somebody in their early forties." One reason Cyrus paired with older men is that he enjoyed "being treated like a prize." Notably, while Justin and Cyrus both described this narcissistic dynamic, they were the only two younger men to do so. Most other men who described the theme of being comforted around older men stated that they felt less anxious around older men or felt flattered that older men found them desirable or interesting.

Feeling Cared for or Protected

Ten younger men noted that they felt protected, cared for, or safe when around older men. DaShawn (27), for instance, noted "a sense of safety" when explaining why he partnered with much older men. Michael (30) similarly noted that "the daddy type" includes men who "can be there to protect you, can be there to provide you insights on life, things of that nature." This safety was primarily emotional but also included a physical component. Referring to a former romantic partner, Michael mentioned, "I could be myself, 100 percent out, I could have any questions I want, but also at night, curling up to him, it made me feel safe." Michael was not the only man who mentioned that cuddling helped him feel safe. Nicholas (30) mentioned that when he is with older men he may be "cared for, in a way" that "can sometimes be paternalistic." One example he gave referred to a situation when he was on the third date with an older man: "For example, one of the last older guys that I was hanging out with, I think our third date I went over to his place and he ordered sushi, I brought beer, and we just hung out for hours. It ended with, I don't know. I much more identify as liking being controlled a lot of times, but in this instance [it proceeded] with us cuddling and me being held in a way that made me secure in a way that I haven't felt in a while. I don't know, like giving up control a little bit." Cuddling felt like a form of protection and emotional intimacy. With this theme we again see that many younger adult men enjoyed emotional intimacy with older men. This intimacy existed in a variety of relationship forms: romantic partnerships, sexual friendships, and casual hookups or dates.

Several younger men explained that their sense of protection was similar to, but different from, protection a father would provide. This feeling is what Anthony (25) referred to several times as "the whole paternal thing." Others elaborated on this concept. "In addition to the maturity level I think there's also that sense of, I don't want to use the word 'fatherhood,' but kind of that sense of security," Benjamin (26) explained. "Whether I recognize it or not, that's definitely something that leads to my attraction, I think, having that sense of security of an older man." Relatedly, one of the most attractive features of older men, John (31) explained, was a feeling of safety. "Maybe it has something to do with safety. Maybe it reminds me of, if I'm in their arms or something I just feel safe, like kind of how I did when I was in my father's arms." This point is related to one Cyrus (25) made about the type of men he found attractive. He wanted older, masculine men to "worry about me" and have "those very father figure aspects that come from dating an older man I love." Many younger men felt safe and comforted around older men because they found older men emotionally mature, stable, and experienced. Additionally, older men had already gone through the unstable years of emerging adulthood, with which the younger men were still coping.

Mentorship or Nurturance

Chapter 3 described mentorship or nurturance as key to daddyness. This section overviews similar themes, except it details more about the mentorship younger men experienced and why they sought the company of older men. Many younger men experienced mentorship that profoundly shaped their lives. When Michael (30) was twenty, he met a man in his late forties online. After talking online for three to four months, they met. "It was intended to truly just be a sexual relationship," Michael said, "but as we got to know each other more and more he would help me with insights on life. He would help me on how to take on different situations that I didn't know where the best route was." These insights included "how to take on different situations, experiences he's gone through that may be something I've gone through, whether it's a breakup or whether it's a certain situation in the workplace, or if it's a certain situation, a social situation. I think it was just I was able to speak to him almost as a therapist, for him to bounce ideas off him and share my thoughts and my emotions and have him to be there to talk to, and he would provide feedback or things that he was in a similar situation, or things of that nature." This early romantic relationship was important for Michael and shaped his young adulthood. Because most of the younger men I talked to had experiences with older men when the younger men were aged nineteen to twenty-one, older men greatly affected their emotional development.

Amir (24) also looked for older men to mentor him, and the mentorship he received was both emotional and financial. "In terms of, emotionally, I usually find them to be better at mentoring, better at being someone to guide you through things you haven't done before or life experiences you haven't had before." He continued,

> Usually what I'm looking for out of a partner is not someone who's as lost as I am about certain things, it's someone who knows a little bit more than I do and is able to give me a nudge in the right direction, so to speak, and give me advice or some sort of insight towards what should I do in this situation, or what should I do to improve my career, or what should I do to resolve this kind of issue. I'm looking for some degree of knowledge or wisdom out of a partner and a lot of times that's something that I'm looking for with an older partner.

Amir gave a specific example from his current romantic relationship.

> I'm not in a purely monogamous relationship. I'm actually in a polyam-
> orous relationship with an older couple. I guess maybe when I was look-
> ing for jobs last year I had a couple of job offers I was looking at and one
> of my partners . . . has, I guess, a fair amount of experience with recruit-
> ing and job offers and that kind of thing. So I showed him the offers I had,
> I told him what I liked and disliked about the companies, and he gave me
> some advice as to the reasons why I should choose each offer, what were
> the pros and cons. He let me make my decision, but it definitely helped
> have someone guide me through the thought process of here's what you
> should be looking for, here's the pros and cons, so to speak.

Mentorship could be emotional, or it could have material consequences,
as in Amir's example of how his partner helped him navigate competing
job offers.

Mentorship could take other concrete forms as well. Jamal (23) explained, "I'd say that what I find most attractive, beyond just the physical
features, is the idea of a person who has their life more secure and put
together than my own is at that point. It's like a mentorship thing, something you can look forward to, so if this person has this together then
they can push me to be a better person myself." He provided examples
of this dynamic from his current relationship with a man ten years older
than himself: "My partner has helped teach me how to drive, he's helped
teach me how to shave my facial hair, he's helped me navigate moving
[between US regions], and as far as how do I look for a job effectively
and that sort of stuff, so overall life skills mentorship."

Mentorship could also be sexual. "The first sexual experience that
I ever had was with an older man," Justin (26) explained. "I originally
looked specifically for older men because I knew that they would know
how to do things and I didn't know how to do things, as opposed to
looking like a fool with one of my peers the first time and not knowing what to do. I think what I did was put an ad on Craigslist saying
someone teach me how to have sex." This fear of "looking like a fool" is
particularly strong in young adulthood; Justin was nineteen or twenty
when he sought his first male-male sexual experience. This experience

helped him learn about sex and he took this knowledge to encounters with men of a variety of ages.

Anthony (25) reported one of the most involved mentoring dynamics, a situation that changed the course of his life. When Anthony was nineteen, he met a man online in his late fifties. At this time in his life Anthony was unhappy because of where he lived, in an isolated rural area. "I absolutely hated it. I was miserable there. I was a recluse and I never left the house, didn't do anything because I had nothing to do. Didn't really have much of a friend group after high school. And my dad was, let's just say, basically being around my house was like walking on eggshells 100 percent of the time. Any potential small thing could set them off and it was a really bad situation for everybody in the house." Anthony considered his options. "I was like all right, I'm absolutely miserable. I was probably a bit suicidal at the time, and if I didn't do something about it I wasn't going to get any better. I didn't really have much in the way of opportunities there. So I took my ex up on his offer to come visit for a few days and ultimately it was one of the best things that ever happened to me." This decision may have saved his life. He explained, "Every now and then I think about where I would have ended up if I hadn't ended up moving in with my ex, and it's not something that I particularly like to think about. It humbles me a bit to realize that even though there were a lot of issues with my ex, it was ultimately a very beneficial experience for me."

Although Anthony and his former partner are no longer together, Anthony gained much from that partnership and remains close to his former partner. "My favorites were how much I learned from him and how much I learned about myself in the time frame, and how many new experiences that I had while we were together." Just as importantly, Anthony's former partner did not attempt to unduly influence him.

> He gave me the opportunity to be individualistic and not rely and depend on [him] for every single little thing, allowed me to be very self-sufficient, as much as we could, and the opportunities that he presented to me by us being together allowed me to go move from the middle of nowhere to a huge city that ultimately shaped who I am now. And he was always super supportive of me, like 99 percent of the time, and he helped me really

move forward as a person and made me a lot happier in my life, and made my life a lot more stable, and felt like I had a support system that would always be there for me.

Thanks in large part to the mentorship he received, Anthony reported that he matured quite a bit during this relationship.

Anthony and his former partner remain close to this day. "We still talk. He's been giving me advice on how to handle certain things in regard to what's going on with the pandemic and everything, financially and in general how to potentially feel a little bit safer like when I have to go out and about and whatnot." This positive early relationship shaped what Anthony looks for in future older-younger pairings, particularly a dynamic in which older men mentor him but do not try to control his choices. "Most attractive is the patern[al] aspect, the fact that they have that experience to not necessarily lead me along, but they can give me suggestions and if they've been through an experience, firsthand knowledge, might give me advice." Anthony makes sure that he retains his sense of independence, much as he did when in his prior partnership. "I like having the advice, but I don't like the whole power thing that comes with it. I prefer having somebody try to guide me rather than try to tell me what I should be doing." Anthony, like most other young men I talked to, was aware that age differences could be associated with power differentials. As a result, he was mindful of the dynamics in his relationships with older men and ensured that he never felt controlled.

Kyle (25) also described mentorship dynamics with his two partners, both of whom are around the age of forty, particularly related to coming out. "Initially it was just friends, and then helping me through the coming-out process, since they were already knowledgeable in it and everything like that and been through hard times and stuff. And then it grew into a romantic relationship." He explained that their help was valuable when he was coming out. "They helped me a lot on the religious side of things. Like my family is very religious, and one of my boyfriends, his family was, too, so he was able to relate and guide me through steps and easing my parents into the whole swing of things." Many younger men benefited from older men's mentorship, and actively sought that mentorship when they paired with older men. Kyle's story demonstrates that older-younger pairings between adults are uniquely important for gay and bisexual men, some of whom need support or advice when they come out to their families.

Younger men's mentorship stories collectively show three main things. First, mentorship was not simply a side effect of older-younger pairings; younger adult men actively sought mentorship. Second, there was not a misunderstanding between older and younger men about the value of mentorship. Younger men did not simply tolerate older men's attempts to mentor them, and older men did not misunderstand the value of their advice. For instance, older men did not think they were being helpful when younger men actually found their advice irritating. That situation was uncommon. Both older and younger men knew that mentorship was an aspect of older-younger pairings and valued this practice. Third, mentorship provided benefits specific to gay and bisexual men, including knowledge about sex and coming out. Mentorship is a key reason why older and younger adult men pair with one another, and it is central to daddyness.

Distinct Interpersonal Dynamics

Several younger men described distinct interpersonal dynamics with older men that did not exist with younger men. These dynamics were difficult to explain but nonetheless made experiences with older men more enjoyable and typically also created stronger connections between older and younger men. As Alejandro (26) described, "Guys around my age, I feel like there's a certain way I'm supposed to behave or act around them, and with older guys I don't feel that way. I feel like I can just be myself with them." Relatedly, Tyler (33) noted, "Age-wise, I almost am slightly unattracted just by hearing the [age] of people that fall close to myself. It's almost like I just assume that it won't happen well or there won't be a lot of common interests or something. Again, there's just something with people my own age group, I tend not to relate too well." Tyler, like several other younger men I talked to, explained that he connected with older men better than men around his age. Aydin (28) detailed a similar feeling. "Aside from the physical attraction there's definitely a deeper kind of romantic feeling once the relationship gets there. And I say that because in the times that I've been in parallel going through the process of exploring whether a relationship would or would not be possible or be a good fit I think I am more inclined to develop feelings for older men as opposed to men my age." Younger men felt as though they connected with older men more strongly than with men around their own age, and this connection led some younger men to develop feelings for older men.

Jacob (27) described a unique dynamic in which older men respect his boundaries more than men around his own age. "They tend to respect the boundaries in a sort of casual way that I think people my generation don't. It maybe has something to do with an experience of cruising culture and how having been cruising pre apps or whatever, I think there's a different sort of social contract to that. Whereas I think for a lot of people of my generation it's just different, and in my mind I feel more assured in that social contract when I'm with older guys than when I am with younger ones." In addition to feeling that older men respected his boundaries more than younger men did, Jacob also noticed a "provider" dynamic related to large age differences. "I think about the other things that define those sexual experiences, whether that's like, daddies typically want you to come to their house instead of them coming to your house. Or after we have sex a lot of times they'll feed me something or give me coffee or a beer. There's sort of a performance beyond the actual act of fucking that's like, I'm the daddy here, I'm the provider here. And I think that's pretty definitive of those experiences to me. Of course to varying degrees." This dynamic was distinct from that which existed with men around his own age. Whether their feelings of connection were due to qualities of older men or difficult-to-describe dynamics that existed in older-younger pairings, or both, younger men felt like they connected to older men better than men around their own age.

Understanding older references or greater levels of comfort with older people in general also made connections with older men more comfortable. "I grew up with my grandparents and I think I've always [been] attracted to people, whether that's friendships or things like that, with older people, whether it's ten or twenty years or more," DaShawn (27) explained. "I think it's just something natural for me because I was always around it since a young age. I think that plays a big part." Similarly, John (31) explained, "I am able to talk to older guys a little easier than guys who are younger than me or my age, mainly because I grew up in an older family." He continued, "I get a lot of the references because I watch a lot of old films and things, so there's that. I don't know, it's just, it's easy. It's something that I don't have to think too hard about all the time, I can just go with it." Shared references and comfort around older people helped John connect with older men better than men around his age. Cyrus (25) touched on similar themes. "They know how to do everything better. They know how to flirt better. They just get me better than guys my age. If I were to talk about, I don't know, *Twin Peaks*, they would get it better than somebody who's twenty-five who doesn't know who Audrey Horne is." Overall, "I really do connect with older guys rather than younger guys."

Several men pointed to older men's better communication to explain why they connected with older men better. Overall, "They usually know what they want and they're more inclined to say that up front when we're meeting or talking," Justin (26) explained. "If they have issues or something, or if something's not going the way that they wanted it to they say something right away and I don't have to pretend like I know what they want, or pretend like I understand them, because I do." This dynamic was not present with younger men. "Versus a lot of times with younger people it's a lot more complicated trying to figure out what, when, where, why, how. Younger people are much more likely to ghost or to drag things along, whereas older men are more to the point." Similarly, Austin (27) explained, "I like how older men, generally, they're quicker to pick up on my communication. . . . If I give a subtle hint or if I even say something they'll usually pick up on it and respond to it quicker, which makes the experience more pleasurable for me because then they are listening to what I'm saying and giving me that either right away or working towards it. Whereas with younger men you have to be a little bit more explicit with your communication, and that can take away from the focus of actually enjoying each other." Better communication made older-younger pairings between adults more enjoyable both sexually and nonsexually. This theme connects to prior ones about greater experience, maturity, and stability. By virtue of those three qualities, older men typically communicate more effectively than younger men.

Sex and Physicality

Physical Attraction

Twenty of twenty-six younger adult men described physical attractions to older men. While this finding may seem obvious given their sexual involvement with older men, a common stereotype is that younger people have older partners *despite* older men's looks rather than *because* of them, for instance because the younger person is a gold digger or has personality issues. While the book up to this point has helped to disprove these ideas, it is worth briefly overviewing younger men's physical attractions—especially because little prior research has examined attraction to people in midlife or older adulthood.[2] Physical attraction often went hand in hand with emotional attraction, as earlier sections detailed. "I think there's always a physical attraction there," Aydin (28) explained, and "I think then it goes beyond that once I get to know them." Younger men did not pair with older men only because of older men's greater experience, emotional maturity, and so on; they also found older men physically attractive. In short, for younger men, older men were fulfilling both physically and emotionally.

Younger men found older men highly physically desirable. Several pointed to specific characteristics associated with aging that they found particularly attractive. Joshua (23) explained, "Physically I really, for some reason, like the aesthetic of graying hair. I'm not exactly sure what it is. Like salt and pepper look, I don't know, it's appealing to me physically." Amir (24) described, "I just find myself more physically attracted to them generally. I guess some wrinkles, silver hair, that kind of thing are attractive traits. They're not strict requirements, but they're definitely a strong preference." Michael (30) noted that he was attracted to "guys that are hairier, muscular-ish" yet not necessarily "super buff," and men who are "a little bit weathered if you will, their skin [has] a little bit of rough to it, beards, goatee facial hair, balding or very little hair." Austin (27) agreed. "I really like receding hairlines," he noted. William (29) went into more detail: "There's some sexual chemistry and sexual attraction that I have towards older men typically. That's not to say that I don't have attraction for people my own age, but it's that there's definitely a through line of being attracted to older men in my life." Overall, he noted, "I love gray hair, I like a beard. Signs of age I find are things that are attractive.

I like men that wear glasses. Those sorts of physical features I find really are the things that draw me most." Gray, silver, or salt-and-pepper hair, receding hairlines, "weathered" skin, and body hair were among the characteristics younger men found attractive.

Other younger men did not describe specific physical characteristics that they found attractive in older men, but nonetheless made clear that they typically preferred older men in part for physical reasons. Nicholas (30) began, "In general, physically there's an aesthetic and maturity." He continued, "Older, hairy men, for whatever reason, do it for me in a way that younger guys tend not to." Tyler (33), relatedly, noted that what he finds most attractive about older men is "physique, because they just look different than younger built guys. So physique. I do especially like faces." More succinctly, DaShawn (27) noted, "Physically I think there's a sex appeal when it comes to maturity." John (31) similarly explained, "I just have never really been attracted to the youth look. Much more rugged, handsome, older guys" are who he finds attractive. Anthony (25) was blunt: "My physical attractions are just not there for younger guys."

Some younger men described characteristics that were not necessarily caused by age, but that in their experience were more common in older men. For instance, Jeffrey (23) explained, "They look more mature. That really attracts me. I tend to go for guys who are really masculine—muscular build, stocky. I like guys with beards and that tends to be a lot of older guys." Benjamin (26) agreed. "There's physical things that I think are attractive about older gentlemen." He continued, "There's just some features like a full beard, more hair on your chest and stuff like that. That stuff I like." Beards, body hair, muscularity, and stockier builds are not limited to men in midlife and older adulthood, but several younger men linked these traits with older men.

The younger men I talked to differed in whether they were physically attracted to guys around their age. Some had absolutely no physical interest in men unless they were in midlife or older adulthood. Other young men were physically attracted to older men in addition to men around their own age, although physical attractions to younger men were not always accompanied by emotional attractions. What younger men shared was physical—and emotional—attraction to older men.

Younger adult men did not pair with older men because they had no other options. Nor did they pair with older men despite their looks. Instead, younger men actively sought pairings with older men due to both physical attraction and emotional compatibility. In short, for many of the younger men I talked to, older men were simply more desirable than men around their own age.

Better Sex or More Sexual Experience

Eleven younger adult men explained that sex with older men was either better or provided more opportunities for sexual exploration. Nine men also noted that older men's greater sexual experience was a factor that shaped their choice to pair with older men. As Joshua (23) put it, "I've noticed the more and more that I've been with older guys that they tend to actually be more compassionate and giving in bed. . . . I have noticed, for instance, like they care more about making sure that their partner is pleasured and they know more ways to do it. They know of more techniques, more things that a person can do to make the other person feel good, and they seem to genuinely care more about the experience and the person than just getting their rocks off. That's the general trend that I've noticed." Older men provided a better sexual experience, both because they are better at sex and because they seem to care about their sexual partner. Sex with older men could be more egalitarian, too. "They are very much into making sure that everybody is satisfied. I mean, I feel like there's always a scoreboard above the bed. If he comes then I have to come, too. So they're very good with that," Cyrus (25) noted. Older men made the entire sexual experience better, including but not limited to the sex itself. "I find a lot of guys around my age are . . ." James (28) began before pausing and laughing. "I don't know how to put this delicately. They're pretty focused on just getting off and then running out, as it were. A lot of older guys, they need a bit more time, and I personally like that." Needing more time meant that encounters with older men could be more intimate.

Better sex extended beyond sex acts, too. Older men are "more intimate, they're more sensual," David (27) explained, including through kissing.

> I think younger guys have a bit more of a casual view of sex, and it's more
> fun to have sex with a younger guy in some ways, but then it's more emo-

tionally connective to have sex with an older guy, from my perspective. I end up kissing with older guys a lot more than I would with guys my own age, for some reason. I find there's a lot more physical closeness and stuff like that. It's not just about the sex act. It's about the whole experience of intimacy. So I do really like that with older men.

Older men were more skilled at establishing intimacy than younger men. One way this intimacy manifested was through more kissing. "I find that I kiss older guys a lot more often. There's a lot more making out, a lot more passionate kissing," David continued. Older men's focus on the entire experience—not just penetration—enhanced emotional connection and made the encounter more enjoyable.

Many younger adult men also noted that older men were more willing to engage in kink practices than men around their own age. "I have a very specific list of kinks [and] I find that older guys are a lot more willing to indulge in freakier things, and I appreciate that a lot," Joshua (23) noted. This willingness included "various small-scale kind of BDSM stuff. Some of the things I've experimented with older guys that I've never heard any younger guy ever mention, or bring up, or want to do is like, there's lots of nipple play, lots of sensation play, things like the use of ice cubes, for instance, is an interesting thing, or hot and cold kind of stuff. What else? Body contact in general. For instance, I'm really big into rimming both ways and I find a lot more older men that are cool with that than younger men." Joshua appreciated the ability to engage in a wide range of sexual practices. He noted, "Sometimes I'm also down to lick somebody's armpits, or down to lick somebody's feet, or vice versa, and I've again noticed that older men are more willing to indulge me in that aspect than younger guys. They're like, 'Yeah, whatever makes you feel good.' And I'm like, 'Man, I appreciate that, thank you.'" Alejandro (26) agreed. "I guess with older guys, they're more comfortable doing more kinky sex, and they're more open to being submissive with me. With guys my age, I feel like there's a lot more butting heads, a lot more negotiation with them, and with older guys it's a lot easier for me." Examples of "kinky sex" included "leather and maybe some role playing," including a "dominant-submissive" dynamic. Amir (24) also appreciated this greater comfort with kinks and sexual experience. "Sexually speaking there's definitely less of me having to be the more experienced or more knowledgeable partner. There's definitely an expectation of common knowledge, generally speaking, when there's a shared kink interest. I don't have to hand-hold someone else through explaining what the kink is and how it works and there's less of a reaction of 'Oh, you're kinky, that's so weird,' or 'That's so neat.' There's less of that novelty attitude and more 'Oh, okay, cool,' if that makes sense." Older men were more knowledgeable about and respectful of kinks, and more willing to engage in kink practices.

A handful of men speculated why older men may be more accepting of kinks. "I feel like there's less judgment involved," David (27) explained. "I don't know if it's just because they've seen more of the world or whatever, but if you're interested in kink or anything like that, you've got a better chance of meeting like-minded men if you're looking older." James (28) explained that another reason may be that older men are less focused on penetration. "I think in general I tend to have more foreplay with older men and I tend to get kinkier with older men. They're less focused on penetration and more on experiences. I would say I've explored kink a lot more with older men than I have with men my own age," including "water sports" and "leather protocol." Older men's focus on the entire experience, rather than penetration, made the encounter better for everyone. Another reason older men were more willing to engage in kinks, according to John (31), is that "they're more into accepting the fetishes that they're actually into." In other words, older men may not have as much internalized stigma about their kink preferences as younger men.

Greater acceptance of kink may result from more life experience that makes older men less self-conscious about kinky sex. Greater willingness to engage in kink may also be due to the fact that older men, on average, were more exposed to nonnormative sexual practices in the 1970s, 1980s, and 1990s, before there was as much of an emphasis on LGBTQ assimilation into mainstream society. In prior decades, gay cultural worlds were more autonomous from mainstream society and developed alternative sexual norms. Distinct norms still exist, but partial assimilation into wider society has led to increased numbers of young men who seek conventional relational arrangements such as monogamy.[3]

Older men's greater experience with sex also made sexual experiences better. "I've thought about this before, actually, and I think it's because when they are older it can be assumed that they have more experience because they've lived longer, and a lifestyle where they're having gay sex, and so what my brain says when I see someone older is, 'Okay, you know what you're doing, this will be fun,'" Austin (27) explained. "I think there's less chance of it being bad because they've had a longer time to learn what they're doing," Jacob (27) added. Experience was particularly beneficial in exploration of new kinks. "I think experience level is something that I really appreciate. It's something I find very attractive," Terry (24) explained. "Especially when I'm working to explore something that is either more dangerous or is just something that's new to me in general, I really tend to value someone who has done it for a long time who can guide me through the activity safely. And so that's one of the things that I tend to appreciate the most." Indeed, as Justin (26) noted when referring to men around his own age, "I guess the inexperience is a little off-putting. I like someone who knows what they want."

Overall, many younger adult men felt that sex with older men was better than sex with men around their own age. Emotional intimacy was more common in older-younger sexual pairings than in age-similar sexual pairings, for one thing. Older men also tended to focus on the pleasure of both partners, were interested in the entire sexual experience rather than just penetration, had the sexual experience to know how to make sex feel good, and were knowledgeable about kinks. Although social science research typically does not examine sexual pleasure, doing so is critical if scholars want to fully understand sexual life.[4]

Being Controlled or Dominated

Nine younger adult men noted that they paired with older men so they could be controlled or dominated in a consensual sexual dynamic. This preference was similar to a dominant-submissive kink. "I can be more submissive with older men," Chris (33) explained. There is "an understanding about, I guess mutual respect and care when it comes to sexual relationships. I like that it frames the relationship as one with someone with more experience, more confidence, more control, but still a respectful and caring relationship."

Submissive-dominant power dynamics were evident in terminology. As David (27) stated about the term "boy," "It's putting on a mildly submissive persona." Overall, "'boy' hits a sweet spot where it's like I'm still my own person, but somebody else knows better and can help me make decisions." This dynamic ties in to how David uses "daddy."

> It's funny. At first it took me some getting used to because it was kind of a weird thing to say. But now I'm just so used to it. I like it because it puts me in a more sub-y mindset, and I like the sense of I guess, confidence that it gives them when you do it. Like when you call somebody "daddy" and then they light up or get horny or whatever, it's just fun to watch the reaction that happens with it. So that's something I really enjoy, seeing what the guy does when you use that term. They tend to get a little more aggressive, get a little bit more dominant, and that's fun for me.

"Daddy"-"boy" language helps to establish a dominant-submissive dynamic for David, which is what he prefers with older men. Indeed, "It's a little bit less reciprocal when I'm with an older guy, but I like that. I like being more the service-oriented one, like I'm here to help get him off, and that's a little bit different than with guys my age. With guys my age I expect it to be more of a give and take. And I still want it to be give and take with an older guy, but I like them to take more." David and several other younger men enjoyed being submissive around older men to fulfill a sexual kink.

Dominance and submission could involve more physical aspects too. "It usually involves the man having a strong grip on me," Austin (27) began. "That to me is taking complete control in the situation, whether it's me being picked up, me being held, me being positioned, where he is doing the physical, like when you're dancing when he's leading, that's the best way to put it. And it could be as simple as like a subtle, like, hand moving my jaw one way or, you know, holding me in a certain grip." These practices require excellent communication, and "not just the physical communication, but also verbal communication." Cyrus (25) agreed and explained, "Sexually they will hold me. I like that. Like hold me down, pin me down. They're very good with that." Additionally, "I think it's a dominance thing, too. I like that. Sexually I like to be more submissive. I find it more common with older guys that they want to be more dominant in bed, so that's also an attraction."

Older men's sexual dominance allowed younger adult men to experience pleasure without having to be in control or worry about whether they were doing something incorrectly. Older men helped younger adult men enjoy sex but without pressures or expectations that would exist if younger men were expected to be dominant. It is likely that age differences helped make the dominant/submissive dynamic feel more natural for younger men who wanted to be submissive. Not all younger men enjoyed being submissive with older men—several, in fact, enjoyed being dominant regardless of the age of their partner—but those who did enjoy being submissive explained that older men were ideal partners.

Distinct Sexual Dynamics

In addition to unique nonsexual dynamics that were present in older-younger pairings between adults, there were also distinct sexual dynamics that were difficult to describe. For instance, William (29) explained why he enjoyed calling older men "daddy." "I think that there's this piece of the way that it changes the dynamics in the room," he described. "I enjoy narrative, I enjoy a story, and I think that adds narrative to what's happening in the bedroom. And I think that there's this piece of how it alters the interaction and adds," he began, "subtle guidelines around what we're doing." He continued, "It changes the interaction" because "it adds more depth to what we're doing."

Several men struggled to articulate how the dynamic with older men was different. "I don't feel comfortable dating people younger than me, for one. Don't know why that is. There's been a lot of things," Joshua (23) explained. In particular, "There's a little bit of an appeal sexually for me being with somebody older. I don't know exactly how to put my finger on it. I think it's like experience is a little bit of a turn-on." Later, Joshua described why he might feel this way. "This is going to sound really gross, but the thing that appeals to me is sometimes this sort of raunchy, lecherous attitude. It's again the confidence of older guys, [they] know who they are and they're not afraid to kind of like be a little more gross and fun and lighthearted in the bedroom. Just that attitude of aggressive, raw, masculine sexuality is something that draws me in, and . . . I don't always see that same assertiveness with people closer to my own age."

In ways he found difficult to describe, Joshua and other younger men considered it arousing to pair with older men. Younger adult men did not pretend that age differences did not exist. Instead, they found these age differences pleasurable.

During sexual encounters, age differences changed interpersonal dynamics in ways that were both playful and arousing. Younger men did not necessarily call older men "daddy," but age differences were obvious, and both parties typically acknowledged them in ways that improved sexual chemistry. Many younger adult men identified distinct dynamics, sexual or nonsexual, that existed in older-younger pairings that did not exist between themselves and men around their age. These dynamics, while varied and difficult to describe, made the experience of being with older men more enjoyable. In short, connections and chemistry with older men were typically better than with men around their own age.

Issues with Biological Fathers?

Most younger men did not describe any issues with their biological fathers that they felt shaped their attractions to older men. Several younger men explicitly denied this possibility and explained that their enjoyment of being around older men did not exist because they had a poor relationship with their own fathers. As David (27) noted, "I had a great family life. I don't really think it has anything to do with replacing a father figure or anything like that. I have supportive parents and they're even supportive of my being gay and all that, so it's nothing familial, really, that I'm trying to replace." Michael (30) similarly explained, "I've always had a very supportive family and I've had a very close relationship with my dad and my grandfather." Attractions to older men, in most cases, had nothing to do with the younger man's relationship with his own biological father. Paternal dynamics were appealing in and of themselves because they helped to form a comforting connection between older and younger adult men. They did not indicate unmet needs for something biological fathers did not provide.

While undoubtedly some younger men have "daddy issues" stemming from problems with their own fathers, few younger men shared stories that even remotely touched on this idea. The belief that older-younger pairings between adults are driven by poor father relationships is a stereotype with little empirical support. As this chapter demonstrates, there were many reasons younger adult men paired with older men. These reasons are not reducible to stereotypes about father-son issues.

Older men in roles that involve mentorship—including archetypical roles such as father, coach, and teacher—are often associated with a paternal warmth. These roles involve helping younger people mature, and perhaps also providing emotional nurturance within the bounds of conventional masculinity. Even men in midlife or older adulthood who are not in these types of roles are quite different from younger men, given that they have had decades longer to mature. Although not all older men are mentors or even good people, older men are often seen as supportive figures. Thus, younger adult men who are attracted to older men may find comfort in the warmth associated with older men (among other traits), but this interest usually does not indicate issues with their own fathers. Given that older men are culturally associated with a range of positive characteristics, it makes sense that younger adult men enjoy involvement with them.

There were, however, three men who speculated that issues with their biological fathers may have shaped their interest in older men. They did not have incest fantasies, but rather described an unfulfilling relationship with their father as a reason for their interest in older men. "I reflect back on my relationship with my father," Juan (25) explained. To earn money for the family, his father lived in a different country for most of Juan's childhood, "so I really didn't have that son-to-father relationship that I would have loved." He continued, "It's crazy to say this, but sometimes I feel like dating older men kind of gets me that ability. Not in terms of that son and father relationship, but in terms of having that older person to kind of be in your life. I don't know if that makes sense, but I share some similarities or feelings about my relationship with my father and how I want my relationship with my partners to be." Juan believed that older romantic partners perhaps fulfilled his desire to have a supportive older person in his life. Juan's relationship with his father was not negative, but it was emotionally distant. This story is similar to findings in studies of transnational fathering.[5]

In contrast, Jamal (23) explained that a negative relationship with his father may have shaped his desires for older men today.

It's really a rough thing to talk about, particularly because nobody wants to feel like they're a stereotype. But there's some things I feel like Dr. Freud was right about in his studies where it's like if you have an absent father figure, that's something that you crave for your healthy development as an adult. And as somebody whose father was a part of my life, but not a positive influence, it's something that I feel like I particularly want in my experience, and as somebody who's involved in leather culture, that's something I specifically need to feel satisfied in relationships.

Jamal's negative relationship with his father is in part due to his father's unhealthy enactments of masculinity and attempts to force a similar understanding of masculinity onto Jamal.

His idea of masculinity is very much wrapped in that kind of militaristic outlook on life. It's very much about achievement and following rules and order, which is something that I crave, but it was enforced upon me. And senses of failure that I had for not reaching those goals in those ways made me feel like a less masculine and less successful person. And so a big example was he really wanted my brother and I to do sports, and my brother was older and muscular and more taller than me because we have different dads, so he had a better genetic setup for doing that kind of thing.

Jamal tried out for sports, but it did not go well.

I tried out for football. It just didn't work for me. I tried out for rugby and that wasn't a thing for me. And I settled on soccer as the most physical sport I could handle, and my dad was never really invested in me doing that, and he was always hypercritical of my performance in the sport, where it's like, "You should be doing better than this, you shouldn't be stuck in the goal box, you should be out there running around chasing the ball with the other kids, you should be not afraid to rough them up to get access to the ball," that kind of thing. So the idea of not being as physical of a person in that kind of stuff really affected my own masculinity.

These childhood experiences were difficult for Jamal and continue to affect him today. "As a child I knew the kind of person that I felt like

I really wanted to be and not having that identity be respected by my father really affected me in the sense that, is it really okay to think these things about myself, and if they aren't, why do I feel this way anyway if it's not the normal thing to do?" Pairing with older men allowed Jamal to experience validation from older people, which he did not experience as an adolescent from his own father.

Benjamin (26) also noted that difficulties with his father may have shaped his interest in older men, although these difficulties only began for him as an adult. "I had a really good upbringing, really good family life," he explained. Unfortunately, Benjamin's relationship with his father soured after Benjamin came out in his early twenties. "It was almost like a night and day break in our relationship." He felt that "everything up until that point was almost staged, because he didn't know the true me." These experiences are why, he explained, "Having that older authority figure both physically attracted to me and invested in my life really is satisfying on multiple levels."

Most of the younger adult men I talked to did not report any issues with their fathers that they felt shaped their attractions to older men. Several men explicitly denied this possibility. A small minority of men— three of twenty-six younger men (11.5 percent)—did, however, report that negative relationships with their fathers shaped their interest in older men. Pairing with older men allowed them to experience connection to or validation from an older man that they did not experience earlier in life, due to either a nonexistent relationship with their father or a negative one. Poor father-son relationships do not appear to be a primary reason that younger adult men pair with older men, but it is a factor that affects a small number of men.

5

Daddyness and Masculinity

Little research has examined how aging or older-younger pairings between adults are related to masculinity, even though masculinity shifts over the life course.[1] Masculinity consists of "the practices, behaviors, attitudes, sexualities, emotions, positions, bodies, organizations, institutions, and all manners of expectations culturally associated with (though not limited to) people understood to be male."[2] Masculinity varies by social context, and individuals reinforce masculinity in different ways. While prior research has clearly shown how masculinity is constructed in adolescence and young adulthood, less research considers how masculinity shifts during or past midlife.[3]

Many life changes can shape how middle-aged men enact masculinity. Involvement in fathering is one example.[4] Men construct masculinity differently as they age: for instance, some heterosexual men reduce heavy drinking, which they did in youth to bond with peers, to instead focus on "breadwinning" for wives and children.[5] Many middle-aged men bolster self-esteem by framing themselves as wiser and more responsible than younger men, and more self-sufficient and physically able than older men.[6] In terms of sexuality, men at or past midlife may take medications to address erectile dysfunction or delink masculinity from sex, focusing instead on nonsexual intimacy.[7] Both strategies bolster men's masculinity when it may otherwise be challenged, given the association between sex and masculinity.

The authors of a comprehensive review of studies about masculinity in older adulthood past midlife explain, "The rules that older men followed were nuanced versions of the idealized masculinity script" and such men did things "to acquire and retain others' respect, to project an aura of toughness and independence, and to be courageous risk takers when necessary."[8] Being a grandfather and working past conventional retirement ages for reasons other than financial necessity also bolster masculinity in older men.[9] Men in older adulthood often find sexual and physical limitations posed by aging to be potential threats to their masculinity,[10] but at the same time they may bolster their masculinity by emphasizing how their bodies nonetheless achieve ideals related to strength, health, and autonomy.[11]

Many heterosexual men know that aging will lead to marginalization in older adulthood, but rather than challenging this marginalization, they try to prevent themselves from becoming "old" for as long as possible, for instance, through exercise and a healthy diet.[12] Even as masculinity shifts over time in response to changes to bodies as well as work and living contexts, how it shifts is not reducible to a simplistic and condescending narrative of "decline."[13]

The nuances of how aging shapes masculinity have been underexplored among gay and bisexual men, who understand masculinity in ways distinct from heterosexual men.[14] Existing research shows that many older gay men experience positive changes as they age, including greater confidence, but also disadvantages, such as disconnection from gay communities and younger gay men.[15] There are both similarities and differences in how gay and bisexual men, on one hand, and heterosexual men, on the other, experience midlife. Both groups report frustration with bodily changes that may make it more difficult to engage in certain physical activities (such as sports) or to recover from injuries, as well as concerns about erectile dysfunction.[16]

However, gay and bisexual men typically report more concern than heterosexual men about becoming unattractive.[17] Additionally, gay men may experience isolation due to ageism in gay communities, particularly in older adulthood.[18] Even middle-aged gay men can experience ageism; as a result, some men view their age negatively and try to look or act younger, whereas others frame their age as a positive attribute that has given them better communication skills, greater perspective, or more accomplishments than younger men.[19] Maintaining sexual activity and perceived desirability also boosts gay men's satisfaction with midlife.[20] Other gay men in or past midlife seek to appear younger by exercising, maintaining a healthy diet, engaging in certain cosmetic practices (such as hair removal or medical interventions to modify skin appearance and body fat), and forming social networks with younger men.[21]

Aging shapes masculinity due to the ways in which bodies, relationships, involvement in institutions, social networks, and social practices change over time. There are many commonalities between gay and bisexual men, on one hand, and heterosexual men, on the other, as well as some key differences, especially those related to perceived physical attractiveness. An underexplored dynamic, however, is how aging—among gay and bisexual men, specifically—may actually *boost* masculinity, rather than being a trait to "overcome," particularly as aging relates to involvement in age-gap pairings between adults.

Related to this point is the fact that few older men discussed ageism. While ageism undoubtedly exists, the increased popularity of daddies over the past decade or so appears to have reduced ageism for many men in their forties through their sixties. A sizable segment of the gay world today values men in midlife and older adulthood. This valuation helps to shield many older men from ageism, even as it still exists.

Many older men felt that daddyness bolstered their masculinity because daddyness went hand in hand with mentoring and feeling desired by younger adult men. Mentorship allowed daddies and younger men to express care and emotional vulnerability in ways both parties felt were masculine. Mentorship also gave men the opportunity to be role models or to feel helpful. The stories of the men I talked to show that daddyness can bolster masculinity in midlife or older adulthood when masculinity is otherwise threatened by aging. Importantly, few older or younger men described feminine daddies. This omission suggests that most men implicitly or explicitly tied daddyness to masculinity.

Stories of younger adult men were more complicated than those of older men. Pairing with older men made some younger men feel *more* masculine because they learned from older men what it means to be a masculine gay or bisexual man, because they felt desired by a masculine man, or simply because they had sex. Other younger men felt *less* masculine because they enacted a submissive sexual role with older men as part of a sexual kink. (Not all younger men tied submissiveness to femininity, however.) Still other young men felt that pairing with a more masculine older man affirmed their feminine traits. In contrast, no older men reported feeling more feminine by pairing with younger men. Older men's masculinity is a blueprint for younger men, and this dynamic had varied effects on how younger men perceived their masculinity. The effects varied depending on the man as well as different personal factors such as the degree to which younger men linked sexual submissiveness to femininity (if they were sexually submissive). These findings parallel research about three cohorts of gay and bisexual men, which shows that men aged eighteen to twenty-five rate themselves as less masculine than men in the other two cohorts, aged thirty-four to forty-one and fifty-two to fifty-nine.[22]

Daddy Masculinity

Twenty-two older men explicitly linked daddyness to masculinity. Mentorship of younger adult men, in particular, boosted their masculinity. Ryan (48) noted that he feels most masculine "definitely in the interactions with the boys, either chatting on the apps or in person does make me feel more masculine." He elaborated, "I think the control and the confidence, almost like they look up to you like a father figure type thing." Ryan continued, "Not having kids of my own I guess also might play into that. It's kind of an outlet for that, for being a father and a role model in a masculine way."

Other men agreed that being a role model to younger men was fulfilling and made them feel more masculine. Jay (58) noted that he feels most masculine "when I am providing what I'll call fatherly or daddy assistance, whether it's my own biological kids or the young men that I meet who are seeking that kind of advice." Relatedly, Jordy (57) explained, "It does make me probably feel more masculine because in some cases it feels like a parental role, which it's like a fatherly role so it makes me feel probably more masculine being in that role." Enrique (62) also noted that being perceived as a daddy bolstered his masculinity: "Since I don't have any children it makes me feel pretty good. So I like to be known as a daddy."[23] Referring to masculinity, Steven (60) too expressed, "It probably boosts it a little bit. You know, that younger guys are looking up to me as a dad figure." Greg (50) went into further detail about why he felt that daddyness boosted his masculinity. He attributed this boost to a "sense of responsibility." Referring to two younger FWBs, he noted that he feels masculine "when I feel responsible for people, when I'm looking out for Jerry with his depression, or thinking about Tim with his job change, for example, I feel like more of a man. I like that. It's very satisfying and very edifying to me."

Many older men felt more masculine because they mentored younger adult men and because younger men looked up to them. Several older men described these dynamics as paternal, not in that they treated younger adult men as substitute sons but rather in that they provided a positive presence in a young man's life. Men who were biological fathers drew parallels between how they felt when they mentored their children and how they felt when they mentored younger adult men, although with obvious differences between the two groups of younger people. Men who were not fathers explained that they felt more masculine by virtue of being a role model to young adult men, which they experienced as daddies.

Cody (59) pointed out gendered terminology related to mentoring or nurturing. "It's interesting, I just realized when I'm talking about my masculine side I use the term 'mentoring.' When I talk about it as a more feminine trait, I'm using the word 'nurturing.'" Other men did not necessarily agree that nurturance was feminine. However, older men made vulnerable emotions and intimate relationships with younger men compatible with masculinity by framing these factors as part of mentorship or paternal nurturance. While people of all genders mentor and nurture younger people, these concepts may take on different meanings depending on the gender of the people involved. Masculinized framings of mentorship or nurturance allow many men to share emotional vulnerability and intimacy with other men that they would not otherwise feel comfortable doing.

Other older men, including Scott (54), felt masculine because of asymmetrical dynamics they had with their much younger partners: "When do I feel most masculine? Wow. Actually, I'd have to say it's when I'm actually with my partner. And I think it's because again it's like, if we're going out, I'm typically the one that's making the decisions about where we're going. But I also see myself as the protector and the leader, the decision maker. But my concern is also that he's enjoying himself and having fun and is happy. So I would say that that's when I feel like the most masculine, is when I'm with my partner." Scott had an asymmetrical relationship with his partner that paralleled gender inequalities in many woman-man relationships. This dynamic made him feel more like a man. Cody (59) also tied daddyness to dynamics in his romantic relationship, saying, "In my mind I'm equating being a man with aspects that are very much daddy to me." He elaborated,

> Being a man is even a little closer than a dovetail to being a dad or a daddy in [that] this is how I handle taking care of my family. This is how it's important to me, these are things that are important to me—to be able to be the one to be the hero, but not like I have [to] take all the credit. Hey, pull the rabbit out of the hat. We got this bill paid and we moved on to a new milestone in the business. We've done whatever it is, but it's never about me, it's about what it does for the family and how it grows the family.

Both Scott and Cody tied daddyness to dynamics in their romantic partnerships, but they differed on the extent to which asymmetries affected how their partnerships operated. Scott's partnership was more explicitly asymmetrical than Cody's, although both Scott and Cody viewed themselves as being a head of the household compared to their younger partners.

Many older men also indicated that one of their favorite parts of daddyness is younger adult men's perception of them as desirable, something Finn (64) connected explicitly to masculinity. "I consider myself very lucky. I never would have predicted, say twenty or thirty years ago, that people would find me so attractive." He continued, saying it "definitely feels really good." Overall, he noted, "Sexuality is part of masculinity for me and to have so many people who are so into me really validates the shallow part of my masculinity." Finn and others felt more masculine in part because they were perceived as desirable by younger adult men. Robert (69) also explained this dynamic. "You know, when you get to be this age, you say 'I'm surprised anyone would find me attractive and want to spend time with me,' and it's somewhat flattering and it's somewhat sexy. And I don't go out seeking it all the time. But occasionally something clicks and it's like, 'Okay, let's go for it.' So to me, it's not amusement, it's not entertainment, but it's affirming that even at the age of sixty-nine, I'm energetic, I'm youthful, I'm sexual, I'm enjoying life." Most men I talked to did not feel as though they were on the decline. Instead, many felt invigorated and desired by younger adult men. Older men felt affirmed that younger adult men found them desirable, and this affirmation helped to reduce the threats aging posed to their masculinity.

Other older men agreed that younger adult men's desire for them boosted their self-image. In Edgar's (46) words, it is "marginally empowering in some way. I guess to say that there's someone younger who finds us appealing is nice." He continued, "The thing that I'm intrigued by and leaning into about being a daddy is that having someone younger be interested in you is flattering. And I've decided I like that." Edgar was not born a daddy; he transitioned into daddyness after a period of hesitancy. Caleb (57) too felt "very masculine when I'm with a younger man, in a sexual role or in a romantic role or whatever, I do feel very masculine at that point." He continued, "I feel more masculine with somebody who is younger, and maybe smaller, maybe not, but definitely maybe less experienced or less worldly or less age or whatever. That's when I feel more masculine." He speculated as to why he might feel that way. "I think it's because I bring an age or an experience level or something to that relationship that they don't have, a masculine situation. Because it's two men having sex or two men being romantic, that it's not necessarily a dominant-submissive role, but it's more of a masculine and I think daddy role." Caleb felt as though he fulfilled a "masculine" and "daddy" role. Although Caleb did not describe this dynamic as dominant, it does contain more similarities than differences with consensual dominant-submissive dynamics that other men described.

Several men noted a sexual history similar to Spencer's (59): "I have hot young boys of legal age, generally speaking, twenty-three to like twenty-eight who are certainly hotter than the men that I was meeting when I was twenty-three to twenty-eight, at the same age." Numerous older men reported that their younger adult sexual partners were more attractive than men with whom the older men had had sex when they were that young—and this pattern existed because younger adult men found older men desirable.

Wyatt (66) too felt that being a daddy bolstered his masculinity, but specifically due to power dynamics in sex. He explained that he feels most masculine "when I'm fucking," and that being a daddy affects his masculinity "at a very deep level, simply because it is who I am." Wyatt continued, "It's a feeling of power in some ways from many respects—

not just the age-wise, but the inherent sexual domination of being the top and really knowing that you are bringing somebody intense pleasure from the role you were playing in that situation. And that's addictive in some ways. I mean, I enjoy it." Consensual sexual dominance over younger adult partners made Wyatt feel more masculine. Neil (51) shared similar thoughts, and said he feels most masculine "when a boy is submitting to me in some way, offering me his submission. And whether that's being fucked or whether it's like licking my boots or massaging my penis, that he's offering it up willingly." Several men who viewed themselves as dominant in sexual encounters with younger adult men linked this preference to masculinity. Only a handful of men specifically described this connection, however. Most of the older men who connected masculinity and daddyness explained that mentorship of or desire from younger adult men was more integral to masculinity.

Several men linked their appearance or other characteristics to daddyness. Jake (52), like several others, connected masculinity and nurturance, although for him masculinity was also linked to his personal aesthetic. "It definitely feeds into your masculine psychology and it definitely feeds into a little bit of a nurturing thing." At the same time, he also explained that he usually wears clothes that are part of his skilled trade occupation. Wearing this type of clothing is not a strategy for Jake to have sex, however. "I don't do it intentionally. That's what I wear. That's what I wear to work. That's what I wear till my husband says 'take that off, you can't go to eat in that.'" He elaborated, "I'm not trying to do it to get laid, it's part of my identity. It's part of my genuine identity." Jake is a rare man who checks multiple daddy boxes:[24] he is muscular and physically attractive, enacts a consensual dominant-submissive dynamic with younger adult men, earns a high income, and has a job that involves manual labor. Relatedly, as Connor (59) described, "I'm a big, mature, masculine guy, so if you're looking for the quasi-typical daddy image, older man, well built, gray haired, and looks like a daddy kind of thing, then that certainly, from a visual standpoint, is an appealing component." A majority of older men described daddies as masculine and felt that their own traits exemplified common ideas about daddyness.

In sum, daddyness boosted the masculinity of many older men as they mentored, felt desired by, or had sex with younger adult men. Mentoring younger adult men made older men feel helpful, valued, and wise.

Older men often felt that sex with younger adult men was invigorating: it made older men feel desired and also knowledgeable, since they often taught younger adult men how to have fulfilling sex. Interestingly, too, several older men noted that they felt more sexually desired at midlife than they had in their young adulthood, thanks to interest from younger adult men. Aging can pose threats to how men perceive their masculinity, but age-gap pairings with men in their twenties and early thirties bolstered older men's masculinity.

Younger Men's Perceptions of Older Men's Masculinity

Several younger men also connected daddyness to masculinity, and most younger men preferred masculinity in their sexual or romantic partners. Both older and younger men described daddies as masculine, but younger men formed a stronger association between daddyness and masculinity. "I tend to be drawn to the masculine men that are bears and older men. I just feel like when I see an older man with a hairy chest and perhaps facial hair, for some odd reason that signals masculinity to me," Michael (30) explained. Other men provided less detail when describing masculinity but were nonetheless clear that daddyness and masculinity go hand in hand. Alejandro (26), for instance, provided his definition of daddyness. "I would say it would be a masculine guy, usually muscular masculine guy, I would say older, like in his late thirties and older than that." On a related note, James (28) mentioned that a daddy is "someone who displays a calm masculinity, like a calmer, gentler, more laid-back sort of masculine energy." Kyle (25) shared these sentiments. "I would definitely say one, it's an older guy, and two, they're kind of a more dominant figure. They're a bigger guy. To me a daddy means a little bit more on the butch side of things, more masculine." Overall, "I would say just basically an older guy who's more of that macho figure that is seen in society." Younger men overwhelmingly viewed daddies as masculine.

Joshua (23) described two daddy archetypes: a distinguished upper-middle-class professional and a rugged mountain man. "Either it's an older gentleman ranging—it could range anywhere between forties and early sixties—but who's a little bit polished and refined, like maybe wears polos or khakis or suits and things like that, and is professional but also has that air about them of like they could very easily switch into being really primal or really visceral if they wanted to be." The other daddy archetype he described is more rugged. "It's either that or what comes to mind is a guy around their midforties that's more rugged, like wears flannels and jeans. Maybe they live in a more rural area or something like that. Not a cowboy aesthetic, but a mountain man kind of aesthetic. Those are the two images that come up in my mind when I think about that term." Archetypical daddies, in Joshua's view, are upper-middle-class professional men or rugged mountain men. These enactments of masculinity are quite distinct but are nonetheless captured under the "daddy" umbrella. One is clearly associated with urban life, whereas the other draws on ideas about rural masculinity.[25] Both are connected to socioeconomic class, in that one archetype is an upper-middle-class professional whereas the other is a rugged, working-class man.

Masculinity could also be evident in the dynamic between older and younger adult men. Benjamin (26) explained that daddies enacted a "masculine role." "I would say that it's a relationship, a two-way relationship with an older man and a younger man, and it could take on forms of just verbal role play and it could take on much more physical roles like sex and dominance versus submissive and serving a more masculine role as the daddy." Whereas Benjamin drew on dominant-submissive dynamics to explain older men's masculinity, Austin (27) described the connection between masculinity and mentorship, as many of the older men did. He thought of a "daddy as someone who is about ten years older and has that manliness to them," and furthermore, "the person in the relationship who is domineering and teaching the boy to become a man." Masculinity is not simply a trait of older men; it is something older men enact through their relationships with younger adult men.

Younger men typically desired masculinity in older men. "I think an older man is by definition manlier than a boyish twenty-year-old, and so that manliness is a turn-on as well," Austin described. These "manlier" characteristics were both physical (for instance, traits such as facial hair) and behavioral. "Behavior-wise I would just say the confidence and wisdom that come with someone who is older and more experienced." Similarly, Jeffrey (23) explained, "When I think of 'daddy' I'm just picturing somebody older, has a masculine look, and honestly, I like guys who look dominant, but are also caring." He later elaborated on characteristics associated with daddyness: "a bear, looks. Pretty well built. I also don't mind somebody who's just an average dad bod kind of type, I also think that that's a turn-on. But yeah, somebody who's masculine, older, beard, scruff." Daddyness, for many of the younger men I talked to, involved masculinity. Although younger men often linked physical characteristics to masculinity, such as facial or body hair (which they connected to older ages), they also specified that masculinity was evident in how older men behaved. Confidence, wisdom, assertiveness, and dominance were among the traits that younger men felt made daddies masculine.

David (27), interestingly, reported different preferences for masculinity in older men compared to younger men. "I tend to be more attracted to more masculine men, I suppose. But there's pretty big variation in there. I think with older guys I do want a more masculine kind of sounding, looking guy." In contrast, "With guys my own age," he went on, "it's a little bit more fluid because it gets back to that weird dynamic I was saying before, where when it's around my own age it's a lot more casual, and it's a lot more egalitarian. It's like we're just two friends fooling around. And so with that scenario I am pretty open to a wide range of masculine-feminine because it's just two people having fun." With older men it is different. "But when it's with an older guy I want it to embody that daddy/boy or father/son kind of dynamic. So when it's like that, masculine plays a bigger role." Both of the scenarios that David described were, notably, pornography tropes.

Although a majority of younger men preferred masculinity in sexual partners regardless of age, several specified that they were more flexible with masculinity in younger partners compared to older. In short, younger men typically wanted daddies to be masculine. Older men's masculinity involved physical attributes such as body hair, personal aesthetics such as how men dressed, and behavioral factors, including how older men interacted with younger men.

Younger Men's Masculinity in Relation to Older Men's

Feeling More Masculine

Overall, fifteen younger men explained that their involvement with older men shaped the way they perceived their own masculinity. Whether this involvement made younger men feel more or less masculine, however, varied. Older-younger pairings do not have uniform outcomes on younger men's masculinity. In contrast, of the twenty-two older men who connected daddyness to masculinity, all felt that pairing with younger adult men made them feel more masculine.

Several younger men explained that they felt masculine with older men because they learned masculinity from them. Daddies provided masculine role models for younger men. Although "I might hook up with the daddies," David (27) noted, "that doesn't make me feel feminine, it actually makes me feel more masculine, even though I would definitely take on a submissive role with them." He continued, "Being with daddies makes me feel more masculine because I feel like I'm growing more into the man that I am."

Austin (27) expressed similar thoughts. "I find boyishness also masculine because of the fact the boy can turn into a man and the daddy helps him do that. Masculinity to me is that power, either physical power or confidence." He explained that partnering with older men "improves my masculinity because I get to learn from a manly person." Austin's understanding of his masculinity stems from his childhood, in which he learned that he was not masculine enough. "Well, when I was young I did enjoy Britney Spears and playing with dolls and was told no, and so I actually made an effort to be better at masculine things like playing catch and stuff like that. So that societal aspect of my growing up did affect my desire to be more masculine." He continued, "And I think partnering with older men has allowed me to learn from them and be more like them in that sense."

Referring to situations in which older men taught him how to top effectively, Tyler (33) noted, "I would expect them to be masculine and when I'm with them to always be the most feminine, [but] it's almost like they've coached me on how to kind of equalize my parts when I've been with them." Learning to top with older men helped Tyler feel more masculine. These stories show that older men provided a masculine blueprint for some younger men. Part of the older-younger mentorship process involved younger adult men learning how to enact an expression of masculinity they admired.

James (28), in contrast to the men I quoted above, did not necessarily feel more masculine when he was with older men, but he did seek to learn from them. He began by clarifying that he feels "a love-hate thing" when he considers his masculinity, "because a lot of masculinity or ideas of masculinity are so unhealthy and rooted in trying to be an impossible ideal. So when I think about my own masculinity I try to model it, I guess, after the men I'm most attracted to. I would like it to be seen as sort of a quiet strength and not an overt aggression." In terms of how that feeling relates to partnering with older men, "I do kind of view myself as innately less masculine than the men I tend to be attracted to. I haven't analyzed that too deeply, but I think it definitely might be that I'm trying to build and model my own masculinity on the men I'm interested in."

Notably, James, like most of the other younger men I talked to, was aware that masculinity could be problematic. Many clarified that they intentionally sought to avoid "toxic" enactments of masculinity, and several described feminine traits of which they were proud. None of the younger men I talked to described stories that suggested that they replicated harmful enactments of masculinity linked to, for instance, gender inequality or poor health behaviors. (Importantly, research shows that even many progressive masculinities reinforce social inequalities in often subtle ways.)[26] Being gay or bisexual means that men necessarily have to challenge certain masculine norms, given the link between heterosexuality and masculinity in most contexts.[27] That factor, combined with recent social developments that have highlighted how masculinity needs to change to be less harmful,[28] encouraged younger men to look to older men to see how they enacted a masculinity that younger men considered healthy.

Admiration of masculinity also meant that many young men distanced themselves from femininity to at least some extent: most preferred masculinity in sexual partners, and many felt that older men enacted a masculinity that younger men found appealing for themselves. Few younger (or older) men made disparaging comments about male femininity, and many described feminine traits of their own, such as emotional expressiveness, that they considered important. Nonetheless, older-younger masculine mentorship does represent an implicit valuation of masculinity over femininity. Not all younger men described older-younger masculine mentorship, but those who did sought to use older men's masculinity as a blueprint for their own.

Jamal (23) compared his experience with older men to mentorship between Roman men in ancient times. "It's definitely a comforting thing to be around men who are older and more masculine than myself," he began. "It's like an archetypical thing that I'm sure can reflect how the Romans handled their gender and relationships back in the older days, where the older, experienced men could take on younger men as their mentors and partners until they reached their own legal adulthood. I think that's a factor that plays, largely in the sense that an older man has a more intense air of masculinity around them and that helps to give you a framework for yourself to model yourself after." Older men provided a masculine "framework" that younger adult men could use to shape their own masculinity. "So I think that being around older men helps me feel the sense that I am less masculine than they are, but it gives me an idea on what masculinity is supposed to look like at the same time, so it's like a very good balance of those two feelings of being less masculine, but also having a goal for what your masculinity should look like." Older men mentored Jamal, and through that process Jamal learned how to enact a type of masculinity he considered appealing.

Some younger men felt more masculine in older-younger pairings specifically because they felt desired, similarly to how older men felt more masculine for this same reason. "It makes me feel more masculine, I guess, because older guys tend to have more traditional views on gender," Chris (33) explained, "and if they're seeing me as desirable, then I feel more masculine." Others felt more masculine because they topped older men. Alejandro (26), for instance, noted, "I think it makes me more masculine" to be with older men, and elaborated, "The older guys that I like, I mean, I'm the one that is always on top."

Feeling More Feminine

Other men felt less masculine in relation to older men because there was a clear contrast between younger men's and older men's gender expression. These younger men did not value masculinity over femininity in the same way as the young men who sought to learn masculinity from older men, but most did find masculinity sexually desirable in older men. Joshua (23) noted, "I'm definitely the more feminine" compared to the older men with whom he usually has sex. Jacob (27) agreed, stating, "It makes me feel very feminine" to have sexual or romantic relationships with older men, but also shared nuance about this attitude. "Honestly, it can feel really conflicting, too, in that I can feel very embodied in my femininity when I'm actually in the act of having sex with an older man, but then oftentimes through conversation, differences in our understanding of masculinity and femininity will come up and oftentimes I'm put into a position to defend my femininity or defend my thinking of myself as something more expansive than a man or whatever. And I think that has a strange effect, or I don't know if it's strange. It's not bad or good or whatever, it just is what it is." Jacob had a complicated understanding of how sex with older men shaped how he perceived his femininity. He continued, "On a surface level I certainly am attracted to more masculine, in whatever way that reads. I'm not only attracted to masculine men by any means, but there's something about a masculine stability that comes with dating or hooking up with or having sex with older men that very much affirms my feminine side." Overall, Jacob felt as though having sex with older, masculine men affirmed his femininity because his gender expression contrasted with theirs. He did tend to prefer masculine men, but this enjoyment was in part rooted in a feeling that older men's masculinity validated his own femininity.

A handful of men framed submissive-dominant power dynamics in terms of masculinity and femininity. Andrew (25) noted that he feels most feminine "when I'm with an older man and bottoming." He continued, "I feel feminine because I feel like a man is dominating me in a lot of ways. But a lot of times when I bottom—one of my favorite positions is being on top—and that still makes me feminine, because I become more submissive when I do bottom. Yeah, and I like, sometimes I like being held afterwards, too, and being the little spoon. I feel kind of feminine when that happens." Enacting a submissive role in sexual encounters made Andrew feel more feminine, but this feeling did not bother him. Similarly, Benjamin (26) explained, "I take on that feminine role when I'm partnering with an older man and I'm acting in a submissive role versus, whether it's a hookup or a relationship with somebody closer to my age or younger than me I may take on a more even role, a less dominant or submissive role and more of a neutral role." Most younger men did not state that being submissive in sexual encounters made them feel more feminine, but a handful of men did. Notably, however, no younger men reported a negative connotation to feeling more feminine. It was simply something they experienced.

DaShawn (27) also felt more feminine at times, but not necessarily because of a dominant-submissive dynamic. Instead, he felt more feminine because "there are some older men who look at younger guys as a, I don't know, what's the word, as a, I don't want to say a piece of meat, but it's something that they, for lack of better words, want to get into." He continued, "And it can make you feel less like a man," since "they want to take advantage of you sexually. They get off on that. And that can kind of make you feel less like a man and more like how, in your traditional picture of society, how men treat women." He continued, "I kind of feel that. As a man I can't say what a woman feels, but I can say it can be similar in some ways. And you're kind of made to feel like you're an object. And sometimes I'll say it's, in a sexual sense it can be exciting, but other times it's like okay, it's kind of gross." DaShawn was one of the only younger men to describe this dynamic, and his experience captures how complex sexuality can be. Men may experience a host of contradictory feelings in response to objectification: they may feel aroused, excited, disgusted, and emasculated, all at once. However, most of the younger men I talked to either did not feel that older men objectified them or did not find objectification bothersome.

What These Stories Tell Us about Masculinity

These stories highlight how masculinity has the potential to be positive. Most research has focused on how masculinity reinforces inequality, either overtly or subtly, and for good reason: often, masculinity reinforces gender inequality as well as inequality between men. It also often harms men themselves. For instance, public health studies show that men typically have poorer health outcomes than women because they are less likely to seek care for mental and physical health issues and are more likely to engage in harmful health behaviors.[29] Yet masculinity does not *always* or *necessarily* have harmful effects.[30] Masculinity is complex, and so too are the ways in which it affects people. The effects of masculinity vary depending on the situation, the people involved, and the specific masculinity people enact. In some circumstances masculinity leads to beneficial outcomes.

The stories of the men I talked to show that masculine dynamics between older and younger adult men can be tender, tied to both emotional connection and mentorship. Older men's masculinity often validated the masculinity *and* femininity of younger men. In some situations, such as the ones this chapter has detailed, masculinity can be beneficial both for the people who enact it and for the people with whom they develop intimate relationships. In short, masculinity is complex, and so too are its effects.

6

Love between Older and Younger Adult Men

Large age gaps can make romantic partnerships complicated. Older and younger partners are at different stages in their careers, and the older partner usually makes more money than the partner in his twenties or early thirties. The two partners may also have a different outlook on life by virtue of having different levels of life experience and having had experiences that are specific to certain cohorts.[1] For instance, Gen Z, Millennial, Gen X, and Baby Boomer young adulthoods were distinct due to different social norms, economic conditions, and Internet availability.

In contrast to stereotypes, few men—either older or younger—described age-gap partnerships with notable power differentials. Most age-gap partnerships functioned similarly to age-similar partnerships, although with some differences related to differences in life direction, interests and attitudes, career stage, and earnings power. Unhealthy dynamics can exist in any type of partnership, and a handful of men did describe age-gap partnerships (usually in the past) that had unhealthy power imbalances and/or poor communication. Nonetheless, these stories were uncommon, and I found little evidence that age-gap romantic partnerships were inherently harmful for either younger or older men.

Age-gap partnerships are complicated, however, because the younger partner will most likely need to caretake for the older partner later in life. Asymmetrical caretaking responsibilities are not much of a problem if there is an age gap of under ten years, but the wider the age gap, the more evident this future caretaking responsibility will be. This reason, among others, helps explain why only a minority of the men I talked to were in romantic partnerships with a man much older or younger than themselves.

Romantic partnerships are not necessarily more meaningful than other types of relationships. People have deeply intimate friendships (platonic or sexual) that are just as important as, if not more important than, their romantic partnerships.[2] Thus, the absence of an age-gap romantic partnership is not an indication that a man cares little about someone much older or younger than himself.

Of older men, seventeen were single, nine were married to a man, three were cohabiting with a man, one was in a cohabiting polyamorous relationship with two men, four were in nonmarital, noncohabiting relationships with a man, four were married to a woman, and one was in a nonmarital, noncohabiting relationship with a woman. All but two man-man relationships were sexually open;[3] most men in relationships with women did not discuss their sex with men with their woman partner. Of older men in romantic partnerships, eleven had a partner within ten years of their own age; ten were ten or more years older than their partner(s), and of them, seven were partnered to a man in his twenties or early thirties; and one was more than ten years younger than his partner.[4] (See table A.1 in the appendix.)

Older men's "daddy" experiences were often associated with nonromantic sexual partners in their twenties and early thirties who may also have been friends. This pattern extended to men I talked to who were in their fifties or sixties but had romantic partners in their forties. These romantic partners were ten or more years younger than they, but they were past the twenties/early-thirties time frame typically associated with daddy dynamics. Again, older men's daddy experiences were usually with nonromantic sexual partners who were in their twenties or early thirties. Similarly, younger men typically discussed daddy dynamics with men who were in their late thirties, forties, fifties, and sixties, with whom they had developed nonromantic sexual relationships in addition to, or in place of, romantic relationships with men closer to their age.

Of younger men, fifteen were single; one was married to a man; two were cohabiting with a man; four were in a polyamorous relationship with one or more men,[5] of which three were noncohabiting and one was cohabiting; and four were in noncohabiting relationships with a man. Of the eleven men in partnerships, seven were ten or more years younger than their partner(s) and four were within ten years of age. (See table A.2 in the appendix.) Eight relationships were open, whereas three were closed.[6]

Demographic research shows that large age gaps are most common among man-man couples, yet the stories of the men I talked to show that romantic partnerships are only the tip of the iceberg of the total number of older-younger pairings. Many older-younger pairings between adults are nonromantic, and of pairings that are romantic, many are nonmarital and noncohabiting. Demographic research about man-man couples substantially underestimates the total number of older-younger pairings between adults, since demographic research typically does not measure nonromantic or noncohabiting relationships.

Older Men's Age-Gap Romantic Partnerships

Notably, most of the older men who were partnered to men substantially younger than themselves did not describe many nonsexual dynamics in their partnerships that were related to the age difference between them. As Neil (51) said about his partner in his late twenties, "The things I appreciate and am challenged by are not necessarily related to our being in a daddy-boy relationship or age, it's just about who we are." Men described a variety of things they liked about their current age-gap partnerships, as well as challenges they experienced. Most topics they discussed were not related to their age gap. Few noteworthy patterns distinguished men in age-gap partnerships from those in age-similar partnerships. (Recall that many of the older men I talked to were in a romantic partnership with someone around their own age, but were also sexually involved with much younger adult men because their partnerships were sexually open.) A handful of men did, however, report relationship dynamics that were shaped by the age difference between themselves and their partner, and this section will focus on those dynamics.

One dynamic that a handful of men described is difficult to describe but can perhaps be stated simply as differences in life direction. Tomas (44), for instance, explained that he and his husband in his midtwenties love one another, yet also experience complications due to their age difference. "Sometimes I definitely feel like there's a certain frustration of 'Okay, we've been together this long and you are still trying to figure out what it is that you want to do with your life' and so forth." He added,

He's still trying to figure out what he wants to do and where he wants to go and how to get there. And it's like well, we can walk through it together, but you have to make a decision. I'm not going to drag you through life. I'd say that's probably, especially since it's been a long-term, it's probably the biggest frustration at this point is, "Okay, you made a big decision. You decided yes, you wanted to be with me. And you wanted to be responsible for me in case of anything happens and you want me to be responsible for you and so we got married. And now let's be responsible. And how are you being responsible?"

Tomas acknowledged that this difficulty exists due to both him and his partner. "Sometimes there's definitely a certain viewpoint on my side of 'You should be more my equal rather than so much younger than me.' And that sometimes can be really hard for me to remember. But he is so much younger than me and he doesn't have the experience that I have and that I can't just make it easy for him to make decisions or anything, that he actually has to make his own mistakes at times and so forth." Tomas found it frustrating that his partner did not have confidence in a life direction, as Tomas did, but Tomas also recognized that his partner needed the opportunity to make mistakes and grow from them.

Jordy (57), relatedly, is in a relationship with a man in his late twenties and often mentors him on various issues. "I often give him advice and I listen to what he's going through in his career." He continued, "Quite often I'm telling him what I went through and saying I went through the same thing, talking to him about it, and just to let him know that it's normal. Things will change, things get better, and just encouraging him." Mentorship dynamics existed in both romantic and nonromantic pairings. On a less positive note, Jordy also explained that there is a generational disconnect. "He doesn't know references that I have being older, that things happened in the '70s and '80s and movie stars and singers and all of those things that he's never heard of." This disconnect could be difficult. "That's kind of challenging because it feels like we don't have things in common when that happens." Many older men noted the issue of generational disconnects in knowledge about popular culture. Fourteen younger men similarly noted this disconnect, as well as differences in attitudes on social issues.

It is instructive to consider men's former age-gap partnerships that ended for various reasons. Brett (43 and currently single), like several older men, noted that he paid for a higher proportion of expenses than his younger partner, given differences in earning power. Reflecting on a recent partnership that involved a twelve-year age gap, he explained, "I liked to be able to be a provider for him, too, because there's no way he could have ever afforded the place we lived in without me. In fact that's why he could only pay about a third of the rent. And I liked being able to pay the other two-thirds." They separated for reasons unrelated to their age gap.

Other men described situations in which the younger partner was not ready to commit to a relationship, causing a separation. Jorge (47 and currently single), for instance, noted that he had recently dated a twenty-one-year-old for several months. "He was kind of looking for a new experience. And I think he was just trying things out." The twenty-one-year-old was unwilling or unable to enter a long-term relationship, and as a result he and Jorge separated.

Charlie (49 and currently single) described different issues with a former partner several decades younger than he, related to social media use. Charlie and this man "hung out for maybe two months, three months." The man's social media narcissism was unbearable. "He's one of these guys who I realized was so self-absorbed in the sense that he would have a Twitter post in the morning that would say, 'Oh look at my cute outfit today.' And I'm a very private person in a way. Maybe it's a self-esteem issue, but I don't feel like everyone needs to know everything about my life. And I don't need to broadcast it out there." Narcissistic social media posts Charlie attributed to generational differences.

> I think a difference between my generation and the younger generation where there's Facebook and Instagram and Snapchat and all of this crap where everyone thinks that everything they're doing is so interesting, they've got to put it out there for everyone to see it. And it drives me crazy. And this guy was doing this. I'd look at Twitter, and I don't post anything, I just subscribe and will look and I rarely ever post anything. But I'll see a Twitter post from this guy that said, "Oh I'm feeling cute today." And I'd be like "Oh God. Just please don't." It drives me crazy.

Frustration with social media narcissism eventually led to the end of their relationship. "I think that's one of the things that stuck with me and was like 'I don't need this. Can't we just fly below the radar a little bit?

And why do you have to post everything you do?' And, or he'd have a rant on Twitter. I'm like it's just not me. So that contributed to it."

While people of all ages can be narcissistic, it is likely true that younger people are more narcissistic online. Younger cohorts are more likely to use social media,[7] and this fact both reflects and reinforces generational differences in norms about sharing personal information online. It is also likely true that there are generational differences in how people perceive narcissism. In any case, several men (both younger and older) perceived younger men as more prone to narcissism than older men. This perception posed challenges for older men who felt that younger men's narcissism weakened connections between them. On the other hand, it also provided opportunities for certain younger men, several of whom stated that they enjoyed the company of older men in part because they perceived older men as less narcissistic than men in their twenties and thirties.

Power Imbalances?

Readers may wonder, understandably, whether there are issues with power imbalances in romantic age-gap partnerships. Notably, few older or younger men described situations in which there was a problematic power imbalance. Most younger men I talked to enjoyed older men being somewhat more dominant or assertive in certain circumstances, as prior chapters detailed. These circumstances are ones in which younger men retain their independence and agency but defer to older men on certain matters to relieve pressures associated with masculinity, to learn from older men, or to act on a pleasurable sexual kink. Survey research has similarly found that age gaps are mostly unrelated to either decision-making power or relationship satisfaction in man-man partnerships.[8] Thus, there is little evidence that age-gap partnerships are more prone to power imbalances than age-similar partnerships.

One older man did, however, have a current romantic relationship that had a power imbalance. The power imbalances in his partnership are similar to gender-based relational inequalities but, in his circumstance, are mapped onto age. On one hand, Scott (54) explained, "I guess in one aspect of it there's a sense of control, but also there's a responsibility there where the guy you're with or I'm with, it's like I lead the relationship, but I recognize that I'm also taking care of him and being responsible for him, and also trying to be aware of what his expectations and needs are." Scott's story highlights asymmetries in his partnership.

> In past relationships a lot of times what is going on is I'm basically the head of the household, as it were, where I feel like I've always been the one who would make decisions about things. Obviously I would include him in, like, if we were going to go take a vacation, where are you interested in going and whatnot. But as far as making, like starting the process, I would be the one that would actually instigate it. That would be what I mean as far as being in control. As far as making sure that bills get paid. That's something that I'm responsible for. Basically I take the lead on things in the relationship. I'm the instigator.

Being the "head of the household" indicates a power imbalance. Indeed, Scott elaborated, "Part of the reason I'm attracted to younger people is because I like to be in control and I like to take the initiative on things, and that's who I'm attracted to." Reflecting on a past partner, he noted, "He moved in with me, so it was my place, and he worked part-time, and basically I made pretty much all the decisions in the relationship. And that was actually one of the reasons we ended up breaking up, because I was literally making all the decisions. He actually had a hard time just standing up for himself."

These asymmetrical dynamics continued in Scott's current romantic partnership with a man in his early thirties.

> [My partner] just started a new job and so he contacted me this morning and he was feeling really frustrated, so I'm walking him through ways to help deescalate this frustration, put things in perspective for him. I'm controlling the conversation and telling him—I guess if you want to be blunt about it, I'm telling him how he should feel and how he can deal with it. And then he let me know that he needed money for gas, so I sent him some money for gas. It's all part of being confident with my experiences and who I am, but also trying to be protective and supportive.

Scott's partnerships (past and present) are asymmetrical, both emotionally and financially.

Another man, Ryan (48), also shared sentiments that indicate a preference for power imbalances: Ryan described daddies as being "more dominant, experienced," and explained, "I like the control of it. I like being the one in the relationship more making the decisions and even not just sexually, but being in charge. And then sexually I like the same thing, being the one in charge, being served in that way." These sentiments are similar to those that some heterosexual men express in their partnerships with women.

Age differences *can* be tied to asymmetrical power arrangements. Importantly, however, few men other than Scott or Ryan, either younger or older, described power imbalances. I found little evidence of widespread power differentials between older and younger men that harmed the younger (or older) man. It is overly simplistic to conclude that age gaps create or exacerbate inequalities in partnerships between two adult men.

Sharing Younger Adult Men

Three older men discussed situations in which they and their partners around the same age shared physically and emotionally intimate relationships with much younger adult men. Two of these three men were married to one another: Graham (51) and Greg (50). (They were the only two men I interviewed who were partnered to one another.) As Graham explained, "A significant amount of the guys that I meet are through my husband." He described an intimate dynamic with a younger man with whom both Graham and Greg spent time. "We have social time together. We have cuddle time. He's twenty-three. He's a cute boy, too, hairy and he's handsome. He's got this beard. And he's having some emotional problems. He's having grownup problems. He's battling depression. He's having some real problems. And we're just offering him a place to come and hang out." Sex was part of the relationship, although more so with Greg. Graham had more of an emotional connection with this man. "He has more sex with my husband than he does with me. But I like to cuddle him and give him aftercare. The deep fucking and stuff, that's with my husband. He's actually smaller than me, too, so he physically fits inside my body. It's really hot and very sweet. But then he'll come over. . . . When we're in my room we'll watch a movie or something and I'll hold him and love on him. It's really sweet and I love it. Then he goes home." Graham later elaborated, "I'm more of like emotional support, we're social," and noted, "I really love that kid." Graham valued the sexual and nonsexual time that he and Greg shared with this younger man. "There are things that we can offer him that he needs or wants. And if it's healthy, that's a turn-on for me, and then my dick gets hard, and I'm like yeah, I want to fuck him every once in a while, but mostly I want him to suck my dick and I want to hug him and squeeze him and stroke his hair, pull him into my armpit, make him smell my Old Spice soap that he says 'Oh, you smell [good].' 'That's sweet, boy, I'm glad I can do that for you.' It's hot." Sharing these moments with young adult men was both arousing and emotionally intimate. Graham and his husband formed mutually beneficial relationships with younger adult men.

Greg (50) shared a similar experience as his husband, but with a different younger man, who is twenty-four years old. "He loves to suck dick, and this is where I feel very daddy and a little bit dom. I love a range of sexual experiences. But if a guy is really good at sucking dick and can deep throat, I can lay back and enjoy that for a long time and he does as well." He continued,

> I'm going to give you some visuals, because to me it relates to the daddy-boy dynamic. There are different positions in which you can suck someone's dick. But with Graham and I, our pattern is I'm laying back and he's between my legs at the foot of the bed. So it has, I don't like the word "service" or "being serviced," but it has that vibe of, "I'm going to lay back here and look at your beautiful, furry body while you go down on my dick." I fucked him for a while. I feel like with he and I that tends to be him riding me more or straddling me. And then at one point, I was fucking him on his back.

This encounter was both sexual and sensual.

> We also cuddle. There's a lot of affection in my sexual interactions, especially with the boys—a lot of cuddling, and a lot of touch, and a lot of, I tell him he's beautiful, and rubbing his beard and rubbing his hair and—true to form in my relationship with my husband—a bit later Graham joined us and they were cuddling for a while. And then I took a break and

came back in and then Graham was fucking him. I would say, if there's such a thing as traditional daddy-boy sex, it fits into that category pretty easily.

Greg and Graham shared both sexual and emotional intimacy with men in their twenties. Having these relationships with younger adult men was fulfilling for all parties. Graham and Greg had sex with their younger friends, and they also enjoyed spending nonsexual time with them.

Their relationships with younger adult men have some characteristics of chosen family,[9] yet not others. Like chosen family, Graham, Greg, and the younger adult men with whom they formed connections were highly emotionally intimate. Unlike chosen family, however, and also unlike in typical gay friendships,[10] sex was a large part of their relationship. The relationships Graham and Greg formed with younger adult men cannot be easily categorized, nor should they be. The two men formed sexually and emotionally meaningful relationships with younger adult men in ways distinct from most other types of relationships.

The dynamic of sharing younger adult men took different forms. Cody (59) was currently in a polyamorous partnership with his husband in his midfifties and a man in his early thirties, who "is the third of three longer-term live-in young men" they have had. Cody was the only older man I talked to who was in a polyamorous partnership. Mentorship was a large component of the relationship Cody had with this younger man. "But to me one of the things that I really try and instill," he began, "is you can't be scared of everything." He continued, "Example, the job that he's working at now, when he started there's all kinds of outward signs that my husband and I were like, 'Wow that's great' and 'Hey, you realize that they're putting you in charge of this now and that they're moving you up to doing direct customer interaction. These are good signs.'" All jobs came with complications, of course, which Cody communicated to his partner. "I used to tell him. 'This isn't the *Princess Bride*. You're not going to go to work and they're going to say, "Goodbye, we'll most likely fire you tomorrow." If you're not doing good, you're not doing good. And [they're] going to have things to tell you. But none of that is out there. Stop being afraid. Start standing up for yourself. Start being proud of yourself for what you're doing.'" Although this partner worked full-time, there was a clear financial difference between him, Cody, and Cody's husband. "Obviously between my husband and I, we make probably eight times at least what he makes. And that's not ever brought up like, 'You're just here and all of this is because of us.' But it also allows him to have an amazing life," including the ability to live in a nice home and drive a fairly new car.

This type of relationship with a younger man was much different from what Greg and Graham described. What all three had in common, however, was a dynamic of shared intimacy between two older men and a younger adult man. The relationship between Cody, his husband, and the younger man is not a sugar relationship, since the younger man had a career and helped pay for household expenses, but the partnership was clearly "sweetened" by the greater earning power of the older men.

Younger Men's Age-Gap Partnerships

As with older men's partnerships, few major patterns were evident in the age-gap partnerships younger men discussed. A few notable themes did, however, emerge, particularly related to independence. As Joshua (23) explained about his long-distance partnership with a man in his midthirties, "I'm very independent, I'm very much a free spirit, and I don't want to have my future decided before I've explored all of the options. And being in his position, he's not actively looking to settle down at the moment, but he is pretty stubborn in his ways, and he wants things to be secure." He continued, "I sometimes had problems with intimacy. I sometimes held myself back a little bit because I was afraid of fully committing to something long-term or fully diving into something long-term. Still am a little bit. And that's the big thing, is I think that we [are] not just at different points in our lives, but we have different priorities. I want to see the world." Joshua implied that his partnership may end soon, since he and his partner have different life goals. These differences likely stem from a multitude of factors, some related to age differences and others not. Juan (25) also maintained independence by living separately from his partner but felt emotionally closer to his partner than Joshua did. As Juan explained about his partner in his early forties, "As far as things that I dislike, it's very hard to pinpoint. I would have to be digging into it to find things I dislike about dating him."

Tyrone (32), who is in a noncohabiting polyamorous relationship with two men (who are not involved with one another), relatedly explained, "Part of just getting older and being trans, I feel like I have a connection with these guys partly because I'm finally coming into myself and I feel like they are, too, like having a round two in life, dating again after being married and shit. So we're both like we're being ourselves finally, this is really fun." The main thing Tyrone has to be aware of is a dynamic related to them being older. "They have [had] entire lives before me, and if I get too self-conscious about that it can be self-sabotaging." For instance, "One of my boyfriends actually has two kids," he explained, and "I need to make sure I'm not all in his business all the time. I have to give him space for that." Being mindful about his partner's parenting responsibilities was important to ensure a healthy partnership.

Amir, the twenty-four-year-old man in a polyamorous partnership with two men around the age of sixty, also did not discuss many issues in his partnership related to age differences. As with other young men who preferred to maintain independence, Amir had his own apartment. "I like having my own space and I like having my own place to call home and a place to sort of make my own, so to speak." He concluded, "They're nice people to spend time with and do couples stuff with and thruples stuff with. I really enjoy the time I get to spend with them, no matter how it is, even if it's just hanging out washing or hanging out and eating breakfast together or what have you. It's all really nice and sweet. It means a lot to me being able to spend that kind of time with them." Not all younger men in age-gap partnerships lived separately from their partners, but those who did appreciated the independence they achieved by living separately.

Kyle (25), the man in a cohabiting closed polyamorous partnership with a married couple in which the men were about fifteen years older than he, noted that they "share the same interests, like they grew up playing video games and stuff like that, and I'm kind of a nerd in the same way." Kyle lives with this couple, and they split the cost of expenses "basically evenly. Pay bills where we can with whoever has what." Notably, Kyle made more than these men: "Honestly, I make more than both of them. Not combined, but job-wise I got into a good position at a younger age and kind of excelled from there." They also get along well. "We tend to get along very well, except for small bouts of little things, but that's normal in any relationship. And I would say my favorite thing, honestly, is their compassion. They tend to be more understanding of certain things and tend to have the same kind of mindset I do on certain topics. They tend to always be there for me when I'm down." Kyle did not describe dynamics in his relationship that were related to the age gap between him and his partners.

DaShawn (27) described a more complicated dynamic than other young men, not only because of the age gap between himself and his partner in his late fifties, Wayne, but also because of a combination of poor communication and the fact that Wayne is not "out" to his family. "This older guy that I've been dating for the last seven years, he's retiring and he's decided that he wants to move [to a different region of the United States]. I was never asked to go along with him. I was never asked to move with him." He continued, "That's part of the manipulation, because it's never a concrete answer. I always feel like things are my fault." DaShawn elaborated, "Every time we have serious conversations it feels like it always is I'm the reason why he didn't consider my feelings. But in turn when I'm upset about something, 'Oh, I don't want to talk about something.' When I explain my reasons he gets upset and then he'll find another reason to either stop talking to me, ignore me, or whatever reason. And that's what I mean about the manipulation. It's kind of like there's no win for me. I don't really get a say in anything." Other communication frustrations were evident in the partnership as well.

> The challenging parts are feeling like I'm not being listened to. And then what I end up doing when I don't feel like I'm listened to is I'll, I don't want to say shut down, but I'll do that, I'll shut down. And then when he's trying to explain himself, I'm upset because I just feel like I can't reach him, and so I feel like he wants all these things from me, and it's draining because I feel like I don't really get much from him. I feel like he wants to receive, but he doesn't really want to give.

In addition to poor communication and what sounds like Wayne's emotional selfishness, DaShawn's partnership was extra complicated because Wayne was not out to his family. "I'm open, but he has kids. They're in their twenties now. But his family doesn't really know about us, and if his kids come over, I have to leave." He continued, "If I want to spend time with him I have to wait till the weekend because he just doesn't really want to spend time with me during the week, or he has kids, or he's working." When I asked what DaShawn foresaw in the future between him and Wayne, he explained, "I don't know. He's moving as soon as all of this stuff [with the coronavirus pandemic] is over with. He's moving to [a different region of the United States]. I really couldn't tell you. Maybe I know and I don't want to say it. And part of me is being hopeful and trying to just see, be optimistic and see what happens. I don't know."

Even with these problems, however, DaShawn described enjoyable aspects of the partnership, particularly in the beginning. Just before DaShawn and Wayne met, DaShawn came out to his family, when he was nineteen. Coming out was not a positive experience because "my grandmother, who I'm really close with, she didn't take it well, and she ignored me for about six, seven months." On top of these family difficulties, DaShawn was dating a man around his own age who broke up with him. As a result of these events, "I kind of felt abandoned with family" and "I was really depressed." But these feelings changed when DaShawn and Wayne spent time together.

> When I met him a few months later, he allowed me to spend weeks at his house with him. Took me places, did things for me. It wasn't about money or things. It was an escapism, escape for me from my life and how I was feeling. We just had fun. We would do things. We'd go to the zoo, go out to eat. He helped me get my first job and things like that. And I think that really helped me during that time because I was going through a lot. And so fast forward a few years later, I still like to go out on dates with him and things like that. I think we have a really good time together. We traveled, going different places. I love that aspect of our relationship.

DaShawn's partnership, like many partnerships, is complicated and sometimes messy. His partnership with Wayne had many difficulties, and likely was not going to last much longer. Yet earlier in life, this partnership had been important for DaShawn, and even at the time when I interviewed him, there were aspects DaShawn enjoyed. Not all partnerships last forever or should last forever, but they can still be meaningful during part of the time (or the entire time) two people are together.

Former partnerships younger men described are also instructive for understanding complications that could arise in age-gap partnerships. As Michael (30 and currently single) described,

> My last relationship that ended [about five years ago], something we always went back and forth on and it never really ended well was the fact that he was twenty-five years my senior, so he would always struggle with looking forward and how his life was going to play out, and I was nonchalantly thinking about that because of the fact of I was just having fun and having sex. And I think something that I came to a realization with, part of the reason it never came to fruition of a true long-term relationship, if you will, is due to the fact that I was in love with the idea of being in love, and I was lusting after him more than trying to figure out if it fit.

Michael was highly self-aware and traced difficulties in his former partnership to him not considering what the future could look like with someone twenty-five years older than himself. Eventually, both realized that a quarter-century age gap posed too many complications for the partnership to continue. Notably, Michael reported that his older partner was most concerned about the age gap.

Cyrus (25 and currently single) described a similar dynamic with his last partner, Kevin, who was in his midfifties when they met.

> This is a man that I'd been seeing on and off for over a year. Yeah, he was the last one. And it ended because the age gap was so large. He thought that it would get in the way of us having a relationship. Honestly, most of these guys will dump me. That's another trend. Because they feel so insecure. Just like this guy. His deal was that . . . he's going to be too old for me, and I'm going to lose interest in him and find interest in somebody else. Which is a valid fear. But give me the benefit of the doubt, like "I won't do that to you because I'm not that type. And if I did, I would not just cheat on you." So a lot of them will do that, will just end the relationship because of their own insecurity.

Overall, Kevin "was kind of ashamed, like embarrassed of dating somebody much younger." Part of this embarrassment stemmed from Kevin's friends. Cyrus explained, "Earlier when we started dating he would talk about how his friends are making jokes about me, and I said, 'What are some of the jokes,' and some of them were like 'Oh, does he have a bedtime?'" He continued, "So that was a conflict. He didn't see me fitting in with his circle of friends. . . . If this is not big enough for you to push those voices out, then I guess we're not meant to be together. They were always [bringing up] the fact that I'm younger and he's older. That was the biggest challenge. He couldn't come to terms with it. But he kept fucking me. He didn't have a problem when he was inside of me that he was older. He had no problem when I was making him laugh and we were literally closing restaurants. Like every day we would close a restaurant." Cyrus found Kevin's hesitancy to commit frustrating. "I was like, 'I like you too much for you to be going back and forth on this issue, so if you're not in this I cannot continue having sex with you, because I'm not here for the sex alone, I'm here for the connection or the companionship also.'"

After their partnership ended, Cyrus did eventually come to understand why Kevin thought about their relationship the way he did.

> Now that I'm out of that fuck fog, whatever you call it, I understand where he was coming from, that this age gap is too large for us. Though I still think we could have made it work. But I understand what he was saying. Because he had a friend who had dated an older man, a female friend, and he kept using her as an example. He kept using her as like, "This is what happens when you date an older man." So I think he had a fear. And I had no fear because I was like, "Let's take it one day at a time, I can't promise I'm going to be with you." Well, I didn't say that in those words, but "I can't promise that I'm going to be with you in ten years, but that has nothing to do with you being older, that has, it's just life. I don't know what's going to happen."

What Cyrus described is the flip side to the fear younger men have about future caretaking responsibilities. After older men invest time building a relationship with someone decades younger than they, they have no guarantee that the relationship will last long term. For older men this possibility is a serious concern. For younger men, like Cyrus, "It's just life," and much less consequential given that younger men have decades longer to find a partner before reaching retirement age. This dynamic is inherently asymmetrical and negatively affects older men.

Despite complications due to the age gap, Cyrus enjoyed Kevin's company.

> He was genuinely interested in other people's lives. He would ask me questions not because it was his turn to find out about me, he was genuinely curious about my feelings and how my week was, and where do I come from, how was my family and all these things. He was a good kisser. . . . He had money. I really love that. Not for me, but for him. I shouldn't have to worry about where your next paycheck is coming from. And he did not. He had no issue there. What else? I think that sums it up. He was very passionate, very sensual. Like even the sex was so, not vanilla, but very, it was passionate, like, "Let's make eye contact instead of like fucking doggy style," right? "I like to look at you when I come." He was very into me.

Although Cyrus and Kevin built—and ended—a complicated partnership, Cyrus did remember much of it fondly. Unfortunately, he noted, "We're not in contact. I wished him a happy birthday [recently], but that's about it. I haven't talked to him because I still have feelings for him and he can't make up his mind." Kevin was too concerned about the age gap for the partnership to last. Although Cyrus came to mostly understand Kevin's reasoning, he did not fully grasp the fact that the consequences of a partnership ending in, say, ten years would be much different for Cyrus than for Kevin. Cyrus would still be young and easily be able to rejoin the dating market. Kevin, on the other hand, would be in his sixties, and would likely have more trouble finding a romantic partner.

Of course, not all former partnerships were positive. Andrew (25 and currently single) described a relationship he considered unhealthy: "I like to be very independent, especially recently being very dependent on an older man that I was . . . almost married to. That was very manipulative. And then as soon as I got out of that I really craved and nurtured my independence physically and financially and all of that stuff. . . . I would really give him all of my money when it came to bills and groceries and stuff like that, so I felt financially dependent on him because he, in a way, controlled my money. And by the time that I had given him all the money that he had asked for I really didn't have much for myself to go out and have a drink with a friend or anything like that." Additionally, Andrew noted, "I feel like my biggest issue with my previous relationship was I had major codependency issues, and that's why it took me, I think, several times to finally leave him when I first did leave him. And I don't ever want to deal with or feel like that again or struggle with codependency."

At the same time, "The stability we had between us was really nice. The idea of being married and having a quote, unquote 'normal life' with someone was really great."

> I grew up a lot, I feel like, in the . . . years that we were together. I felt very connected to him most times. I felt like he tried really hard to show what's best for me through all of the arguments and yelling and stuff. So looking back at that, I guess that was kind of a thing that kept me in that relationship. I loved the fact that I was never worried about my life or the future when I was with him. Everything seemed to be there and be good, and not have to worry about am I going to die alone, am I going to be able to eat tonight, or this or that, which are things that I felt and realized once I left, because I left him and had nothing. I could barely afford rent, I had no bed, I had no furniture. It was just me and my dog, my clothes, and a blow-up mattress. So really enjoying the things that I had with him materialistically . . . I really liked that. I felt like that really molded our bond together.

Andrew also enjoyed their interpersonal connection. "I loved at night we would always be holding one another. I always loved that. Even when we would fight. I loved the fact that even if I was mad at him in the morning, he would make me kiss him goodbye when he would go to work, or when I would go to work." In a different partnership that also had a large age gap, Andrew explained, "With my ex it was, I felt like a kid. A lot of times I felt like I was his trophy boy." Treatment as a "trophy boy"—as with a "trophy wife"—may feel demeaning to some, arousing to others, and a complicated mixture of both feelings to many.

Andrew had experienced a range of issues with older men in romantic partnerships. These issues were not necessarily caused by the age gap between him and the other man, but the age gap did exacerbate relational inequalities or provide a justification for the other (older) man to control Andrew or dismiss his concerns. Nonetheless, even in these partnerships, which involved many troubling power dynamics, Andrew felt as though he matured quite a bit. These partnerships also, later, taught him what to avoid in future relationships. Andrew's partnerships were more negative than what most other young men described (except DaShawn, who noted similar levels of concern). This finding itself indicates that emotionally manipulative dynamics can exist in age-gap partnerships but are not necessarily more common compared to other partnership types.

Other partnerships were not negative, but ended because of a lack of compatibility. Anthony (25 and currently single) described a fulfilling partnership with a man in his late fifties whom Anthony had met when he was nineteen, as a previous chapter detailed. Anthony described issues stemming from their age difference.

> [A] lot of the challenges just came from the general things that come with generation gaps. Him being so much older than me. I think the only reason we were together as long as we were was because he was in general a very open-minded person about things that I liked and the things that I enjoyed for hobbies. He would never look at something that I enjoyed for a hobby and either dismiss it or just be like, "Wow, that's stupid," which is something that I find is very common when talking to older people. But I think him being like that allowed us to find more common ground, even if it wasn't anything more than on a superficial or basic level.

Anthony did, however, experience difficulties connecting with his partner at times. "There were a lot of times that we would find ourselves arguing over very different generational mindsets." Additionally, "I guess overall I would say things that he was taught growing up often superseded his ability to work with me on the way that the things that I grew up learning, which made it difficult to connect on a lot of things, so there was a lot of agreeing to disagree, and probably more than a typical relationship would have with somebody my age. And eventually those were the things that kind of weighed me down so much that I was not happy anymore and ultimately ended up being a big reason on why we broke up." Anthony noted that this partnership was beneficial for him, particularly given that it helped him move away from his isolated

rural area, but it was not sustainable. The two men remained emotionally connected, however.

> I fell out of love with him. Right now it's more of a familial relationship. I
> still love him as a friend. But part of the experience was because I learned
> so much about myself while we were together. For a long time I was in
> denial about the fact that I didn't love him anymore, and that was one of
> the things that I learned about myself in that process. I still think he's a
> great guy and I'm glad that we ended it in a way that allows us to still be
> friends. But we're just not compatible anymore.

Anthony continued, explaining that his partnership "absolutely shaped
who I am today and I can't imagine where I'd be at if I wasn't there, or if
I hadn't been there."

This partnership, while not permanent, nonetheless greatly changed
Anthony as a person in ways he felt were for the better. Anthony's story
shows one possible outcome of age-gap partnerships: younger men can
change so much during the partnership that the two partners are no
longer romantically compatible. People can change at any age, but huge
changes are particularly common during emerging adulthood—and
these changes have implications for partnership stability.

Sharing Older Men

A handful of younger men in partnerships with someone around their
own age shared intimacy with their partner and an older man, much as
some older men described doing with younger adult men. David (27)
was one such man. He described a positive partnership with his boyfriend in his early thirties, with whom he had been in a partnership for
several years. He explained, "My favorite thing about him or about our
relationship, he's very quiet and a little reserved, but he's really sweet
and we have a very kind relationship. I really need that because I need
somebody to ground me and be patient with me because I can get manic
sometimes. So he's very stable and supportive, and I like that. He's very
chill, which I need. He's kind of a stoner, which I like. Our relationship
is very relaxing and calm and good." David and his partner also "shared"
an older man in sexual encounters.

He actually has a long-standing relationship with this guy who's, I'd say, forty, so not a huge difference, but enough where they do the daddy-boy role play. And they've had a long-standing relationship for like five years where they hook up every week. And this guy's really, really hot, like he's pretty incredible. Usually our schedules don't line up . . . and it's very complicated. But we actually got to hook up all three of us, and that was really fun, because I got to join in their daddy-boy dynamic and become the second boy in the scenario. And so that was fun and a cool experience for me and my boyfriend to have together with this guy. And he took care of both of us and it was a good time.

David explained what happened during the sexual encounter.

We started out making out and blow jobs, all that stuff in the living room. And there was a lot of cuddling and getting intimate with each other, because it was my first time with him, so it was getting used to each other first. And then we moved to the bedroom and I remember—I've got a really bad memory, so it's kind of blurry—but I remember this guy was doing something with my boyfriend, I guess probably sucking his dick, and I got to eat his ass, which was really fun, because I wasn't expecting I'd be able to do that, and that's one of my favorite things. But with the dynamic it's usually the top does that. But he enjoys it, so I got to do that, and that was a lot of fun. And then he did top my boyfriend. I didn't bottom in that scenario. But I was just watching and enjoying that. And then he, I think, fingered me while I got off or something like that at the end.

While David and his partner also had sex with older men separately, they sometimes shared enjoyable sexual experiences with older men. Doing so did not threaten their partnership. In fact, it strengthened their partnership because both men were able to have a range of fulfilling sexual experiences.

Tyler (33) also described sharing an older man with his boyfriend. The situation was enjoyable in and of itself, but Tyler's boyfriend also learned things about Tyler that he did not know previously. This situation involved a hookup with a man in his midforties. "It was a three-way with him and then my boyfriend and I. It was a nicer time. We did a little bit of everything." Tyler elaborated,

One thing he did that I hadn't really done with someone before—he was masculine enough. He said he had to take a piss, so I was like, "Okay, I'll go with you." Because I don't know, I like that. [Laughs.] So I sometimes, if someone's taking a piss, I'll eat them out at the toilet while they're pissing. In this case I sat in the bathtub so he could piss on me. It was funny because my live-in boyfriend didn't know that I enjoy that, so it was a fun exposure for him to see that. I mean, so nothing like—no crazy boundaries were pushed. It wasn't the best sex I've ever had, but it was a nice time.

Tyler explained that there is a "triangle" between him, his boyfriend, and this older man. "It's funny, we have this little triangle going. I like him physically a little bit more than my live-in boyfriend. On the physical spectrum. Emotionally I'm not as attached to this guy. So this guy really enjoys my live-in boyfriend. Then of course my live-in boyfriend wants more emotionally from me than I am ready to give, so we have this little love triangle. . . . So he's around, and we'll go over to his house every once in a while, but he's not in my daily life. But he's definitely accessible." While complicated, the relationship the three of them shared was enjoyable because each was able to get his emotional or physical needs met without harming Tyler and his boyfriend's existing partnership. Having romantic partnerships with someone around their own age, alongside hookups with older men, was ideal for many younger men.

Younger Men's Hesitancy about Age-Gap Romantic Partnerships

Younger men explained what the ideal age gap would be between themselves and a romantic partner (men in a partnership described a hypothetical ideal age gap, if they were to be single in the future). Twelve preferred a gap of under ten years; four preferred a gap of around ten years; nine either preferred a gap of more than ten years or were open to men of a variety of ages; and one was unsure. Their answers are revealing. While most younger men preferred older men for sexual encounters, a majority also felt that romantic partnerships with much older men may be too complicated to work. Of course, as Joshua (23) noted, "It's difficult to say because I think it changes when people get older. I think that time and age matters less and less the older you get." Still, many young men considered reasons why a particular age gap would be preferable to them. Many knew that there was a disconnect between their attraction to older men and their preferred romantic partners. "I guess it's kind of weird that I like older guys sexually," Jeffrey (23) noted, "but younger guys around my age romantically." It was, nonetheless, how he and several other young men felt.

Young men who preferred a partner around their own age typically had concerns about differences in life goals, shared interests, or social stigma. Jacob (27) noted, "More than ten years, you have that added pressure of people thinking about you, looking at you funny and thinking, that societal pressure to be like, 'This is weird.' But also I think those age differences can really define different life goals, or where you are in life." James (28) noted similar reasons as Jacob when he described a preference for a partner around his own age. "I do prefer to date around my own age. Like for long-term partner-wise I do prefer to be with someone who's my age, just because then things are on equal footing more so than if I was dating someone much older than me long-term." "Equal footing" meant several things. "Financially, emotionally. There's quite a bit of difference when age becomes a factor. Usually, not always, but usually an older person is usually a lot more financially established, and they know themselves a lot better, and they're at a different point in their lives. And I really like that for casual dating and friendships and sex, but for long-term partners I prefer to have someone who's at the same place that I am." James, like other younger men, preferred to learn from older men in sexual friendships or hookups, but have a romantic partnership with someone around his age who was similarly becoming established in life.

David (27), relatedly, explained that a partnership with a man around his own age was ideal in part because of shared generational experiences. "In terms of dating, I pretty much only do long-term relationships with guys who are my age, just because I like that we have shared childhood connections and we remember the same TV shows and stuff, whereas I can't say that about older men." Tyler (33) agreed that a man around his own age—not much younger, and not more than five years older—was ideal, because "what I would look for is emotional maturity or we're both at the same phase of life at the same time, so a realistic relationship." Tyler could see a short-term partnership with someone over the age of thirty-eight, but nothing long-term "because I just feel like something would break it apart."

Several younger men preferred someone around their own age to avoid possible power imbalances in an age-gap partnership. Notably, few young men other than Andrew or DaShawn who had experienced age-gap partnerships described a noticeable power dynamic. In short, many younger men were wary about the potential for power differentials between themselves and an older man, but most had not actually experienced these differentials in a romantic partnership. John (31) explained, "At that point, it stops becoming more of a partner aspect and more of a, I lead, you follow type thing. I give you this, you have to give this in return." Austin (27) agreed but described this dynamic in different terms. "I actually find that I am more inclined to have romantic relationships with people around my age, but I am more inclined to have friends-with-benefits relationships with older men." He feels this way "because of the power-equality thing. I feel more equal power-wise with someone who is around my age, whereas when there is that daddy-boy relationship he is the one with more power, and I don't enjoy that in a romantic relationship."

Some younger men acknowledged that their preference for a partner around their own age posed difficulties, given that they enjoyed the company of older men. "Well, that's where the problem is," Alejandro (26) began, "because if I'm looking for a long-term romantic relationship, I find doing that with someone much older than me would be a problem. So when I think about looking for a romantic relationship I will probably only be looking for guys around my age." Concerns about life expectancy were at the forefront of his mind.

> I guess our likes and dislikes would eventually be too much. And I also have this—I mean, it sounds bad and selfish—but if I'm in a long-term romantic relationship with them and they're much older than me, I don't know, I feel like they would eventually get too old and I would still be kind of young-ish, and that would cause more problems. I know it sounds kind of ridiculous, but in the extremes in my imagination I'm thinking, "Oh, what if they die and then I just used up all this time with them and now I'm by myself."

This concern is not unfounded. If younger men partner with men decades older than themselves, they will (most likely) outlive their partner and potentially spend their old age with no partner. David (27) echoed these concerns.

> I don't think I have a set number, but for a long-term relationship I guess I'd like that age gap to be under ten years. And honestly that's just a practical concern. I don't know if I'm looking to get married someday. I don't know if I'm looking for a relationship that lasts the rest of my lifetime. But if you're dating somebody who's more than ten years older than you, you should expect a significantly different life expectancy. If I'm looking to marry somebody, I want us to be at least roughly planning to live the same amount of time from here on out. That seems kind of like calculating and sort of a little too numbers-y, but I feel like I want to make sure that the expectation is the same. I don't think I would be in a long-term relationship with somebody who is too much, like more than maybe fifteen years older than me. But anything in that range is fine.

Realities about different life expectancies were a key issue for David. "I would love it if a fifteen-year age gap was ideal," Tyrone (32) began, but "realistically if you're going to be with someone forever, or for a really, really long time, I want there to not be an answer to that, but probably not that much more than ten years. I know people make it work, but it can be a little bit scary to think about someone you love getting older." Tyrone, like several other men, knew that sooner or later the issue of different life expectancies would emerge if he dated someone more than a decade older than he. While the issue of life expectancy was far in the future, several men knew that if they entered a romantic partnership with a man much older than themselves, it would eventually arise.

A handful of men identified an age gap of around ten years as ideal. An age gap of ten years adequately fulfilled younger men's physical and emotional attraction to older men but did not pose the same complications as a gap of fifteen to thirty years. Jamal (23) described this dynamic clearly. "I think that for romance specifically that ten is probably a very good number for that because it satisfies my attraction needs, but also it gives us enough space to be able to connect on things that otherwise we wouldn't be able to if he were much older. I think as far as attraction physically, twenty years is probably the peak that would be the most effective. But I think as far as romance goes, ten is a pretty good number." A ten-year age gap was a good compromise for Jamal, even though he was most physically attracted to men in their early forties. A ten-year gap was also nice because, in Chris's (33) words, "I think the different levels of experience and different experiences growing up, it's still close, but definitely you have different experiences to draw on, lived through different things, lived through the same things at different times in your lives." Ten years was enough of a gap for men to share different experiences, but not so large that men had little in common. Thinking about this topic was difficult for some men, including Michael (30), who explained, "It's something that I battle time in and time out. I've been with men mostly twenty or thirty years my [senior], which can present a real issue for someone who's looking for a long-term relationship as they look into the future. But at the same time, you live in the moment." Still, he mentioned, "If something struck that was just remarkable and I couldn't pass it up, I'd date him no matter the age gap. But if we're speaking ideally, I'd rather them be closer in age. So if you're talking five to fifteen, or ten to twelve. It's not an answer I can put a definitive answer on. But to generalize an answer, I'd rather them be closer in age than farther apart."

In contrast, a few men explicitly desired a large age gap in a romantic partnership. "I think I'd go as young as maybe a ten-year difference, so that would put that person in his late thirties. I think ideal probably would be closer to fifteen to twenty, a fifteen- to twenty-year age gap," Aydin (28) explained. "I don't think there's any one ideal age gap, but I usually find myself most—I guess the sweet spot is around twenty years, fifteen to twenty years." He continued, "I'm sure there's a younger guy who could potentially blow me off my feet, some guy who's just like a year or two older than me who could blow me off my feet. But generally speaking I prefer someone who is more mature than my cohort is on average. And so guys who are maybe ten to twenty years older than I am, that's when that difference starts to get a result." Aydin emphasized emotional connection when thinking about an age gap. Cyrus (25) agreed that a fifteen- to twenty-year age gap was ideal. "I think realistically I would say like fifteen to twenty years." He continued, "I see myself with someone who is definitely older. I cannot see myself dating somebody who's my age or just like five years older, ten years older. You've got to be a little bit more established when it comes to that." Because his most recent partnership, with a man in his midfifties, ended because that man was concerned about the age difference, Cyrus did not want a gap any larger than fifteen to twenty years.

Anthony (25) reported that he had so little attraction to men around his age that a romantic partnership with someone around his age would be difficult. "I would say my bare minimum the overwhelming major-ity of time is people over forty, like between forty and fifty. In terms of a relationship, I would say my oldest is probably midforties. Ideally I would end up with somebody in the early thirties or very early forties. But the overwhelming majority of the time my physical attraction is so limited that it makes it difficult. Ideal would be late thirties, early for-ties." Anthony knew that his limited physical attraction, to older men, made the thought of a romantic partnership with a man around his own age much less appealing. Kyle (25) agreed. "That's kind of a tough one. I would say, like if it were to happen right now, probably twelve years. Ten to twelve years tends to be the majority of the men I am attracted to, at least based on SCRUFF's stats that I 'Woof' that age group more often, late thirties to early forties."[11]

In short, the younger men I talked to reported a variety of prefer-ences for age gaps in romantic partnerships. There was a fairly even dis-tribution of men who preferred a partner around their age, a partner about ten years older than themselves, a partner more than ten years older than themselves, or a partner of just about any age. Only seven were currently romantically involved with men ten or more years older than themselves. Men who preferred someone around their own age discussed concerns related to life expectancy, disconnects with shared interests, or concerns about power differentials in age-gap partnerships. Notably, only a handful of men who had actually experienced age-gap romantic partnerships described concerning power dynamics—and these issues were not necessarily caused by the age difference between the two, but rather emotional manipulation from the older partner that may exist in partnerships regardless of the age gap. Several men acknowledged a dilemma: they are attracted to older men, but are also concerned about romantic partnerships with older men because they fear what the future may look like.

Enrique: What the Future Holds for Younger Men

Younger men shared understandable concerns about the future of a romantic partnership with a large age gap. For an example of how a partnership of this type would work, we can turn to Enrique, a sixty-two-year-old who is in a partnership with a man about twenty years older than himself. Enrique had preferred older men for most of his life but began to be perceived as a daddy around age sixty because "I started to open up more after I turned sixty" and began to feel "more confident in myself." Both shifts, along with interest from younger men, led Enrique to increase his sexual involvement with much younger men. Enrique explained, "I don't have a choice" but to be a daddy because he had aged into the daddy category whether or not he wanted to do so. He had mixed feelings about being seen as a daddy. Unlike most other men, Enrique described little association between daddyness and age, and even described younger sexual partners as daddies on the basis of their personality and physique. (Few other men shared similar stories.)

Enrique, at the time of the interview, had just celebrated a multide-cade anniversary with his husband. Enrique noted that they do not have sex "at all anymore, for the last two or three years" because of health issues. "He's having some trouble, physical problems, heart problems, and he's diabetic. His libido has gone, completely gone, but he still mastur-bates. But we don't have sex." This lack of marital sex is one reason why Enrique has sex with other men.

His partnership is challenging due to their age difference, but they make it work. "I think the main challenge is to get him healthy. I've been doing that for the last three years and it's getting stressful and a little harder every day practically, so. I'm just living with it as well to [fulfill vows for] richer, poorer, sicker, sick and health so I think that's my thing of staying with him." But, he added, "I still love him so it's okay."

Enrique is not miserable. His partnership does have notable chal-lenges due to his husband's health issues, but Enrique takes care of him and, at the same time, has sex with other men because they are in an open relationship. Both have their needs met in this way. Thus, it is un-fair to portray Enrique's partnership as a "warning" to younger men who consider involvement with much older men. At the same time, his expe-rience does offer lessons.

Younger men need to be aware (and usually are aware) that there is a strong possibility that their much older partners will require caretaking and will likely die decades before them. This scenario does not mean that age-gap romantic partnerships are inadvisable. It simply means that everyone should be aware of what the future holds. Some men I talked to did not think caretaking responsibilities would be much of an issue. Others, however, foresaw the future, and wanted to avoid asymmetrical caretaking responsibilities even as they enjoyed sexual pairings with men substantially older than themselves. Older partners of younger men—for instance, Cyrus's former partner—were understandably concerned that the younger man could leave them when life became more complicated. Overall, older and younger men should be aware of future asymmetrical caretaking responsibilities. Younger men should also not make guarantees to caretake for an older partner but then change their minds later. This topic is one that requires open communication and fair expectations, given its complexities.

Do Older Men Desire a Younger Romantic Partner?

Most of the seventeen currently single older men, like the single younger men, did not seek an age-gap romantic partnership. Of these seventeen single older men, six wished to remain single, three sought an age-similar romantic partnership, three wanted an age-gap romantic partnership, one man stated that he wanted a partnership but vacillated about whether he would like it to be with a younger man or a man around his own age, and three offered ambiguous answers about whether they sought a romantic partnership. These findings, combined, demonstrate that there was not a large mismatch between the goals of younger and older men. Within each group there was a diversity of relationship statuses, desires for romantic involvement, and hopes (or lack thereof) for age-gap romantic partnerships. Most currently single older and younger men did not seek a romantic partner much different in age from their own.

Three older men sought a romantic partnership with someone around their own age. Hunter (49) wanted a "peer": "I probably wouldn't date younger guys. It would be more my peer," he explained. "I mean, there will be some good ones, of course, but I'd rather be with a peer in that regard." Hunter preferred a partner who was similarly emotionally mature and stable in life. Two other men reported concerns about whether an age-gap partnership would last long-term. Santiago (43) explained, "Even though I feel strong satisfaction taking care of younger guys, I don't think I will pursue them romantically. It freaks me out to think of that. So I would like to have a relationship with a guy who is closer to my age," and specifically an open relationship. He continued,

> I like hooking up with guys who are way younger than me, definitely. But if I am also looking to have a relationship with someone, I'm looking at having a boyfriend, but I don't want to have a boyfriend who is twenty-two. I don't want to have a boyfriend who is twenty-five. I would like to have a boyfriend who is very close to my age. If I'm going to have a relationship with someone that is durable and is going to be a long-term thing, eventually probably get married or something like that, it's going to be with a guy who is way closer to my age.

In addition to concerns about partnership stability, Santiago was concerned about having enough shared interests. "I feel like we don't have a lot of things in common anyway. And I'm very sexually attracted to them," he began, and "we can have nice conversations or whatever, but I kind of [run] out pretty quickly. And so I don't see myself dating a younger guy for long-term." Santiago wanted to continue to have sex with younger men, but in the context of an open relationship with a romantic partner around his own age.

Steven (60) also reported a preference for an age-similar partner because "I shut myself off to the idea that it [an age-gap partnership] could actually turn into anything serious, although I know it still does happen." He did, in fact, have a friend in his late twenties and another in his early sixties who were in a partnership with one another. Nonetheless, "I don't see myself getting involved with somebody under the age of forty as a long-term relationship. And part of that is because I just don't. It just doesn't really work for me. I'm flattered in many ways having these younger guys, and it's fun hanging out with them and keeping up with what's going on." Despite his enjoyment of the time he spent with younger men, Steven was concerned that younger men would be unfairly burdened in an age-gap partnership.

I always ask the young guys about that and I bring that up to my guys that I'm involved with that are younger, like counting the cost as far as, "If you do get into a relationship with an older man who you consider a daddy, but who is significantly older, there is going to be a cost as that person ages, that while you're in your prime of life you're going to take care of this person that's not doing well healthwise. And then when that person passes you again will have to start over. You will now have to find another relationship because you'll be forty years old." So those are questions I always challenge young guys. And some are fine with it, and most of them have thought about that. But again, love is love, right? If it's meant to be it's meant to be and people are going to be okay with that.

Although Steven knew that some people were happily involved in age-gap romantic partnerships, and although he accepted other men's choices to form them, he himself remained skeptical about their long-term stability and benefit for both partners.

In contrast, three other men wanted a much younger partner. Matthew (55) stated that he desired a younger partner, but "realistically, not as young as eighteen to twenty-five or whatever." Brian (61) similarly wanted a partner in his "early thirties." Ryan (48), who enjoyed asymmetrical partnerships as previous sections detailed, wanted a younger partner in part so he could be "in charge." On one hand, he desires someone "on the more submissive side, too, sexually and somewhat in the regular part of the relationship, too." He continued, "This is just like if I could make an ideal one, right, not being kind of realistic. Where I would be the one in charge. I'm the one picking the movie or where we go to dinner, being in charge. They kind of want to cater to me and please me. But then also where I'm fun, too, maybe take them out or buy them presents and stuff like that." While Ryan knew that this specific arrangement was unlikely, he did desire it. Ryan, unlike most of the men I talked to, explicitly desired an asymmetrical partnership.

Brett (43) was more conflicted about whether he wanted an age-similar partner or one much younger than he. "I wish I could relate more to guys my age," Brett explained.

I get on Grindr or SCRUFF or whatever, and to my credit in trying to change this, I message guys and I find guys my age attractive, I do. And

I message them and it's like never hear anything back from anybody that is thirty-three or older. It's the weirdest thing. Guys that are thirty to twenty-two, I have to beat them away with a stick. It's so weird. It's like this weird thing that I just cannot explain. I guess one of the reasons why that I normally date younger guys is because it's so much easier because there's so many more options for me personally. And a lot of guys that are my age either don't take care of themselves, they are jaded from terrible life experiences or whatever, or they're just really fucking boring. Pardon my language. They're just really boring, you know what I mean? I feel like I'm really young at heart. I still, from time to time, like to go out to the clubs till two o'clock, three o'clock in the morning and I'm forty-three years old. It's very rare that it happens, but I can pull it together from time to time.

Brett experienced more interest from younger men than men around his own age, and he related to younger men better too. At the same time, younger men posed challenges as well.

One thing I hate about it is I want that long-term relationship, but I kind of, not sabotage it, but kill it in my head before it starts because I remember how I was when I was in my twenties, and I didn't want a long-term thing, and then maybe it's like a defense mechanism. I don't know. It's just a lot different with guys my age, I think, in terms of starting a relationship with them. Just from what I've seen my friends do. It's like you meet someone in their early forties, and they've been through it, and they just click right away, and everybody's mature, and there's no fighting about bullshit, and they just work. With a guy in their twenties, it's like all this drama and shit.

Brett had concerns about whether a partnership with a younger man would last, and also found younger men's immaturity irritating. Yet he nonetheless connected with younger men better than men around his own age. His hesitancy about men younger than himself *and* men his own age created a difficult dynamic in which he was ambivalent about a romantic partnership with anyone, even though he did desire a partnership.

How Culture Affects Age-Gap Romantic Partnerships

Most of the men I talked to were not currently involved in a romantic partnership with a man much older or younger than themselves, nor did most want to be. A majority wanted to avoid the complications they associated with age-gap partnerships, including differences in life expectancy, asymmetrical caretaking responsibilities, differences in maturity level, and (for younger men) concerns about personal autonomy. Most men instead formed sexually and emotionally fulfilling age-gap pairings of different types, such as FWBs.

Notably, most men who were in romantic age-gap partnerships reported that they were satisfied with their partnership, and they reported few issues related to the gap between partners' ages. Other men were in open romantic partnerships with a man around their own age and enjoyed sexually intimate and nonromantic but emotionally meaningful age-gap pairings. Although some younger men reported past romantic partnerships with an older man that they perceived as unequal, this dynamic was rare. Similarly, only a handful of older men reported asymmetrical age-gap partnerships. In short, most men who were currently involved in a romantic age-gap partnership (or had been in the past) enjoyed them, despite some complexities, and there was little evidence of widespread power differentials between older and younger men that harmed either party.

In many societies, particularly countries in the Americas, Europe, and eastern Asia, it is expected that a man will partner with a woman, and specifically a woman around his own age (usually, a few years younger).[12] Even in highly individualistic Western societies, men who are attracted to other men must consciously rework cultural expectations around romantic relationships, which assume heterosexuality, so that they can form a partnership with another man. This process is doubly complicated for men who are attracted to other adult men much older or younger than themselves.

The way men navigate sexual desire and romantic attachment amidst cultural expectations for how relationships should look highlights how culture affects partnership formation. The fact that most of the men I talked to were not in a romantic partnership with someone much older or younger—and often intentionally avoided this possibility—highlights how expectations around age similarity affect whether two people become partners. Age gaps are far more common in man-man partnerships than in any other couple type, yet the stories of the men I talked to suggest that a large proportion of men channel their desires into other types of relationships that are nonromantic yet still meaningful.

Additionally, cultural expectations affect how partnerships function. Even though age-gap pairings are usually distinct both sexually and emotionally—for instance, many involve a mentorship component—most of the men I talked to described age-gap romantic partnerships that functioned like age-similar partnerships. Most men who formed age-gap romantic partnerships used existing cultural tools to form partnerships that were egalitarian, as is the cultural ideal, and tried to ensure that the younger partner maintained a sense of personal autonomy. In short, the men I talked to navigated existing cultural expectations around egalitarian, age-similar partnerships to either avoid age-gap romantic partnerships or to carefully shape the functioning of the ones they did form.[13]

Conclusion

This book focused on the stories of thirty-nine daddies as well as twenty-six younger adult men who paired with much older men. The findings defy stereotypes about sugar daddies and gold diggers. Both older and younger men described relationships that involved mutual emotional enrichment, and most men in both groups took steps to ensure that finances did not substantially affect their relationships.

Nonromantic yet emotionally intimate older-younger pairings between adults are not easy to categorize. Some of them, like friendships the married couple Graham and Greg developed with younger men, are in some ways similar to chosen families common among LGBTQ people.[1] What constitutes family is subjective,[2] and although not all LGBTQ people consider friends to be family, many do.[3] "Family" in this context does not necessarily refer to relationships that replace or mimic legal/biological familial relationships. Rather, "chosen family" describes close relationships, of various types, between two or more people. Most of the men I talked to did not describe their older-younger pairings as chosen family, however.

"Friend" also does not completely describe emotionally intimate older-younger pairings between adults. While it is common for gay men to have had sex with friends, such sexual involvement often happens at the beginning of a friendship and usually does not last—although it certainly can.[4] Gay men often describe sex as something that can make friendships too messy.[5] Unlike the majority of friendships between gay men, most of the older-younger pairings men discussed with me were sexual and involved intergenerational transmissions of knowledge. Some older-younger pairings eventually became nonsexual friendships, much as in other gay friendships, whereas other pairings continued to be sexual. While "friend" may be the closest term to describe emotionally intimate but nonromantic sexual relationships between adults, older-younger friendships were distinct from age-similar friendships, at least according to past research about gay friendships.[6]

Many older-younger pairings between adults are unique in either form or function, and often do not fit under the umbrella of any existing term.[7] Some older-younger pairings were unique enough that no term does them justice, such as pairings between Graham, Greg, and the younger adult men with whom they developed intimate connections. Other pairings could be described as emotionally close friendships, casual sexual friendships, or hookups, yet they too often contained qualities unlike those between two men of a similar age, given the mentorship or distinct sexual dynamics typically involved. In short, older-younger pairings between adults are a distinct aspect of gay and bisexual men's social lives and deserve special analysis.

The Puzzle

Now we return to the puzzle I posed in the introduction: in the Western world, why are large age gaps more common among man-man couples than woman-woman couples when people in both groups experience limited dating pools?[8] It is not a mystery as to why woman-man couples in the West are the least likely to have large age gaps. Heterosexuals have more dating options than LGBTQ people, heterosexual social norms encourage similar-age partnerships, and most heterosexuals have children and want their partner to be around the same age. On the other hand, LGBTQ people have limited dating pools, they challenge relationship norms more often than heterosexuals, and they are less likely to have children. Thus, it makes sense that age gaps are more common among same-sex couples. Yet these explanations do not fully account for why age gaps would be more common among man-man couples than woman-woman couples.

The stories from this book show that men's older-younger pairings are not always the result of a limited dating pool but rather preferences for much older or younger adult men. Limited dating pools partially explain the commonality of age gaps among man-man romantic partnerships, but other factors are at play. Older-younger pairings between adults are an important part of the cultural life of gay and bisexual men's communities. Not all gay and bisexual men form sexual or romantic age-gap pairings (I only talked to those who did), but many of those who do find these pairings emotionally meaningful, socially important, and sexually exciting.

But why would age gaps be more common among man-man couples than woman-woman couples? I did not talk to LGBTQ women, so I cannot say for sure. Prior research does offer some clues as to why LGBTQ women have lower rates of age-gap partnerships than men, however.

LGBTQ women historically—and today—have had fewer physical spaces such as bars and bathhouses in which to meet.[9] For instance, there have always been far fewer bars specifically catering to LGBTQ women than to men.[10] Recent decades have accelerated this disparity, such that there are only a handful of bars today that cater specifically to LGBTQ women.[11] There are about two dozen left in the United States,[12] compared to hundreds of bars that cater specifically to gay and bisexual men.[13] There are also many bathhouses that cater to men, but almost none for women.[14] The lack of institutions such as bars and bathhouses means that LGBTQ women have fewer opportunities than men to meet potential sexual or romantic partners of different ages.

Women have also had fewer "cruising" grounds than men. "Cruising" is a practice in which people meet anonymously in a public or semi-public place (like a park) to engage in sex, often secretly. Men have had greater access to public spaces than women. As one historian wrote, "Gay men as men also enjoyed greater freedom of movement than lesbians did as women, since many of the public spaces where gay men met, from street corners to bars, were culturally defined as male spaces."[15] Even today, it is often safer for men than women to cruise,[16] given that it is more common for women to experience catcalling and other forms of street harassment that can quickly escalate.[17]

There are also far more dating and hookup apps that cater to gay and bisexual men than to LGBTQ women.[18] The lack of digital spaces for LGBTQ women reduces their chances to meet potential romantic or sexual partners who belong to a different age cohort. Relatedly, institutions such as bars and bathhouses, as well as cruising grounds and apps, both create and reflect social norms about age-gap pairings between adults. Men historically, and today, have had exposure to spaces in which age-gap pairings between adults could form relatively easily. The greater ease of meeting much older or younger adult partners, and the resulting increase in age-gap pairings, also likely changed social norms such that age-gap pairings between adults became more accepted among gay and bisexual men relative to other groups. Today, mobile dating and hookup apps, which connect adult men of different age-segregated social networks, appear to have greatly increased the prevalence of age-gap pairings and daddy identities.

Additionally, due to societal gender inequality, women are devalued much more as they age than men.[19] Consequently, it is more likely that men rather than women will be perceived as desirable as they age.[20] Some women are referred to as "MILFs" as they age,[21] but it is less common for women than men to be perceived as attractive as they age. Furthermore, terms such as "cougar" are often used in a derogatory manner and are not exactly equivalent to the term "daddy." "Cougar," for instance, suggests sexual predation. These facts help explain why woman-older different-sex pairings are less common than man-older different-sex pairings *and* why age gaps are less common among woman-woman couples than man-man couples.

Gay men also have far higher rates of open relationships than lesbians: 33 percent of coupled gay men in the United States are currently in an open relationship, compared to 5 percent of lesbian women.[22] This pattern means that men have many more opportunities to form age-gap pairings than women do, since a same-age romantic partnership does not prevent sexual friendships or hookups with a much older or younger adult partner. Recall, for instance, that many of the coupled men I talked to had romantic partners around their same age, but sexual friends in different age cohorts. Being available for sex regardless of partnership status means gay men will have more opportunities to have sex with adult men much older or younger than themselves.

Gay men have, furthermore, historically pioneered new relationship forms and sexual practices. In recent decades gay men increased the visibility of open relationships, and some of the earliest BDSM communities were gay leather communities.[23] Gay men have also historically been accepting of practices that later gave rise to entire subcultures (for instance, pups). Given this history, it makes sense that gay men are more involved in other sexual practices, like age-gap pairings between adults, that are less common in wider society or more stigmatized.

It is also possible that greater rates of age-gap pairings among men are attributable in part to social changes in the nineteenth and twentieth centuries that led to the emergence of sexual identification as a concept. Men historically had greater opportunities than women to live independent lives, and it was also more acceptable for men to remain unmarried than it was for women to do so.[24] As a result of these two factors, men were able to form communities that societies would later understand as "gay" much earlier than women could. These communities may have developed norms and mentorship practices that have existed, in different forms, up to today, including older-younger pairings that allowed older men to teach younger adult men how to have sex or integrate themselves in gay communities. Additionally, many of the most visible "gayborhoods" have historically, and today, been dominated by men,[25] which means that men who lived in them had more opportunities to meet other adult men of different ages. Gayborhoods may have increased the commonality of men's age-gap pairings and led to greater social acceptance of these pairings among gay and bisexual men compared to other groups.

Other reasons help explain why age-gap pairings are less common among LGBTQ women than men. Man-man couples have more education, race, and age differences between partners than woman-man and woman-woman couples.[26] This pattern suggests that gay and bisexual men are more interested in potential partners who are different from themselves compared to other groups. Child-rearing intentions partially explain this trend. Individuals usually partner with someone of their own race/ethnicity and age group when they plan to have children.[27] Because man-man couples are far less likely to have children than woman-man and woman-woman couples,[28] they are more likely to choose partners different from themselves. To use a term from demography, gay and bisexual men have different patterns of "assortative mating" than other groups.

Limited dating pools are clearly not the only explanation for the commonality of age gaps among man-man couples. Gay and bisexual men approach dating differently than other groups because they are culturally distinct. Within the wider LGBTQ community, there are distinct subgroups that have their own unique cultures. Gay and bisexual men are one such group. Part of their cultural distinctiveness involves interest in sexual arrangements uncommon among other groups, including open relationships and age-gap pairings between adults.

Theoretical Implications

Masculinity

This book has shown that certain enactments of masculinity can have positive effects in some circumstances, both for the people who enact masculinity and for the people with whom they build relationships. The older men I talked to emotionally supported and mentored young adult men in tender ways that they considered compatible with masculinity. Young men appreciated older men's masculinity for different reasons: it validated younger men's masculinity *or* their femininity; it helped several younger men learn how to enact a masculinity they found appealing; and it helped younger adult men who enjoyed being sexually submissive feel comfortable in sexual situations.

It is notable that whereas many older men felt that their masculinity was *boosted* through their older-younger pairings, many younger adult men instead felt that they experienced a *break* from the pressures of masculinity, for instance because they deferred to older men on certain matters or were sexually submissive. Not all men described this pattern, but those who did offer evidence that the effects of masculinity can be both asymmetrical and positive.

Age-gap pairings provided both older and younger adult men the opportunity to explore gender expression outside of constraints posed by heteronormative gender expectations. This flexibility was especially pronounced for younger men, many of whom described the ability to embrace femininity—as well as masculinity—when they paired with older men. On the other hand, age-gap pairings made many older men feel more masculine, and therefore challenged the widespread association between femininity and gayness in wider American culture.[29]

These findings challenge the common scholarly conclusion that masculinity is necessarily bad. As one author wrote, gender scholars who discuss masculinity "tend to focus on its regressive aspects and ignore its progressive potential," paying attention "to expressions of sexism and homophobia, or legitimation of patriarchy" but not to enactments of masculinity that have positive effects.[30] Gay and bisexual men have had to rethink the relationship between masculinity and sexuality, as well as between emotional intimacy and masculinity. Older-younger pairings between adults often involve emotional tenderness and mentorship. The avoidance of tender emotions is not a necessary component of masculinity, and daddies are one group of men who prove this point.

Other scholars have written about what they call "caring masculinities," which involve the "integration of values of care, such as positive emotion, interdependence, and relationality, into masculine identities."[31] Daddies often display these characteristics in their relationships with younger adult men. Some men enact caring masculinities in other contexts as well, such as when parenting,[32] although caring masculinities are not limited to fatherhood.[33]

Scholars should continue to study the many ways in which masculinity can harm people, for instance by reinforcing gender inequalities or by encouraging behaviors that negatively affect people's well-being. It is also, however, worthwhile to examine how masculinity can sometimes be positive. Masculinity is complex and takes many forms, so it makes sense that its effects are varied too.

Exchange Theory

The stories of the men I talked to show that differences between people do not always lead to inequality in the way sociologists usually use the term, to refer to negative situations. People can build relationships around difference, and these relationships may be highly fulfilling for both people not *despite* the differences but *because* of them. Some people unfamiliar with the topic of age-gap pairings between adults may be tempted to assume that most such pairings necessarily advantage one person at the expense of the other. In contrast, I found that many such pairings are emotionally meaningful, sexually fulfilling, and important to both parties. Age-gap pairings can be complicated, particularly when they are romantic, but this complexity does not mean that they are necessarily bad for one or both people involved.

Relationships built around difference can be as positive as relationships in which both partners are similar. The differences between two people do not determine the quality of the relationship, even as differences may add complexity. Scholars should continue to study the ways in which differences between partners may lead to relationship inequalities. All types of relationships can be unequal, of course, and age-gap romantic partnerships are no exception. We should also keep in mind that not all relationships are unequal, even if they appear to be from an outsider's perspective.

Related to the above point, the stories of the men I talked to provide further insight into what social scientists call "exchange theory." The theory argues that "persons who have a lower status than their partner in one respect tend to have a higher status than their partner in another. A relative disadvantage in one domain is 'exchanged' for a relative advantage in another domain."[34] The theory examines factors such as education, occupation, physical attractiveness, race, nationality, and age. Exchange theory does help to explain partnership formation between men and women.[35]

Although most work about "status exchange" has not examined same-sex partnerships due to data limitations, there is reason to believe that exchange theory does not apply to man-man couples in the same way as to woman-man couples. Man-man couples are more likely to have differences along the axes of age, education, and race compared to other couple types.[36] Those patterns, in combination with the stories of the men I talked to, show that partnership formation works differently among gay and bisexual men. What they find desirable in a partner, and how they date, are often different from both heterosexuals and LGBTQ women.

Daddies are popular among gay and bisexual men, and daddies do not necessarily have to "compensate" for their age through, for instance, sugar dynamics. Additionally, the fact that many older and younger adult men avoided age-gap romantic partnerships yet enjoyed sexually and emotionally fulfilling relationships of different types shows that younger men do not necessarily seek to "trade" their youth for older men's financial security (or other characteristics).

It is common for there to be many differences between partners in man-man partnerships, but how exchange theory applies to these partnerships is an open empirical question. We cannot assume that status exchange will operate similarly among gay and bisexual men as among heterosexuals, even among heterosexuals in age-gap partnerships. Exchange theory could help to explain man-man partnership formation, but the exact patterns will likely be different from studies about heterosexuals. Only future research that uses nationally representative survey data will be able to examine this possibility.

LGBTQ Assimilation

In the Western world, the past several decades have seen a massive increase in public acceptance of LGBTQ people, an expansion of legal equality, and greater institutional inclusion of LGBTQ people. A typical assumption among scholars is that LGBTQ people will assimilate into wider society because of these changes. According to this logic, LGBTQ people will look, act, and think more like straight, cisgender people, and will lose many of the characteristics that make them unique. In other words, as LGBTQ people are more integrated into society, distinct LGBTQ cultures will fade.

It is undeniably true that LGBTQ people in the Western world are more integrated into wider society than they were several decades ago. This pattern is especially true for certain people, such as cisgender white gays and lesbians who are economically middle-class or above. The more advantaged someone is in terms of gender, race, and class, the more likely they are to integrate into mainstream institutions. Despite uneven patterns of inclusion and continued discrimination, LGBTQ people as a group are more integrated into mainstream institutions today than ever before.

In contrast to what many scholars have assumed, increased inclusion has not led to the elimination of distinct LGBTQ cultural practices. Ironically, "queer theory"—which supposedly rejects binary thinking—often explains complex social developments as leading to either assimilation or nonassimilation. Through the lens of queer theory, LGBTQ people either reject social norms or embrace them. Queer theorists have criticized marriage equality, in particular, for reinforcing the value of conventional marriage and monogamy among LGBTQ people. There is some evidence to support ideas about assimilation: for instance, younger LGBTQ people seem to be more interested in monogamy than older cohorts,[37] many LGBTQ institutions such as bars are disappearing,[38] and gayborhoods are changing.[39]

Yet assimilation is not a binary phenomenon. LGBTQ people have only *partially* assimilated into mainstream society. Distinct LGBTQ institutions and cultural practices continue to exist even as LGBTQ people do mainstream things like get married and (especially for woman-woman couples) have children. In terms of physical locations, it is true that gayborhoods are changing, but at the same time, "The spatial expressions of sexuality are becoming more diverse and plural."[40] Queer pop-up events have emerged as permanent physical spaces have declined.[41] In terms of practices, gay men are vastly more likely than all other groups to be in open relationships.[42] As this book has shown, many gay and bisexual men are in a similar-age partnership (or are single) yet also form sexually exciting and often emotionally tender older-younger pairings between adults. In other words, yes, more LGBTQ people are getting married—but what is happening in their private lives cannot be neatly described as assimilation.

Gay and bisexual men continue to form unique relationships, even as they can get legally married and are accepted in institutions that once rejected them. Challenging norms about heterosexuality goes hand in hand with challenging other norms as well, such as monogamy and age similarity, particularly for men.

While some LGBTQ assimilation has occurred, particularly with regard to marriage, we cannot describe patterns in LGBTQ life as *either* assimilationist *or* nonassimilationist. Doing so ignores the unique practices of many LGBTQ people and the complexity of social life. Today, LGBTQ assimilation is only partial, and the stories of the men I talked to suggest that assimilation will remain partial for the foreseeable future. Distinct LGBTQ cultural life persists even as LGBTQ people are more integrated into mainstream institutions.

Practical Implications

This project's findings add context to health studies that show that gay and bisexual men's age-gap pairings are associated with a greater risk of HIV transmission and higher rates of condomless sex.[43] (Not all studies find these associations, however, and other factors are associated with HIV transmission and condomless sex—not just age-gap pairings.)[44] By virtue of having been sexually active for a longer period of time, older men have a greater likelihood of having contracted HIV, which means they could potentially transmit HIV to younger partners.[45] Thus, it makes sense that age-gap pairings may be associated with higher rates of HIV transmission.

The possibility of HIV transmission is much reduced today, however, as consistent treatment for HIV makes it impossible for people living with HIV to sexually transmit HIV.[46] Other medications, such as preexposure prophylaxis (PrEP), which people take to prevent themselves from contracting HIV if they are HIV negative, are 99 percent effective at preventing sexual transmission.[47] The combination of these two medications makes it such that sexual HIV transmission could be almost eliminated if these medications were available to all who need them (which, sadly, they are not).[48]

The current project builds on past public health research to show that age-gap pairings among adult gay and bisexual men are meaningful to the men who form them and should thus be acknowledged as an important source of emotional and social support for both older and younger men.[49] In other words, while it is important to study the possible sexual risks associated with age-gap pairings between adults, scholars should also consider how these pairings may improve mental health by fostering emotionally meaningful connections. Paying attention to these positive dynamics can help address what two scholars called a "joy deficit" in the social sciences.[50] While it is important to focus on inequality and other social problems, it is equally important to research what brings people pleasure, happiness, and fulfillment. Older-younger pairings between adults are an important aspect of cultural life for gay and bisexual men.

What Can Daddy-Younger Pairings Teach Us?

Although the subject of older-younger pairings between adults seems like a niche topic, these pairings help show us what a less ageist society can look like. All throughout history it was common and necessary for community members to be involved in one another's lives, regardless of age. Even throughout most of the history of the United States, age did not organize social life nearly as much as it does today.[51] Today many industrialized societies, including the United States,[52] are highly age segregated. People rarely have friendships with adults outside of their age cohort and even many residential areas are segregated by age.[53] Age segregation makes it difficult to understand people who came of age during different historical periods and reduces community cohesiveness. It is not normal, historically speaking, for adults to have friendships only with people their own age.

Daddy-younger pairings help to buck the trend of age segregation. These pairings lead to fulfilling relationships between adult men of different cohorts, help build a sense of community, and transmit knowledge intergenerationally. It is certainly not necessary for people to have sexual relationships with adults much younger or older than themselves, as the men I talked to did. Instead, daddies and the men who admire them show us that tender relationships between older and younger adults are not only possible but also fulfilling. Benefits such as intergenerational transmissions of knowledge can happen in platonic older-younger friendships, and it would strengthen communities if more people had platonic friendships with adults much older or younger than themselves.

What Does the Future Hold?

Demographic shifts may affect the prevalence of daddy identities and older-younger pairings between adults. Over the past several decades fertility rates in North America, Europe, and eastern Asia have plummeted, and many countries in other regions such as Latin America and South Asia similarly have fertility rates at or below the rate necessary for a population to grow.[54] Put simply, many regions around the world are "graying." As these populations age and younger people have fewer dating options around their own age, older-younger pairings between adults may become more common. It is difficult to know for sure, however, and so far there is little evidence that such a shift is occurring.[55]

On the other hand, the growing percentage of people who identify as LGBTQ may seem to suggest that older-younger pairings between adults will become more common. After all, woman-woman and, especially, man-man partnerships have higher rates of age gaps than woman-man partnerships. In a recent poll, Gallup found that 7.1 percent of Americans identify as LGBTQ.[56] There are huge variations by age cohort, gender, and specific sexual identity. About 20.8 percent of Generation Z (born 1997–2003) identify as LGBTQ, compared to 10.5 percent of Millennials (born 1981–1996), 4.2 percent of Generation X (born 1965–1980), 2.6 percent of Baby Boomers (born 1946–1964), and 0.8 percent of Traditionalists (born before 1946).[57] Clearly, LGBTQ identification has exploded among young Americans, similarly to other Western countries.

A closer look at these patterns reveals that growing LGBTQ identification will likely have minor effects on the commonality of age-gap pairings. Most of the increase in LGBTQ identification is among women, rather than men.[58] Among American high schoolers, 17.8 percent of girls identified as lesbian, gay, or bisexual in 2019, compared to 5.7 percent of boys.[59] The difference between how girls and boys identify will almost certainly persist into adulthood, given that there are similar gender differences among adults today.[60] Woman-woman partnerships have higher rates of age gaps compared to woman-man couples, but much lower rates compared to man-man couples.

Additionally, most of the increase in LGBTQ identification is attributable to women who identify as bisexual, specifically.[61] Most bisexual people who are coupled are in a woman-man partnership,[62] and woman-man partnerships are the least likely to have large age gaps. Bisexual people are more likely than heterosexuals and lesbian women to be in an open relationship—and people in open relationships could hypothetically have sexual encounters with adults much older or younger than themselves, as the men I talked to did—but bisexual people's likelihood of being in an open relationship is much lower than gay men's.[63] Thus, while age-gap pairings between adults will likely increase due to growing numbers of people who identify as LGBTQ, the increase will probably be small.

Other changes related to dating-app use, however, may increase the commonality of age-gap pairings—at least among gay and bisexual men. One survey study of very young gay and bisexual men found that of sexual partners met offline, 22.5 percent were two or more years older, compared to 66.8 percent of partners met online (more detailed age differences were not presented).[64] In that study, 17 percent of men met partners offline only, 53.3 percent met them online only, and 29.7 percent met partners both online and offline. Relatedly, about 65 percent of American same-sex couples who met in 2017 (the most recent data available) met online.[65] Overall, 55 percent of lesbian, gay, and bisexual Americans of any age, gender, or relationship status have used dating apps (figures specifically for men are not available).[66] Most American gay and bisexual men use apps at some point in their lives. Given that apps allow adult gay and bisexual men of different ages to meet one another, high rates of app use will likely continue to bring together younger and older men. Daddies, I suspect, will serve important roles for quite some time.

ACKNOWLEDGMENTS

This book was made possible thanks to the support of my colleagues and loved ones. Thank you to Héctor Carrillo for helping me begin this project and to Gregory Ward for discussions that deepened analysis. I also wish to thank the Sexualities Project at Northwestern (SPAN) for funding the postdoctoral fellowship that allowed me to conduct this project, and the Graduate School at Northwestern University for awarding me a Graduate Research Grant that partially funded research expenses. Thank you to David John Frank, Amin Ghaziani, Tom Kemple, and Ash Woody for helpful feedback on drafts, as well as to the participants at UBC's Sociology Research Forum who provided thought-provoking suggestions. I also wish to thank my editor, Ilene Kalish, who supported this project at all stages of the process, as well as to other folks at NYU Press whose hard work made this book a reality. Of course, I am also deeply grateful to the men I interviewed, who trusted me with intimate details about their lives. Many thanks also to my loved ones, in no particular order: Mom and Dad, Kari, Shon, Tanya, Ash, and Janeth.

APPENDIX

TABLE A.1. Characteristics of Older Men

Pseudonym	Age[a]	Partnership status	Approximate age of romantic partner(s)
Brett	43	Single	
Diego	43	Cohabiting with a man	Early thirties
Santiago	43	Single	
Tomas	44	Married to a man	Midtwenties
Edgar	46	Single	
Jorge	47	Single	
Ryan	48	Single	
Charlie	49	Single	
Hunter	49	Single	
Greg	50	Married to a man	Early fifties
Graham	51	Married to a man	Early fifties
Neil	51	Cohabiting with a man	Late twenties
Jake	52	Married to a man	Mid fifties
Luis	54	Married to a man	Late fifties
Scott	54	Noncohabiting partnership with a man	Early thirties
Mateo	55	Single	
Matthew	55	Single	
Brendan	56	Single	
Caleb	57	Cohabiting with a man	Mid forties
Jordy	57	Noncohabiting partnership with a man	Late twenties
Todd	57	Single	
Jay	58	Noncohabiting partnership with a man	Mid sixties
Cody	59	Cohabiting polyamorous partnership with two men, one of whom is Cody's husband	Husband is mid fifties and his other partner is in his early thirties
Connor	59	Noncohabiting, nonsexual, nonmarital partnership with a woman[b]	Mid forties

a. To preserve confidentiality, I slightly changed the ages of Greg and Graham, since they were the only two men who were married and both participated in the study.

b. Connor was in a nonmarital, noncohabiting, and nonsexual relationship with a woman over ten years his junior, which he described as "a coparenting relationship, as close as possible to traditional marriage without cohabitation."

TABLE A.1. (*cont.*)

Pseudonym	Age[a]	Partnership status	Approximate age of romantic partner(s)
Spencer	59	Single	
Zachary	59	Married to a man	Early sixties
Aram	60	Married to a woman	Mid sixties
Ethan	60	Married to a woman	Approximately the same age as Ethan[c]
Logan	60	Married to a man	Early sixties
Steven	60	Single	
Brian	61	Single	
Enrique	62	Married to a man	Husband is about twenty years older than Enrique
Brad	64	Single	
Finn	64	Married to a woman	Early sixties
Seth	65	Single	
Wyatt	66	Married to a man	Mid forties
Luke	68	Noncohabiting partnership with a man	Early twenties
Robert	69	Married to a woman	Late sixties
Dustin	70	Single	

a. To preserve confidentiality, I slightly changed the ages of Greg and Graham, since they were the only two men who were married and both participated in the study.

c. Ethan did not specify his wife's age, but everything he stated in the interview about his marriage and history of raising children suggests that the two are around the same age.

TABLE A.2. Characteristics of Younger Men

Pseudonym	Age	Partnership status	Approximate age of romantic partner(s)
Jamal	23	Noncohabiting polyamorous partnership; Jamal is in a relationship with a man who has two other partners, but Jamal is not in a relationship with those two men	Early thirties
Jeffrey	23	Single	
Joshua	23	Noncohabiting partnership with a man	Mid thirties
Amir	24	Noncohabiting polyamorous partnership; Amir's two partners are in a relationship with one another	Both partners are around the age of sixty
Terry	24	Single	
Andrew	25	Single	
Anthony	25	Single	
Cyrus	25	Single	
Juan	25	Noncohabiting partnership with a man	Early forties
Kyle	25	Cohabiting polyamorous partnership. Kyle's two partners are married to one another	Both partners are around the age of forty
Alejandro	26	Single	
Benjamin	26	Single	
Justin	26	Single	
Austin	27	Single	
DaShawn	27	Noncohabiting partnership with a man	Late fifties
David	27	Noncohabiting partnership with a man	Early thirties
Jacob	27	Single	
Aydin	28	Single	
James	28	Cohabiting with a man	Mid twenties
William	29	Single	
Michael	30	Single	
Nicholas	30	Single	
John	31	Single	
Tyrone	32	Noncohabiting polyamorous partnership; Tyrone's two partners are not in a relationship with one another	One man is in his early fifties and the other man is in his early sixties
Chris	33	Married to a man	Early thirties
Tyler	33	Cohabiting with a man	Mid twenties

NOTES

INTRODUCTION

1 Dewey 2016; Levinson 2016.
2 There is even academic DILF research: Oswald et al. 2022.
3 Description is from the Google Play Store, accessed on November 4, 2022.
4 See also Ellis 2021.
5 Farhi 2005; Lighter 1994.
6 Farhi 2005; Lighter 1994.
7 Kirkland 2018; Albo 2013.
8 Hale 1997; Bauer 2018. See Minkowitz 1994 for an early discussion of daddy identities among lesbians.
9 Andersson et al. 2006; Boyd and Li 2003; Ciscato, Galichon, and Goussé 2020; Lengerer and Schroedter 2022; Schwartz and Graf 2009; Verbakel and Kalmijn 2014.
10 See for instance Randall 2019.
11 Individuals in the Western world today tend to have similar partners in terms of race, education, and age regardless of the gender composition of the couple (Jepsen and Jepsen 2002)—i.e., *patterns* of homogamy are similar—but the *prevalence* of heterogamy of same-sex couples on these dimensions is much higher compared to different-sex couples. Put differently, at the population level, patterns of homogamy among same-sex couples (particularly man-man couples) are significantly weaker than patterns of homogamy among different-sex couples. This discussion relates to the scholarly term "assortative mating." "Assortative mating" refers to "the non-random matching of individuals into relationships" (Schwartz 2013:452); see also Luo 2017. To make this book more readable, I avoid this term but use the concept. See also Levine 1998 and Orne 2017 for their ethnographic observations of gay and bisexual men's sexual pairings that cross race and socioeconomic class lines. Barrett 2017 argues that "crossing lines of social difference in sexual interactions is often highly valued within gay sexual markets" (222), even as inequalities remain.
12 Scholars use different terms to refer to partnerships with large age gaps, including "age-heterogamous," "age-discordant," "age-dissimilar," and "age-heterogenous." This manuscript uses the term "age-gap partnership" or "age-gap pairing" to enhance readability.
13 Arrington-Sanders et al. 2013 provide an exception, although they interviewed seventeen very young men who were mostly involved with other men

in their mid- to late twenties. Franklin, Bourne, and Lyons 2022 interviewed fifteen men about gay subcultural identities (e.g., geek, queer, bear, otter, twink), and of them, four identified as a daddy. While the article briefly discussed daddy identities, they were not the main focus of the study. See also Olson's 2020 *Psychology Today* blog post about gay and bisexual men's age-gap pairings.

14 Ausubel 2020.

15 Ausubel 2020. In many developing nations, the more education a woman receives, the smaller the age gap between herself and her husband (Carmichael 2011).

16 Choi and Vasunilashorn 2014; Lamidi, Brown, and Manning 2015.

17 Esteve, Cortina, and Cabré 2009; Kolk 2015; Lawton and Callister 2010; Mansour and McKinnish 2013; Poppel et al. 2001.

18 Syrett 2021.

19 Syrett 2021.

20 England and McClintock 2009; Hu and Qian 2019.

21 See also Qian and Qian 2014, Mu and Xie 2014, and Qian, Shen, and Cai 2022 for a discussion of how age-related partnering is shaped by gender inequality in China.

22 England and McClintock 2009. See also Šetinová and Topinková 2021 for an analysis of how age affects dating behaviors in gendered ways.

23 Balistreri, Joyner, and Kao 2017; Elwert 2020; Feighan 2018; Guetto and Azzolini 2015; Gustafson and Fransson 2015; Levchenko and Solheim 2013; Niedomysl, Östh, and van Ham 2010; Tsai 2011. Partner age gaps are much smaller among children of immigrants (Uggla and Wilson 2021). Although partner age differences of six to nine years are associated with increased marital conflict in cross-border man-older marriages, financial stress rather than age heterogamy is more strongly related to marital conflict (Choi and Cheung 2017).

24 Dribe and Nystedt 2017; Feighan 2018; Gustafson and Fransson 2015; Mansour and McKinnish 2013. For an exception, see Coles and Francesconi (2011) for how women with higher education or incomes may partner with younger men, and how systemic gender inequality, which disadvantages women, may affect the formation of these types of romantic partnerships.

25 Dribe and Nystedt 2017; Mansour and McKinnish 2013; Oksuzyan et al. 2017. Relatedly, age gaps between partners are not substantially associated with a woman's earnings (Carollo et al. 2019). In contrast, there is evidence that partner age differences modestly shape eventual retirement ages for each partner (Kridahl and Kolk 2018; Gustafson 2017).

26 Mansour and McKinnish 2013.

27 Choi and Vasunilashorn 2014; Drefahl 2010; Kim, Park, and Lee 2015.

28 Mansour and McKinnish 2013.

29 Lee and McKinnish 2018; Silva 2019; Zhang, Ho, and Yip 2012.

30 Skentelbery and Fowler 2016.

31 Lehmiller and Agnew 2008; Silva 2019. Relatedly, in rural Tanzania, spousal age gap is not associated with fertility, divorce rates, women's mental health, or autonomy in household decisions (Lawson et al. 2021).

32 Perceived level of friend and family disapproval of a relationship is associated with relationship dissolution (Lehmiller and Agnew 2007).

33 Silva 2019.

34 Alarie and Carmichael 2015.

35 Alarie and Carmichael 2015.

36 Gunnarsson and Strid 2021, 2022; Scull 2020, 2022. See also Nayar 2017 and Upadhyay 2021 for content analyses of sugar arrangements and Kirkeby, Lehmiller, and Marks 2022 for a quantitative exploration of the relationship between sugar dating and STI diagnoses, STI testing, and condom use. Lastly, for a discussion of sugar pairings in Africa, see Kadandara 2018 and Kuate-Defo 2004.

37 McKenzie 2015.

38 McKenzie 2015.

39 Jurva 2018.

40 Alarie 2019, 2020.

41 Alarie 2019, 2020. See also Warren 1996.

42 Villar et al. 2019.

43 Banister 2018.

44 Banister 2018.

45 Banister 2018. The full quotation reads,

> For the younger members in the couple, some of the benefits that they reported were being able to ask their partner for advice, having a mentor, feeling protected, having someone take care of them, having access to money, being able to travel, being able to participate in experiences that would not be possible in a similar age relationship, learning how to plan for retirement and manage finances. Older members in the relationship reported being able to live vicariously through their partners, a renewed sense of life, having more energy, keeps them younger, learning about new technology, and having someone who is able to look after their well-being. (131)

46 Andersson et al. 2006; Boyd and Li 2003; Ciscato, Galichon, and Goussé 2020; Lengerer and Schroedter 2022; Schwartz and Graf 2009; Verbakel and Kalmijn 2014.

47 Verbakel and Kalmijn 2014.

48 Ciscato, Galichon, and Goussé 2020.

49 Choi and Tienda 2017; Joyner, Balistreri, and Kao 2018; Schwartz and Graf 2010. Relatedly, age gaps are higher in interracial man-man partnerships (white men partnered to Black, Latino, or Asian men) compared to interracial woman-woman pairings (Joyner, Balistreri, and Kao 2018). This finding suggests that age heterogamy in man-man romantic partnerships is often tied to other forms of differences between partners.

50 Rosenfeld and Kim 2005.

51 Franklin, Bourne, and Lyons 2022; Lyons and Hosking 2014; Prestage et al. 2015; Schnarrs et al. 2021; Silva 2022a.

52 Berlinger 2006; Childs 2016; Hennen 2008; Mosher, Levitt, and Manley 2006; Moskowitz et al. 2011; Rubin 2000; Van Doorn 2016.

53 Hennen 2005; Moskowitz et al. 2013; Quidley-Rodriguez and De Santis 2019; Wright 1997, 2001.

54 Barrett 2017; Ghaziani and Cook 2005; Stillwagon and Ghaziani 2019.

55 Lawson and Langdridge 2020; Langdridge and Lawson 2019; Montgomery 2019; Wignall and McCormack 2017.

56 Mercer 2012.

57 Barrett 2017 (91) analyzed bear terminology identified by Donahue and Stoner 2013.

58 Adam 2000.

59 Adam 2000:432.

60 Albo 2013.

61 Mosher, Levitt, and Manley 2006:105.

62 Mosher, Levitt, and Manley 2006:120.

63 See also *Drummer* magazine, which in the 1970s and 1980s disseminated information and images about gay leather subcultures—and featured many men in midlife.

64 Hale 1997:224.

65 Bauer 2018.

66 Ghaziani 2009, 2014b.

67 "Daddyness" is a term one participant (Luis) used, and I adopt it because it is more succinct than the term "being a daddy."

68 DaddyHunt, Twitter, accessed October 13, 2022. https://twitter.com/Daddyhunt.

69 *DaddyHunt: The Serial*, Vimeo, accessed October 13, 2022. https://vimeo.com.

70 The DILF Party, accessed October 13, 2022. www.thedilfparty.com.

71 The app SCRUFF is spelled with all capital letters.

72 This figure is according to SCRUFF's website (accessed October 13, 2022): www.scruff.com.

73 SCRUFF has more users than DaddyHunt, which caters to men interested in much older or younger adult men. The DaddyHunt Twitter account reports over five million users. There are other apps that cater to older men, but they report fewer users than SCRUFF. SCRUFF is also larger than GROWLr, which reports over ten million users and shares overlap with SCRUFF, but also caters specifically to the bear community. The application Grindr likely has more users than SCRUFF, and it does have a "daddy" option users can endorse, but Grindr does not target specific types of men and has a large share of young men who are not necessarily interested in older men. Several of the men I talked to were currently, or had been, active on Grindr, and there were no notable differences between them and the men who had never or rarely used Grindr. Thus, it is unlikely that recruiting men from Grindr would yield substantively different results. There are

a variety of other applications that cater to gay and bisexual men, but none that focus primarily on older men that have the number of users SCRUFF does. (All user estimates, as provided by the app companies on their Twitter accounts or websites, were gathered in November 2022.)

74 The Leather Archives & Museum (LA&M).

75 See also Orne 2017.

76 See also Ghaziani 2014a.

77 Stewart-Winter 2016; see also Brodyn and Ghaziani 2018.

78 This coding process is similar to how Deterding and Waters 2021 suggest coding.

79 Attride-Stirling 2001; Ryan and Bernard 2003.

80 Connor explained, "I've chosen gay and bisexual. I'm clearly not straight. I don't pick that one. Unless I'm somehow forced into that box for the survey's purposes. But I'm clearly gay or bisexual." Greg reported, "Somewhere between gay and bi."

81 Transgender men aged thirty-five or older were welcome to participate but none responded to the research advertisement.

82 See Donovan 2020 for analysis of how the term "gold digger" came into existence and gained its current meaning.

83 Carrington 1999; Cohen 2020; Hammack, Frost, and Hughes 2019; Weston 1991.

84 Nardi 1999; Stacey 2004.

85 Kemple 2022.

86 Levine et al. 2018.

CHAPTER 1. BECOMING A DADDY

1 Levinson 2016.

2 Macapagal et al. 2021.

3 See Sueyoshi 2018 for historical evidence and Schwartz and Graf 2009 for US Census data for the years 1990 and 2000.

4 Mosher, Levitt, and Manley 2006.

5 Levine, Nardi, and Gagnon 1997; Rosenfeld, Bartlam, and Smith 2012.

6 See also Green 2014.

CHAPTER 2. WHAT IT MEANS TO BE A DADDY

1 Mosher, Levitt, and Manley 2006.

2 Arnett 2014.

3 Many men take medications that either prevent HIV infection (PrEP) or prevent HIV from being sexually transmitted if they are HIV positive (treatment as prevention: TasP). Thus, condomless sex is not as dangerous as it first sounds due to pharmaceutical technologies that can prevent HIV transmission.

4 Andrew (25) mentioned that he would prefer older men to be versatile, but that in his experience most are tops. Interestingly, Jamal (23) is the opposite. He usually bottoms regardless of the age of his partner, but mentioned, "It's definitely a thing that I experience where I feel like as a person who identifies primarily as a bottom, I don't find the idea of topping guys who are closer to

my age to be as appealing because I feel like it's not as fun. It doesn't feel as psychologically comfortable. But if I have an older man who wants to be the bottom I can conceptualize that more because I can experience that power dynamic at the same time through my sexual experience where it doesn't feel as stressful for my psychology."

5 "Generous" propositions were more common on Grindr than SCRUFF, according to the men I interviewed, but in neither case were they interested.

6 See also Adams 2012; Maimann 2015; Nayar 2017; Upadhyay 2021.

7 James et al. 2021.

8 Lever, Frederick, and Hertz 2015; Safdar 2017.

9 Schnarrs et al. 2021.

10 Chong and Kim 2021; Han, Proctor, and Choi 2014; Kao, Balistreri, and Joyner 2018; Morgan 2021.

11 Collins 2004; Demby 2018; Oeur 2016.

12 Petsko and Rosette 2022; Sy et al. 2010.

13 Miller 2022:5.

14 Noël 2018.

15 Noël 2018.

16 Kao, Balistreri, and Joyner 2018.

17 Lawson and Langdridge 2020; Langdridge and Lawson 2019; Montgomery 2019; Wignall and McCormack 2017.

CHAPTER 3. CONNECTIONS BETWEEN OLDER AND YOUNGER ADULT MEN

1 Relatedly, James et al. 2021 conducted a survey study and found that gay and bisexual men were likely to provide emotional support to younger men, and much more likely to offer emotional support than financial support.

2 Jones et al. 2022.

3 Moore et al. 2021.

4 Homelessness Policy Research Institute 2019; Robinson 2020.

5 Rosenfeld, Bartlam, and Smith 2012.

CHAPTER 4. DADDY DESIRABILITY

1 One of the few studies that has examined why younger men partner with older men found that emotional maturity, experience (sexual and nonsexual), and emotional support were key reasons behind this choice (Arrington-Sanders et al. 2013). Importantly, that study focused on adolescents or very young adults, most of whom were partnered to men in their mid- to late twenties, meaning its sample is very different from this book's sample.

2 In a review article about age-related preferences among men, Seto 2017 writes, "I am not aware of any empirical research on individuals attracted to middle-aged persons" (15).

3 Adam 2006.

4 See also Jones 2019.

5 Johansson and Andreasson 2017; Parreñas 2008.

CHAPTER 5. DADDYNESS AND MASCULINITY

1 Jackson 2016; Levant et al. 2020; Springer and Mouzon 2019; Thompson 2018; Tannenbaum and Frank 2011.

2 Pascoe and Bridges 2015:4.

3 The following research examines masculinity in adolescence: Duckworth and Trautner 2019; Oeur 2016; Pascoe 2011; Rios and Sarabia 2015; Unnever and Choudy 2021. Other research analyzes masculinity in young adulthood: Diefendorf 2015; Munsch and Gruys 2018; Gruys and Munsch 2020; Orenstein 2020. There is less research about masculinity in midlife, just as there is little research about midlife more broadly (Lee 2022).

4 Allen 2016; Andreasson and Johansson 2016; Brandth 2016, 2019; Johansson and Klinth 2008; Kim and Pyke 2015; Petts, Shafer, and Essig 2018; Pini and Conway 2017; Pribilsky 2012; Shafer, Petts, and Scheibling 2021.

5 Keenen et al. 2015.

6 Pietilä and Ojala 2011.

7 Hurd Clarke and Lefkowich 2018; Loe 2001; Marshall 2006; Wentzell 2013, 2017; see also Cornwell and Laumann 2011. See also Sandberg 2013, 2016 for how heterosexual men aged sixty-seven to eighty-seven experience and understand sexual desire and intimacy.

8 Thompson and Langendoerfer 2016:136. See also Tannenbaum and Frank 2011. Researchers define various points for the transition from midlife to older adulthood, but they typically define older adulthood as beginning somewhere between one's late fifties (at the earliest) and age sixty-five. For instance, one of the largest nationally representative surveys of older adults, the longitudinal National Social Life, Health, and Aging Project (Suzman 2009), includes individuals as young as fifty-seven, whereas many US government entities use age sixty-five.

9 Foweraker and Cutcher 2015; Hasmanová Marhánková 2020.

10 Hurd Clarke and Lefkowich 2018; Hurd and Mahal 2021.

11 Hurd and Mahal 2021.

12 King et al. 2021.

13 Thompson 2018.

14 Winer 2022.

15 Lyons et al. 2015.

16 Lodge and Umberson 2013. See Montemurro 2021 for an extended analysis of how sexuality changes over heterosexual men's life course.

17 Lodge and Umberson 2013; Lyons et al. 2015. See Montemurro 2021 for exceptions.

18 Slevin and Linneman 2010; Lyons et al. 2015. One study found that Black gay men reported more ageism than white men (David and Knight 2008).

19 Hajek 2014. See also Simpson 2016.

20 Erol and Ozbay 2018; Hajek 2014.

21 Erol and Ozbay 2018.

22 Silva 2022a. See also Savin-Williams 2021 for an exploration of how many young people experience their sexuality and gender in diverse, flexible ways.

23 Enrique continued and said, "But I don't have a choice." Enrique had previously been interested in older men before he himself aged into daddyness. He enjoyed being perceived as a daddy in some ways, but he also recognized that younger men imposed this "role" onto him now that he was sixty-two—and that he could not change younger men's perception of him as a daddy even if he wanted to. Overall, he had mixed feelings about being perceived as a daddy.

24 Jake identifies as a dad rather than as a daddy. As he explained, "The term 'daddy' is a little light for what they're actually playing with," and noted that "dad" dynamics involve more intense role playing and power dynamics.

25 See also Silva 2021, 2022b.

26 Abelson 2019; Arxer 2011; Bridges 2014; Bridges and Pascoe 2014; Elliott 2019; Eisen and Yamashita 2019; Gruys and Munsch 2020.

27 Connell 2005; Dean 2014; Mishel, Bridges, and Caudillo 2022; Pascoe 2011; Silva 2021.

28 Orenstein 2020.

29 Baker et al. 2014.

30 See also Yang's (2020) theoretical reformulation of hegemonic masculinity, which argues that scholars should be attentive to how certain configurations of hegemonic masculinity have the potential to be progressive and to challenge social inequalities such as sexism and homophobia.

CHAPTER 6. LOVE BETWEEN OLDER AND YOUNGER ADULT MEN

1 See Meyer et al. 2020 for details about a national probability study of three cohorts of lesbian, gay, bisexual, and queer Americans. (There is a separate but parallel national probability study that surveyed transgender Americans, specifically.) Publications that analyze this data set have explored cohort differences in numerous outcomes.

2 Cohen 2020. See also Rotundo 1989; Smith-Rosenberg 1975.

3 Cody was in a polyamorous relationship with his husband in his midfifties and another man in his early thirties, all of whom lived together. Their relationship was not sexually open, but they had considered the hypothetical possibility of another younger man joining the relationship. Fifty-four-year-old Scott was in a noncohabiting relationship with his partner in his early thirties. While they were sexually closed, Scott also reported sex with a FWB within the previous year that he did not disclose to his partner.

4 Sixty-two-year-old Enrique was married to his husband, who was about twenty years older than himself.

5 Jamal (23) was in a partnership with a man who had two other partners, Amir (24) was in a partnership with two men who were partnered to one another, Kyle

(25) was in a partnership with two men married to one another, and Tyrone (32) was dating two men who were not partnered to one another. See table A.2 for more information.

6 Juan (25) and DaShawn (27) were in monogamous partnerships whereas Kyle (25) was in a closed polyamorous partnership.

7 Auxier and Anderson 2021.

8 Perry et al. 2016. These researchers did, however, find an interaction between age and relationship length: younger men reported *less* decision-making power than older men in shorter relationships but *more* power in longer relationships. These effects were fairly small, however.

9 Carrington 1999; Weston 1991.

10 Nardi 1999.

11 SCRUFF has a "Woof" feature that allows users to alert another user that they are interested in him.

12 Ausubel 2020.

13 See also Swidler 2001.

CONCLUSION

1 Carrington 1999; Weston 1991. See also Dewaele et al. 2011.

2 Powell et al. 2010.

3 Carrington 1999; Weston 1991.

4 Nardi 1999.

5 Nardi 1999.

6 Nardi 1999.

7 See also Hammack, Frost, and Hughes 2019.

8 Andersson et al. 2006; Ciscato, Galichon, and Goussé 2020; Lengerer and Schroedter 2022; Schwartz and Graf 2009.

9 Communities of people who would later be understood as "gay" or "bisexual" first emerged among men in large part because men had more opportunities to create these communities. In the nineteenth and early twentieth centuries, men were paid more than women and more often worked outside the home. Their greater economic freedom and self-sufficiency allowed them to organize lives around same-sex partners (or singledom in gay communities) much earlier than women. It was also more acceptable for men to live independent lives; women, in contrast, were expected to organize their lives around being a wife and mother. See for instance Chauncey 1994; Duder 2011; and Faderman 1991.

10 Mattson 2019.

11 Mattson 2019.

12 Compton 2020; Marloff 2021. See also the Lesbian Bar Project, accessed October 14, 2022. www.lesbianbarproject.com.

13 Mattson 2019.

14 See Shahzad 2016 for a story about a police raid on a bathhouse event specifically for LGBTQ women in Toronto in 2000.

15 Chauncey 1994:27.

16 Clements 2018.

17 Men's cruising has declined in many areas in recent years (Goodman 2019), although it does still occur in many locations in cities across the world.

18 One of the largest existing apps for LGBTQ women and nonbinary people, Her, launched several years after major apps for gay and bisexual men were developed (Lomas 2013).

19 England and McClintock 2009; Miller, Garcia, and Gesselman 2021.

20 See also Alarie 2019, 2020.

21 MILF stands for "mother I'd like to fuck."

22 Levine et al. 2018. Relatedly, 23 percent of bisexual men and 22 percent of bisexual women are in open relationships—still lower than gay men's 33 percent open-relationship figure.

23 Hennen 2008; Simula 2019.

24 Chauncey 1994; Faderman 1991.

25 Chauncey 1994; see also Ghaziani 2014a, 2015; Spring and Charleston 2021.

26 This observation is based on analysis I am conducting with my colleague Christine Percheski of 2015–2019 American Community Survey (ACS) data.

27 Ciscato, Galichon, and Goussé 2020.

28 Manning and Payne 2021; Statistics Canada 2022.

29 Hennen 2008 calls this association the "effeminacy effect."

30 Yang 2020:329–30. Yang focused specifically on "hegemonic masculinity," which is an important theoretical concept but one that, to enhance readability, I do not discuss in depth.

31 Elliott 2016: 241. See also Elliott 2020.

32 Shafer, Petts, and Scheibling 2021.

33 Elliott 2020.

34 Kalmijn 2010:1252.

35 Gullickson and Fu 2010; Kalmijn 2010; Schwartz, Zeng, and Xie 2016; Torche and Rich 2017; Xie and Dong 2021; see also Gullickson 2017.

36 This observation is based on analysis I am conducting with my colleague Christine Percheski of 2015–2019 ACS (American Community Survey) data.

37 Adam 2006.

38 Mattson 2019.

39 Ghaziani 2014b.

40 Ghaziani 2019:5.

41 Stillwagon and Ghaziani 2019.

42 Levine et al. 2018.

43 Studies that examine HIV transmission and age-gap pairings include Coburn and Blower 2010; Ding et al. 2018; Hurt et al. 2010; and Joseph et al. 2011. Higher rates of HIV transmission between older and younger partners compared to age-similar partners may also help explain racial/ethnic differences in HIV prevalence among gay and bisexual men (Newcomb and Mustanski 2013; Mustanski

and Newcomb 2013). Studies that examine condomless sex and age-gap pairings include Choi et al. 2003; Janulis et al. 2018; Miller, Forney, and McNall 2014; Mustanski, Newcomb, and Clerkin 2011; Oidtman et al. 2017; and Zhang, Wu, and Scott 2019. Relatedly, emotional and physical satisfaction from one's first same-sex sexual experience may differ according to the age at which the experience occurred and the age of that person's sexual partner (Vasilenko, Exten, and Rosenberger 2021).

44 Anema et al. 2013.

45 Chamberlain et al. 2017.

46 "HIV Undetectable=Untransmissable (U=U), or Treatment as Prevention." National Institute of Allergy and Infectious Diseases, National Institutes of Health, May 21, 2019. www.niaid.nih.gov.

47 See this webpage from the US Centers for Disease Control and Transmission: "Pre-Exposure Prophylaxis (PrEP)," July 5, 2022. www.cdc.gov.

48 Hammack et al. 2018.

49 One survey found that older gay and bisexual men are likely to offer emotional support and encouragement to engage in health practices, like testing for STIs (James et al. 2021).

50 Shuster and Westbrook 2022.

51 Chudacoff 1989.

52 Freedman and Stamp 2018.

53 Winkler 2013.

54 "Fertility Rate, Total (Births per Woman)," World Bank, accessed October 14, 2022. https://data.worldbank.org.

55 The prevalence of age heterogamy has slightly increased among woman-man couples over the past several decades. In 2000 about 11.3 percent of married woman-man couples had an age difference of eight or more years (Mansour and McKinnish 2013) compared to 13.59 percent in the 2015–2019 period. This observation is based on analysis I am conducting with my colleague Christine Percheski of 2015–2019 ACS (American Community Survey) data.

56 Jones 2022.

57 Jones 2022.

58 England, Mishel, and Caudillo 2016; Rapoport, Athanasian, and Adesman 2021.

59 Rapoport, Athanasian, and Adesman 2021.

60 England, Mishel, and Caudillo 2016; Silva and Evans 2020.

61 England, Mishel, and Caudillo 2016; Jones 2022. The increase in bisexual identification on nationwide surveys over the past several years is partially attributable to the lack of a "mostly straight" option on most surveys. See Savin-Williams 2017 for an explanation. See also Savin-Williams and Vrangalova 2013, Savin-Williams 2022, and Wignall and Driscoll 2020 for research about "mostly straight" individuals. It is currently unknown how common it is for "mostly straight" individuals to be in open relationships or to form pairings with adults much older or younger than themselves.

62 Parker 2015.
63 Levine et al. 2018.
64 Macapagal et al. 2021.
65 Rosenfeld, Thomas, and Hausen 2019.
66 Vogels 2020.

BIBLIOGRAPHY

Abelson, Miriam. 2019. *Men in Place: Trans Masculinity, Race, and Sexuality in America*. Minneapolis: University of Minnesota Press.

Adam, Barry D. 2000. "Age Preferences among Gay and Bisexual Men." *GLQ: A Journal of Lesbian and Gay Studies* 6(3):413–33. https://doi.org/10.1215/10642684-6-3-413.

———. 2006. "Relationship Innovation in Male Couples." *Sexualities* 9(1):5–26. https://doi.org/10.1177/1363460706060685.

Adams, Guy. 2012. "The Rise and Rise of the American Sugar Daddy." *Independent*, February 19. www.independent.co.uk.

Alarie, Milaine. 2019. "'They're the Ones Chasing the Cougar': Relationship Formation in the Context of Age-Hypogamous Intimate Relationships." *Gender & Society* 33(3):463–85. https://doi.org/10.1177/0891243219839670.

———. 2020. "Sleeping with Younger Men: Women's Accounts of Sexual Interplay in Age-Hypogamous Intimate Relationships." *Journal of Sex Research* 57(3):322–34. https://doi.org/10.1080/00224499.2019.1574704.

Alarie, Milaine, and Jason T. Carmichael. 2015. "The 'Cougar' Phenomenon: An Examination of the Factors That Influence Age-Hypogamous Sexual Relationships among Middle-Aged Women." *Journal of Marriage and Family* 77(5):1250–65. https://doi.org/10.1111/jomf.12213.

Albo, Mike. 2013. "Rise of the 'Daddies': A New (and Sexy) Gay Niche." *New York Magazine*, June 14. https://www.thecut.com.

Allen, Quaylan. 2016. "'Tell Your Own Story': Manhood, Masculinity, and Racial Socialization among Black Fathers and Their Sons." *Ethnic and Racial Studies* 39(10):1831–48. https://doi.org/10.1080/01419870.2015.1110608.

Andersson, Gunnar, Turid Noack, Ane Seierstad, and Harald Weedon-Fekjær. 2006. "The Demographics of Same-Sex Marriages in Norway and Sweden." *Demography* 43(1):79–98. https://doi.org/10.1353/dem.2006.0001.

Andreasson, Jesper, and Thomas Johansson. 2016. "Global Narratives of Fatherhood: Fathering and Masculinity on the Internet." *International Review of Sociology* 26(3):482–96. https://doi.org/10.1080/03906701.2016.1191245.

Anema, Aranka, Brandon D. L. Marshall, Benjamin Stevenson, Jasmine Gurm, Gabriela Montaner, Will Small, Eric A. Roth, Viviane D. Lima, Julio S. G. Montaner, David Moore, and Robert S. Hogg. 2013. "Intergenerational Sex as a Risk Factor for HIV among Young Men Who Have Sex with Men: A Scoping Review." *Current HIV/AIDS Reports* 10(4):398–407. https://doi.org/10.1007/s11904-013-0187-3.

Arnett, Jeffrey Jensen. 2014. *Emerging Adulthood: The Winding Road from the Late Teens through the Twenties*. Second edition. New York: Oxford University Press.

Arrington-Sanders, Renata, Lori Leonard, Durryle Brooks, David Celentano, and Jonathan Ellen. 2013. "Older Partner Selection in Young African-American Men Who Have Sex with Men." *Journal of Adolescent Health* 52(6):682–88. https://doi.org/10.1016/j.jadohealth.2012.12.011.

Arxer, Steven L. 2011. "Hybrid Masculine Power: Reconceptualizing the Relationship between Homosociality and Hegemonic Masculinity." *Humanity & Society* 35(4):390–422. https://doi.org/10.1177/016059761103500404.

Attride-Stirling, Jennifer. 2001. "Thematic Networks: An Analytic Tool for Qualitative Research." *Qualitative Research* 1(3):385–405. https://doi.org/10.1177/146879410100100307.

Ausubel, Jacob. 2020. *Globally, Women Are Younger Than Their Male Partners, More Likely to Age Alone*. Washington, DC: Pew Research Center. www.pewresearch.org.

Auxier, Brooke, and Monica Anderson. 2021. *Social Media Use in 2021*. Washington, DC: Pew Research Center. www.pewresearch.org.

Baker, Peter, Shari L. Dworkin, Sengfah Tong, Ian Banks, Tim Shand, and Gavin Yamey. 2014. "The Men's Health Gap: Men Must Be Included in the Global Health Equity Agenda." *Bulletin of the World Health Organization* 92(8): 618–20. https://doi.org/10.2471/BLT.13.132795.

Balistreri, Kelly Stamper, Kara Joyner, and Grace Kao. 2017. "Trading Youth for Citizenship? The Spousal Age Gap in Cross-Border Marriages." *Population and Development Review* 43(3):443–66. https://doi.org/10.1111/padr.12072.

Banister, Leon, Jr. 2018. "May–December: Navigating Life as an Intergenerational Gay Couple." Dissertation, Barry University, Miami Shores, FL.

Barrett, Rusty. 2017. *From Drag Queens to Leathermen: Language, Gender, and Gay Male Subcultures*. New York: Oxford University Press.

Bauer, Robin. 2018. "Bois and Grrrls Meet Their Daddies and Mommies on Gender Playgrounds: Gendered Age Play in the Les-Bi-Trans-Queer BDSM Communities." *Sexualities* 21(1–2):139–55. https://doi.org/10.1177/1363460716676987.

Berlinger, Cain. 2006. *Black Men in Leather*. Tempe, AZ: Third Millennium Publications.

Boyd, Monica, and Anne Li. 2003. "May–December: Canadians in Age-Discrepant Relationships." *Canadian Social Trends* (70):29–33. www150.statcan.gc.ca.

Brandth, Berit. 2016. "Rural Masculinities and Fathering Practices." *Gender, Place & Culture* 23(3):435–50. https://doi.org/10.1080/0966369X.2015.1013454.

———. 2019. "'Tough and Tender'? Agricultural Masculinities and Fathering Activities." *NORMA: International Journal for Masculinity Studies* 14(4):223–38. https://doi.org/10.1080/18902138.2019.1654725.

Bridges, Tristan. 2014. "A Very 'Gay' Straight? Hybrid Masculinities, Sexual Aesthetics, and the Changing Relationship between Masculinity and Homophobia." *Gender & Society* 28(1):58–82. https://doi.org/10.1177/0891243213503901.

Bridges, Tristan, and C. J. Pascoe. 2014. "Hybrid Masculinities: New Directions in the Sociology of Men and Masculinities." *Sociology Compass* 8(3):246–58. https://doi.org/10.1111/soc4.12134.

Brodyn, Adriana, and Amin Ghaziani. 2018. "Performative Progressiveness: Accounting for New Forms of Inequality in the Gayborhood." *City & Community* 17(2):307–29. https://doi.org/10.1111/cico.12298.

Carmichael, Sarah. 2011. "Marriage and Power: Age at First Marriage and Spousal Age Gap in Lesser Developed Countries." *History of the Family* 16(4):416–36. https://doi.org/10.1016/j.hisfam.2011.08.002.

Carollo, Angela, Anna Oksuzyan, Sven Drefahl, Carlo Giovanni Camarda, Linda Juel Ahrenfeldt, Kaare Christensen, and Alyson van Raalte. 2019. "Is the Age Difference between Partners Related to Women's Earnings?" *Demographic Research* 41(15):425–60. https://doi.org/10.4054/DemRes.2019.41.15.

Carrington, Christopher. 1999. *No Place like Home: Relationships and Family Life among Lesbians and Gay Men*. Chicago: University of Chicago Press.

Chamberlain, Nicholas, Leandro A. Mena, Angelica Geter, and Richard A. Crosby. 2017. "Is Sex with Older Male Partners Associated with Higher Sexual Risk Behavior among Young Black MSM?" *AIDS and Behavior* 21(8):2526–32. https://doi.org/10.1007/s10461-017-1699-4.

Chauncey, George. 1994. *Gay New York: Gender, Urban Culture, and the Making of the Gay Male World, 1890–1940*. New York: Basic Books.

Childs, Andrew. 2016. "Hyper- or Hypo-Masculine? Re-Conceptualizing 'Hyper-Masculinity' through Seattle's Gay, Leather Community." *Gender, Place & Culture* 23(9):1315–28. https://doi.org/10.1080/0966369X.2016.1160033.

Choi, Kate H., and Marta Tienda. 2017. "Marriage-Market Constraints and Mate-Selection Behavior: Racial, Ethnic, and Gender Differences in Intermarriage." *Journal of Marriage and Family* 79(2):301–17. https://doi.org/10.1111/jomf.12346.

Choi, Kate H., and Sarinnapha Vasunilashorn. 2014. "Widowhood, Age Heterogamy, and Health: The Role of Selection, Marital Quality, and Health Behaviors." *Journals of Gerontology: Series B* 69B(1):123–34. https://doi.org/10.1093/geronb/gbt104.

Choi, Kyung-Hee, Don Operario, Steven E. Gregorich, and Lei Han. 2003. "Age and Race Mixing Patterns of Sexual Partnerships among Asian Men Who Have Sex with Men: Implications for HIV Transmission and Prevention." *AIDS Education and Prevention* 15(Supplement A):53–65. https://doi.org/10.1521/aeap.15.1.5.53.23609.

Choi, Susanne Y. P., and Adam Ka-Lok Cheung. 2017. "Dissimilar and Disadvantaged: Age Discrepancy, Financial Stress, and Marital Conflict in Cross-Border Marriages." *Journal of Family Issues* 38(18):2521–44. https://doi.org/10.1177/0192513X16653436.

Chong, Kelly H., and Nadia Y. Kim. 2021. "'The Model Man': Shifting Perceptions of Asian American Masculinity and the Renegotiation of a Racial Hierarchy of Desire." *Men and Masculinities*. Advance online publication. https://doi.org/10.1177/1097184X211043563.

Chudacoff, Howard P. 1989. *How Old Are You? Age Consciousness in American Culture*. Princeton, NJ: Princeton University Press.

Ciscato, Edoardo, Alfred Galichon, and Marion Goussé. 2020. "Like Attract Like? A Structural Comparison of Homogamy across Same-Sex and Different-Sex Households." *Journal of Political Economy* 128(2):740–81. https://doi.org/10.1086/704611.

Clements, Mikaella. 2018. "Looking for Women." *Hazlitt*, July 26. https://hazlitt.net.

Coburn, Brian J., and Sally Blower. 2010. "A Major HIV Risk Factor for Young Men Who Have Sex with Men Is Sex with Older Partners." *JAIDS: Journal of Acquired Immune Deficiency Syndromes* 54(2):113–14. https://doi.org/10.1097/QAI.0b013e3181d43999.

Cohen, Rhaina. 2020. "What If Friendship, Not Marriage, Was at the Center of Life?" *Atlantic*, October 20. www.theatlantic.com.

Coles, Melvyn G., and Marco Francesconi. 2011. "On the Emergence of Toyboys: The Timing of Marriage with Aging and Uncertain Careers." *International Economic Review* 52(3):825–53. https://doi.org/10.1111/j.1468-2354.2011.00651.x.

Collins, Patricia Hill. 2004. *Black Sexual Politics: African Americans, Gender, and the New Racism*. New York: Routledge.

Compton, Julie. 2020. "Few Lesbian Bars Remain in the U.S.: Will They Survive COVID-19?" *NBC News*, May 1. www.nbcnews.com.

Connell, R. W., and James W. Messerschmidt. 2005. "Hegemonic Masculinity: Rethinking the Concept." *Gender & Society* 19(6):829–59. https://doi.org/10.1177/0891243205278639.

Connell, Raewyn. 1987. *Gender and Power: Society, the Person, and Sexual Politics*. Stanford, CA: Stanford University Press.

———. 2005. *Masculinities*. 2nd ed. Berkeley: University of California Press.

Cornwell, Benjamin, and Edward O. Laumann. 2011. "Network Position and Sexual Dysfunction: Implications of Partner Betweenness for Men." *American Journal of Sociology* 117(1):172–208. https://doi.org/10.1086/661079.

David, Steven, and Bob G. Knight. 2008. "Stress and Coping among Gay Men: Age and Ethnic Differences." *Psychology and Aging* 23(1):62–69. https://doi.org/10.1037/0882-7974.23.1.62.

Dean, James Joseph. 2014. *Straights: Heterosexuality in Post-Closeted Culture*. New York: NYU Press.

Demby, Gene. 2018. "When Boys Can't Be Boys." *Code Switch*, NPR, November 2. www.npr.org.

Deterding, Nicole M., and Mary C. Waters. 2021. "Flexible Coding of In-Depth Interviews: A Twenty-first-Century Approach." *Sociological Methods & Research* 50(2):708–39. https://doi.org/10.1177/0049124118799377.

Dewaele, Alexis, Nele Cox, Wim Van den Berghe, and John Vincke. 2011. "Families of Choice? Exploring the Supportive Networks of Lesbians, Gay Men, and Bisexuals." *Journal of Applied Social Psychology* 41(2):312–31. https://doi.org/10.1111/j.1559-1816.2010.00715.x.

Dewey, Caitlin. 2016. "What Is the 'Daddy' Meme, and Why Are Actual Adults Fighting about It?" *Washington Post*, April 22. www.washingtonpost.com.

Diefendorf, Sarah. 2015. "After the Wedding Night: Sexual Abstinence and Masculinities over the Life Course." *Gender & Society* 29(5):647–69. https://doi.org/10.1177%2F0891243215591597.

Ding, Yingying, Yanqiu Zhou, Chunxin Liu, Xing Liu, and Na He. 2018. "Sex with Older Partners, Condomless Anal Sex, and Unrecognized HIV Infection among Chinese Men Who Have Sex with Men." *AIDS Care* 30(3):305–11. https://doi.org/10.1080/09540121.2017.1349275.

Donahue, Bob, and Jeff Stoner. 2013. "The Natural Bears Classification System: A Classification System for Bears and Bearlike Men Version 1.10." Pp. 149–56 in *The Bear Book: Readings in the History and Evolution of a Gay Male Subculture*. New edition, edited by L. Wright. New York: Routledge.

Donovan, Brian. 2020. *American Gold Digger: Marriage, Money, and the Law from the Ziegfeld Follies to Anna Nicole Smith*. Chapel Hill: University of North Carolina Press.

Drefahl, Sven. 2010. "How Does the Age Gap between Partners Affect Their Survival?" *Demography* 47(2):313–26. https://doi.org/10.1353/dem.0.0106.

Dribe, Martin, and Paul Nystedt. 2017. "Age Homogamy, Gender, and Earnings: Sweden, 1990–2009." *Social Forces* 96(1):239–63. https://doi.org/10.1093/sf/sox030.

Duckworth, Kiera D., and Mary Nell Trautner. 2019. "Gender Goals: Defining Masculinity and Navigating Peer Pressure to Engage in Sexual Activity." *Gender & Society* 33(5):795–817. https://doi.org/10.1177/0891243219863031.

Duder, Cameron. 2011. *Awfully Devoted Women: Lesbian Lives in Canada, 1900–65.* Vancouver: University of British Columbia Press.

Eisen, Daniel B., and Liann Yamashita. 2019. "Borrowing from Femininity: The Caring Man, Hybrid Masculinities, and Maintaining Male Dominance." *Men and Masculinities* 22(5):801–20. https://doi.org/10.1177/1097184X17728552.

Elliott, Karla. 2016. "Caring Masculinities: Theorizing an Emerging Concept." *Men and Masculinities* 19(3):240–59. https://doi.org/10.1177/1097184X15576203.

———. 2019. "Negotiations between Progressive and 'Traditional' Expressions of Masculinity among Young Australian Men." *Journal of Sociology* 55(1):108–23. https://doi.org/10.1177/1440783318802996.

———. 2020. *Young Men Navigating Contemporary Masculinities*. Cham, Switzerland: Springer International Publishing. https://doi.org/10.1007/978-3-030-36395-6.

Ellis, Philip. 2021. "What Does It Even Mean to Have a 'Dad Bod' Anymore?" *Men's Health*, January 29. www.menshealth.com.

Elwert, Annika. 2020. "Opposites Attract: Assortative Mating and Immigrant–Native Intermarriage in Contemporary Sweden." *European Journal of Population* 36:675–709. https://doi.org/10.1007/s10680-019-09546-9.

England, Paula, and Elizabeth Aura McClintock. 2009. "The Gendered Double Standard of Aging in US Marriage Markets." *Population and Development Review* 35(4):797–816. https://doi.org/10.1111/j.1728-4457.2009.00309.x.

England, Paula, Emma Mishel, and Mónica Caudillo. 2016. "Increases in Sex with Same-Sex Partners and Bisexual Identity across Cohorts of Women (but Not Men)." *Sociological Science* 3:951–70. https://doi.org/10.15195/v3.a42.

Erol, Maral, and Cenk Ozbay. 2018. "No Andropause for Gay Men? The Body, Aging, and Sexuality in Turkey." *Journal of Gender Studies* 27(7):847–59. https://doi.org/10.1080/09589236.2017.1329715.

Esteve, Albert, Clara Cortina, and Anna Cabré. 2009. "Long-Term Trends in Marital Age Homogamy Patterns: Spain, 1922–2006." *Population* 64(1):173–202. https://doi.org/10.3917/popu.901.0183.

Faderman, Lillian. 1991. *Odd Girls and Twilight Lovers: A History of Lesbian Life in Twentieth-Century America*. New York: Columbia University Press.

Farhi, Paul. 2005. "Conception of a Question: Who's Your Daddy?" *Washington Post*, January 4. www.washingtonpost.com.

Feighan, Kelly A. 2018. "A Quantitative Analysis of Marital Age Gaps in the U.S. between 1970 and 2014." Dissertation, Temple University, Philadelphia, PA.

Foweraker, Barbara, and Leanne Cutcher. 2015. "Work, Age, and Other Drugs: Exploring the Intersection of Age and Masculinity in a Pharmaceutical Organization." *Gender, Work & Organization* 22(5):459–73. https://doi.org/10.1111/gwao.12085.

Franklin, Jake D., Adam Bourne, and Anthony Lyons. 2022. "Characteristics and Functions of Subcultural Identities in the Lives of Gay, Bisexual, and Queer-Identifying Men in Australia." *Psychology & Sexuality* 13(3):459–73. https://doi.org/10.1080/19419899.2020.1856172.

Freedman, Marc, and Trent Stamp. 2018. "The U.S. Isn't Just Getting Older. It's Getting More Segregated by Age." *Harvard Business Review*, June 6. https://hbr.org.

Ghaziani, Amin. 2009. "An 'Amorphous Mist'? The Problem of Measurement in the Study of Culture." *Theory and Society* 38(6):581–612. https://doi.org/10.1007/s11186-009-9096-2.

———. 2014a. "Measuring Urban Sexual Cultures." *Theory and Society* 43(3):371–93. https://doi.org/10.1007/s11186-014-9225-4.

———. 2014b. *There Goes the Gayborhood?* Princeton, NJ: Princeton University Press.

———. 2015. "Lesbian Geographies." *Contexts* 14(1):62–64. https://doi.org/10.1177/1536504214567848.

———. 2017. *Sex Cultures*. Malden, MA: Polity Press.

———. 2019. "Cultural Archipelagos: New Directions in the Study of Sexuality and Space." *City & Community* 18(1):4–22. https://doi.org/10.1111/cico.12381.

Ghaziani, Amin, and Thomas D. Cook. 2005. "Reducing HIV Infections at Circuit Parties: From Description to Explanation and Principles of Intervention Design." *Journal of the International Association of Physicians in AIDS Care* 4(2):32–46. https://doi.org/10.1177/1545109705277978.

Goodman, David J. 2019. "Sex in New York City Parks? It's Less of a Thing Than It Used to Be." *New York Times*, February 22. www.nytimes.com.

Green, Adam Isaiah. 2014. *Sexual Fields: Toward a Sociology of Collective Sexual Life*. Chicago: University of Chicago Press.

Gruys, Kjerstin, and Christin L. Munsch. 2020. "'Not Your Average Nerd': Masculinities, Privilege, and Academic Effort at an Elite University." *Sociological Forum* 35(2):346–69. https://doi.org/10.1111/socf.12585.

Guetto, Raffaele, and Davide Azzolini. 2015. "An Empirical Study of Status Exchange through Migrant/Native Marriages in Italy." *Journal of Ethnic & Migration Studies* 41(13):2149–72. https://doi.org/10.1080/1369183X.2015.1037725.

Gullickson, Aaron. 2017. "Comments on Conceptualizing and Measuring the Exchange of Beauty and Status." *American Sociological Review* 82(5):1093–99. https://doi.org/10.1177%2F0003122417724001.

Gullickson, Aaron, and Vincent Kang Fu. 2010. "Comment: An Endorsement of Exchange Theory in Mate Selection." *American Journal of Sociology* 115(4):1243–51. https://doi.org/10.1086/649049.

Gunnarsson, Lena, and Sofia Strid. 2021. "Varieties of Sugar Dating in Sweden: Content, Compensation, Motivations." *Social Problems*. Advance online publication. https://doi.org/10.1093/socpro/spab063.

———. 2022. "Chemistry or Service? Sugar Daddies' (Re)Quest for Mutuality within the Confines of Commercial Exchange." *Journal of Sex Research* 59(3):309–20. https://doi.org/10.1080/00224499.2021.1952155.

Gustafson, Per. 2017. "Spousal Age Differences and Synchronised Retirement." *Ageing & Society* 37(4):777–803. https://doi.org/10.1017/S0144686X15001452.

Gustafson, Per, and Urban Fransson. 2015. "Age Differences between Spouses: Sociodemographic Variation and Selection." *Marriage & Family Review* 51(7):610–32. https://doi.org/10.1080/01494929.2015.1060289.

Hajek, Christopher. 2014. "Gay Men at Midlife: A Grounded Theory of Social Identity Management through Linguistic Labeling and Intra- and Intergenerational Talk." *Journal of Language and Social Psychology* 33(6):606–31. https://doi.org/10.1177/0261927X14545344.

Hale, C. Jacob. 1997. "Leatherdyke Boys and Their Daddies: How to Have Sex without Women or Men." *Social Text* (52/53):223. https://doi.org/10.2307/466741.

Hammack, Phillip L., David M. Frost, and Sam D. Hughes. 2019. "Queer Intimacies: A New Paradigm for the Study of Relationship Diversity." *Journal of Sex Research* 56(4–5):556–92. https://doi.org/10.1080/00224499.2018.1531281.

Hammack, Phillip L., Ilan H. Meyer, Evan A. Krueger, Marguerita Lightfoot, and David M. Frost. 2018. "HIV Testing and Pre-Exposure Prophylaxis (PrEP) Use, Familiarity, and Attitudes among Gay and Bisexual Men in the United States: A National Probability Sample of Three Birth Cohorts." *PLoS One* 13(9):e0202806. https://doi.org/10.1371/journal.pone.0202806.

Han, Chong-suk, Kristopher Proctor, and Kyung-Hee Choi. 2014. "I Know a Lot of Gay Asian Men Who Are Actually Tops: Managing and Negotiating Gay Racial Stigma." *Sexuality & Culture* 18(2):219–34. https://doi.org/10.1007/s12119-013-9183-4.

Hasmanová Marhánková, Jaroslava. 2020. "Being a (Grand)Father: (Re)Constructing Masculinity through the Life-Course." *Journal of Family Issues* 41(3):267–87. https://doi.org/10.1177/0192513X19876064.

Hennen, Peter. 2005. "Bear Bodies, Bear Masculinity: Recuperation, Resistance, or Retreat?" *Gender & Society* 19(1):25–43. https://doi.org/10.1177/0891243204269408.

———. 2008. *Faeries, Bears, and Leathermen: Men in Community Queering the Masculine*. Chicago: University of Chicago Press.

Homelessness Policy Research Institute. 2019. *LGBTQ Youth Experiencing Homelessness*. Los Angeles: University of Southern California. https://socialinnovation.usc.edu.

Hu, Yang, and Yue Qian. 2019. "Educational and Age Assortative Mating in China: The Importance of Marriage Order." *Demographic Research* 41(3):53–82. https://doi.org/10.4054/DemRes.2019.41.3.

Hurd, Laura, and Raveena Mahal. 2021. "'I'm Pleased with My Body': Older Men's Perceptions and Experiences of Their Aging Bodies." *Men and Masculinities* 24(2):228–44. https://doi.org/10.1177/1097184X19879188.

Hurd Clarke, Laura, and Maya Lefkowich. 2018. "'I Don't Really Have Any Issue with Masculinity': Older Canadian Men's Perceptions and Experiences of Embodied Masculinity." *Journal of Aging Studies* 45:18–24. https://doi.org/10.1016/j.jaging.2018.01.003.

Hurt, Christopher B., Derrick D. Matthews, Molly S. Calabria, Kelly A. Green, Adaora A. Adimora, Carol E. Golin, and Lisa B. Hightow-Weidman. 2010. "Sex with Older Partners Is Associated with Primary HIV Infection among Men Who Have Sex with Men in North Carolina." *JAIDS: Journal of Acquired Immune Deficiency Syndromes* 54(2):185–90. https://doi.org/10.1097/QAI.0b013e3181c99114.

Jackson, David. 2016. *Exploring Aging Masculinities*. London: Palgrave Macmillan.

James, Drexler, Kris Rosentel, Alicia VandeVusse, Darnell N. Motley, and Brandon J. Hill. 2021. "Psychosocial Support, Sexual Health, and HIV Risk among Older Men Who Have Sex with Younger Men." *Journal of Homosexuality* 68(14):2490–2508. https://doi.org/10.1080/00918369.2020.1809890.

Janulis, Patrick, Brian A. Feinstein, Gregory Phillips, Michael E. Newcomb, Michelle Birkett, and Brian Mustanski. 2018. "Sexual Partner Typologies and the Association between Drug Use and Sexual Risk Behavior among Young Men Who Have Sex with Men." *Archives of Sexual Behavior* 47(1):259–71. https://doi.org/10.1007/s10508-016-0909-x.

Jepsen, Lisa K., and Christopher A. Jepsen. 2002. "An Empirical Analysis of the Matching Patterns of Same-Sex and Opposite-Sex Couples." *Demography* 39(3):435–53. https://doi.org/10.1353/dem.2002.0027.

Johansson, Thomas, and Jesper Andreasson. 2017. *Fatherhood in Transition: Masculinity, Identity, and Everyday Life*. London: Palgrave Macmillan.

Johansson, Thomas, and Roger Klinth. 2008. "Caring Fathers: The Ideology of Gender Equality and Masculine Positions." *Men and Masculinities* 11(1):42–62. https://doi.org/10.1177/1097184X06291899.

Jones, Angela. 2019. "Sex Is Not a Problem: The Erasure of Pleasure in Sexual Science Research." *Sexualities* 22(4):643–68. https://doi.org/10.1177/1363460718760210.

Jones, Jeffrey M. 2022. "LGBT Identification in U.S. Ticks Up to 7.1%." Washington, DC: Gallup. https://news.gallup.com.

Jones, Robert P., Natalie Jackson, Diana Orcés, Ian Huff, and Maddie Snodgrass. 2022. "Americans' Support for Key LGBTQ Rights Continues to Tick Upward." Washington, DC: Public Religion Research Institute. www.prri.org.

Joseph, Heather A., Gary Marks, Lisa Belcher, Gregorio A. Millett, Ann Stueve, Trista A. Bingham, and Jennifer Lauby. 2011. "Older Partner Selection, Sexual Risk Behaviour, and Unrecognised HIV Infection among Black and Latino Men Who Have Sex with Men." *Sexually Transmitted Infections* 87(5):442–47. https://doi.org/10.1136/sextrans-2011–050010.

Joyner, Kara, Kelly Balistreri, and Grace Kao. 2018. "Racial/Ethnic Hierarchies in Same-Sex and Different-Sex Mate Markets." Paper presented at the Population Association of America annual conference, April 10–13, Austin, TX. https://paa2019.populationassociation.org.

Jurva, Raisa. 2018. "Independence and Vulnerability: Affective Orientations in Imagining Futurities for Heterosexual Relationships." Pp. 127–40 in *Affective Inequalities in Intimate Relationships*, edited by T. Juvonen and M. Kolehmainen. New York: Routledge.

Kadandara, Nyasha. 2018. "Sex and the Sugar Daddy." BBC, August. www.bbc.co.uk.

Kalmijn, Matthijs. 2010. "Comment: Educational Inequality, Homogamy, and Status Exchange in Black-White Intermarriage." *American Journal of Sociology* 115(4):1252–63. https://doi.org/10.1086/649050.

Kao, Grace, Kelly Stamper Balistreri, and Kara Joyner. 2018. "Asian American Men in Romantic Dating Markets." *Contexts* 17(4):48–53. https://doi.org/10.1177/1536504218812869.

Keenan, Katherine, Lyudmila Saburova, Natalia Bobrova, Diana Elbourne, Sarah Ashwin, and David A. Leon. 2015. "Social Factors Influencing Russian Male Alcohol Use over the Life Course: A Qualitative Study Investigating Age-Based Social Norms, Masculinity, and Workplace Context." *PLOS ONE* 10(11):e0142993. https://doi.org/10.1371/journal.pone.0142993.

Kemple, Thomas. 2022. "Milestones and Cornerstones: Queering the Life Course." *Journal of Classical Sociology* 22(1):100–106. https://doi.org/10.1177/1468795X211048800.

Kim, Allen, and Karen Pyke. 2015. "Taming Tiger Dads: Hegemonic American Masculinity and South Korea's Father School." *Gender & Society* 29(4):509–33. https://doi.org/10.1177/0891243215584602.

Kim, Jae-Hyun, Eun-Cheol Park, and Sang Gyu Lee. 2015. "The Impact of Age Differences in Couples on Depressive Symptoms: Evidence from the Korean Longitudinal Study of Aging (2006–2012)." *BMC Psychiatry* 15(1):10. https://doi.org/10.1186/s12888-015-0388-y.

King, Neal, Toni Calasanti, Ilkka Pietilä, and Hanna Ojala. 2021. "The Hegemony in Masculinity." *Men and Masculinities* 24(3):432–50. https://doi.org/10.1177/1097184X20981759.

Kirkeby, Kimberley M., Justin J. Lehmiller, and Michael J. Marks. 2022. "Sugar Dating, Perceptions of Power, and Condom Use: Comparing the Sexual Health Risk

Behaviours of Sugar Dating to Non–Sugar Dating Women." *Journal of Sex Research* 59(6):731–41. https://doi.org/10.1080/00224499.2021.1962782.

Kirkland, Justin. 2018. "Here's an Outrageously Comprehensive Guide to the Term 'Daddy.'" *Esquire*, June 15. www.esquire.com.

Kolk, Martin. 2015. "Age Differences in Unions: Continuity and Divergence among Swedish Couples between 1932 and 2007." *European Journal of Population* 31(4):365–82. https://doi.org/10.1007/s10680-015-9339-z.

Kridahl, Linda, and Martin Kolk. 2018. "Retirement Coordination in Opposite-Sex and Same-Sex Married Couples: Evidence from Swedish Registers." *Advances in Life Course Research* 38:22–36. https://doi.org/10.1016/j.alcr.2018.10.003.

Kuate-Defo, Barthelemy. 2004. "Young People's Relationships with Sugar Daddies and Sugar Mummies: What Do We Know and What Do We Need to Know?" *African Journal of Reproductive Health* 8(2):13. https://doi.org/10.2307/3583175.

Lamidi, Esther, Susan L. Brown, and Wendy D. Manning. 2015. *Assortative Mating: Age Heterogamy in U.S. Marriages, 1964–2014*. Bowling Green, OH: Bowling Green State University, National Center for Family & Marriage Research. https://scholarworks. bgsu.edu.

Langdridge, Darren, and Jamie Lawson. 2019. "The Psychology of Puppy Play: A Phenomenological Investigation." *Archives of Sexual Behavior* 48(7):2201–15. https://doi. org/10.1007/s10508-019-01476-1.

Lawson, David W., Susan B. Schaffnit, Anushé Hassan, and Mark Urassa. 2021. "Shared Interests or Sexual Conflict? Spousal Age Gap, Women's Wellbeing, and Fertility in Rural Tanzania." *Evolution and Human Behavior* 42(2):165–75. https://doi. org/10.1016/j.evolhumbehav.2020.08.009.

Lawson, Jamie, and Darren Langdridge. 2020. "History, Culture, and Practice of Puppy Play." *Sexualities* 23(4):574–91. https://doi.org/10.1177/1363460719839914.

Lawton, Zoe, and Paul Callister. 2010. *Older Women–Younger Men Relationships: The Social Phenomenon of "Cougars." A Research Note*. Wellington, Australia: Institute of Policy Studies.

Lee, Soomi. 2022. "Midlife May Begin at Different Times and Brings Opportunities, Challenges." *Washington Post*, February 27. www.washingtonpost.com.

Lee, Wang-Sheng, and Terra McKinnish. 2018. "The Marital Satisfaction of Differently Aged Couples." *Journal of Population Economics* 31(2):337–62. https://doi. org/10.1007/s00148-017-0658-8.

Lehmiller, Justin J., and Christopher R. Agnew. 2007. "Perceived Marginalization and the Prediction of Romantic Relationship Stability." *Journal of Marriage and Family* 69(4):1036–49. https://doi.org/10.1111/j.1741-3737.2007.00429.x.

———. 2008. "Commitment in Age-Gap Heterosexual Romantic Relationships: A Test of Evolutionary and Socio-Cultural Predictions." *Psychology of Women Quarterly* 32(1):74–82. https://doi.org/10.1111/j.1471-6402.2007.00408.x.

Lengerer, Andrea, and Julia H. Schroedter. 2022. "Patterns and Trends of Same-Sex Partner Choice in Germany." *Journal of Comparative Family Studies* 53(2):161–88. https://doi.org/10.3138/jcfs.53.2.020.

Levant, Ronald F., Britney A. Webster, Jennifer T. Stanley, and Edward H. Thompson. 2020. "The Aging Men's Masculinity Ideologies Inventory (AMMII): Dimensionality, Variance Composition, Measurement Invariance by Gender, and Validity." *Psychology of Men & Masculinities* 21(1):46–57. https://doi.org/10.1037/men0000208.

Levchenko, Polina, and Catherine Solheim. 2013. "International Marriages between Eastern European–Born Women and U.S.-Born Men." *Family Relations* 62(1):30–41. https://doi.org/10.1111/j.1741–3729.2012.00746.x.

Lever, Janet, David A. Frederick, and Rosanna Hertz. 2015. "Who Pays for Dates? Following versus Challenging Gender Norms." *SAGE Open* 5(4):1–14. https://doi.org/10.1177/2158244015613107.

Levine, Ethan Czuy, Debby Herbenick, Omar Martinez, Tsung-Chieh Fu, and Brian Dodge. 2018. "Open Relationships, Nonconsensual Nonmonogamy, and Monogamy among U.S. Adults: Findings from the 2012 National Survey of Sexual Health and Behavior." *Archives of Sexual Behavior* 47(5):1439–50. https://doi.org/10.1007/s10508-018-1178-7.

Levine, Martin P. 1998. *Gay Macho: The Life and Death of the Homosexual Clone*. New York: NYU Press.

Levine, Martin P., Peter M. Nardi, and John H. Gagnon, eds. 1997. *In Changing Times: Gay Men and Lesbians Encounter HIV/AIDS*. Chicago: University of Chicago Press.

Levinson, Anna. 2016. "Fifty Shades of Daddy." *Mel Magazine*, June 14. https://mel-magazine.com.

Lighter, J. E., ed. 1994. *Random House Historical Dictionary of American Slang*. New York: Random House.

Lodge, Amy C., and Debra Umberson. 2013. "Age and Embodied Masculinities: Midlife Gay and Heterosexual Men Talk about Their Bodies." *Journal of Aging Studies* 27(3):225–32. https://doi.org/10.1016/j.jaging.2013.03.004.

Loe, Meika. 2001. "Fixing Broken Masculinity: Viagra as a Technology for the Production of Gender and Sexuality." *Sexuality & Culture* 5(3):97–125. https://doi.org/10.1007/s12119-001-1032-1.

Lomas, Natasha. 2013. "Dattch, a Pinterest-Inspired Dating App for Gay Women, Closes $160K to Fuel Its UK Beta." *Tech Crunch*, September 22. https://techcrunch.com.

Luo, Shanhong. 2017. "Assortative Mating and Couple Similarity: Patterns, Mechanisms, and Consequences." *Social and Personality Psychology Compass* 11(8):e12337. https://doi.org/10.1111/spc3.12337.

Lyons, Anthony, Samantha Croy, Catherine Barrett, and Carolyn Whyte. 2015. "Growing Old as a Gay Man: How Life Has Changed for the Gay Liberation Generation." *Ageing & Society* 35(10):2229–50. https://doi.org/10.1017/S0144686X14000889.

Lyons, Anthony, and Warwick Hosking. 2014. "Health Disparities among Common Subcultural Identities of Young Gay Men: Physical, Mental, and Sexual Health." *Archives of Sexual Behavior* 43(8):1621–35. https://doi.org/10.1007/s10508-014-0315-1.

Macapagal, Kathryn, Kevin Moran, Michael E. Newcomb, David A. Moskowitz, Christopher Owens, and Brian Mustanski. 2021. "Patterns of Online and Offline

Partnering, Partnership Characteristics, and Condomless Sex among Adolescent Sexual Minority Males in the USA." *AIDS and Behavior* 25(7):2033–45. https://doi.org/10.1007/s10461-020-03133-4.

Maimann, Kevin. 2015. "As Education Costs Rise, Students Seek Out 'Sugar Daddies.'" *Toronto Sun*, January 27. https://torontosun.com.

Manning, Wendy, and Krista Payne. 2021. *Same-Sex Married and Cohabiting Couples Raising Children*. Bowling Green, OH: Bowling Green State University, National Center for Family and Marriage Research. https://doi.org/10.25035/ncfmr/fp-21-08.

Mansour, Hani, and Terra McKinnish. 2013. "Who Marries Differently Aged Spouses? Ability, Education, Occupation, Earnings, and Appearance." *Review of Economics and Statistics* 96(3):577–80. https://doi.org/10.1162/REST_a_00377.

Marloff, Sarah. 2021. "The Rise and Fall of America's Lesbian Bars." *Smithsonian Magazine*, January 21. www.smithsonianmag.com.

Marshall, Barbara L. 2006. "The New Virility: Viagra, Male Aging, and Sexual Function." *Sexualities* 9(3):345–62. https://doi.org/10.1177/1363460706065057.

Mattson, Greggor. 2019. "Are Gay Bars Closing? Using Business Listings to Infer Rates of Gay Bar Closure in the United States, 1977–2019." *Socius* 5. https://doi.org/10.1177/2378023119894832.

McKenzie, Lara. 2015. *Age-Dissimilar Couples and Romantic Relationships: Ageless Love?* New York: Palgrave Macmillan.

Mercer, John. 2012. "Coming of Age: Problematizing Gay Porn and the Eroticized Older Man." *Journal of Gender Studies* 21(3):313–26. https://doi.org/10.1080/0958923 6.2012.681187.

Messerschmidt, James W. 2018. *Hegemonic Masculinity: Formulation, Reformulation, and Amplification*. Lanham, MD: Rowman & Littlefield.

———. 2019. "The Salience of 'Hegemonic Masculinity.'" *Men and Masculinities* 22(1):85–91. https://doi.org/10.1177/1097184X18805555.

Meyer, Ilan H., Stephanie Marken, Stephen T. Russell, David M. Frost, and Bianca D. M. Wilson. 2020. "An Innovative Approach to the Design of a National Probability Sample of Sexual Minority Adults." *LGBT Health* 7(2):101–8. https://doi.org/10.1089/lgbt.2019.0145.

Miller, Lisa R., Justin R. Garcia, and Amanda N. Gesselman. 2021. "Dating and Sexualities across the Life Course: The Interactive Effects of Aging and Gender." *Journal of Aging Studies* 57:1–11. https://doi.org/10.1016/j.jaging.2021.100921.

Miller, Paula K. 2022. "Hegemonic Whiteness: Expanding and Operationalizing the Conceptual Framework." *Sociology Compass* 16(4). https://doi.org/10.1111/soc4.12973.

Miller, Robin Lin, Jason C. Forney, and Miles A. McNall. 2014. "Recent Sexual Partnerships among Adolescent and Emerging Adult Black Men Who Have Sex with Men: The Role of Age and Race Discordant Partnerships in Risk-Taking Behavior." *Journal of HIV/AIDS & Social Services* 13(3):252–70. https://doi.org/10.1080/1538150 1.2012.748584.

Minkowitz, Donna. 1994. "Daddy Is a Dyke." *Village Voice*, June 25. www.village-voice.com/.

Mishel, Emma, Tristan Bridges, and Mónica L. Caudillo. 2022. "Google, Tell Me. Is He Gay? Masculinity, Heterosexuality, and Gendered Anxieties in Google Search Queries about Sexuality." *Sociological Perspectives* 65(2):241–61. https://doi.org/10.11 77%2F07311214211001906.

Mize, Trenton D., and Bianca Manago. 2018. "Precarious Sexuality: How Men and Women Are Differentially Categorized for Similar Sexual Behavior." *American Sociological Review* 83(2):305–30. https://doi.org/10.1177/0003122418759544.

Montemurro, Beth. 2021. *Getting It, Having It, Keeping It Up: Straight Men's Sexuality in Public and Private*. New Brunswick, NJ: Rutgers University Press.

Montgomery, Blake. 2019. "We Live in Packs." *New York Times*, April 26. www.nytimes.com.

Moore, Laura M., Amy Adamczyk, J. Michael Ryan, and Seth Ovadia. 2021. "Shifting Religious Influences on Attitudes towards Same-Sex Behavior and Civil Liber-ties: A Multilevel Across-Time Analysis." *Journal for the Scientific Study of Religion* 60(2):400–423. https://doi.org/10.1111/jssr.12718.

Morgan, Richard. 2021. "Asian American Masculinity Is Being Increasingly Celebrated. But Many Men Still Face Stereotyping." *Washington Post*, June 22. www.washington-post.com.

Mosher, Chad M., Heidi M. Levitt, and Eric Manley. 2006. "Layers of Leather." *Journal of Homosexuality* 51(3):93–123. https://doi.org/10.1300/J082v51n03_06.

Moskowitz, David A., David W. Seal, Lance Rintamaki, and Gerulf Rieger. 2011. "HIV in the Leather Community: Rates and Risk-Related Behaviors." *AIDS and Behavior* 15(3):557–64. https://doi.org/10.1007/s10461-009-9636-9.

Moskowitz, David A., Jonathan Turrubiates, Hector Lozano, and Christopher Hajek. 2013. "Physical, Behavioral, and Psychological Traits of Gay Men Identify-ing as Bears." *Archives of Sexual Behavior* 42(5):775–84. https://doi.org/10.1007/s10508-013-0095-z.

Mu, Zheng, and Yu Xie. 2014. "Marital Age Homogamy in China: A Reversal of Trend in the Reform Era?" *Social Science Research* 44:141–57. https://doi.org/10.1016/j.ssresearch.2013.11.005.

Munsch, Christin L., and Kjerstin Gruys. 2018. "What Threatens, Defines: Tracing the Symbolic Boundaries of Contemporary Masculinity." *Sex Roles* 79(7):375–92. https://doi.org/10.1007/s11199-017-0878-0.

Mustanski, Brian, and Michael E. Newcomb. 2013. "Older Sexual Partners May Contribute to Racial Disparities in HIV among Young Men Who Have Sex with Men." *Journal of Adolescent Health* 52(6):666–67. https://doi.org/10.1016/j.jadohealth.2013.03.019.

Mustanski, Brian, Michael E. Newcomb, and Elise M. Clerkin. 2011. "Relationship Characteristics and Sexual Risk-Taking in Young Men Who Have Sex with Men." *Health Psychology* 30(5):597–605. https://doi.org/10.1037/a0023858.

Nardi, Peter M. 1999. *Gay Men's Friendships: Invincible Communities*. Chicago: University of Chicago Press.

Nayar, Kavita Ilona. 2017. "Sweetening the Deal: Dating for Compensation in the Digital Age." *Journal of Gender Studies* 26(3):335–46. https://doi.org/10.1080/095892 36.2016.1273101.

Newcomb, Michael E., and Brian Mustanski. 2013. "Racial Differences in Same-Race Partnering and the Effects of Sexual Partnership Characteristics on HIV Risk in MSM: A Prospective Sexual Diary Study." *JAIDS: Journal of Acquired Immune Deficiency Syndrome* 62(3):5. https://doi.org/10.1097/QAI.0b013e31827e5f8c.

Niedomysl, Thomas, John Östh, and Maarten van Ham. 2010. "The Globalisation of Marriage Fields: The Swedish Case." *Journal of Ethnic & Migration Studies* 36(7):1119–38. https://doi.org/10.1080/13691830903488184.

Noël, Reginald A. 2018. "Race, Economics, and Social Status." Washington, DC: US Bureau of Labor Statistics. www.bls.gov.

Oeur, Freeden. 2016. "Recognizing Dignity: Young Black Men Growing Up in an Era of Surveillance." *Socius* 2:1–15. https://doi.org/10.1177/2378023116633712.

Oidtman, Jessica, Susan G. Sherman, Anthony Morgan, Danielle German, and Renata Arrington-Sanders. 2017. "Satisfaction and Condomless Anal Sex at Sexual Debut and Sexual Risk among Young Black Same-Sex Attracted Men." *Archives of Sexual Behavior* 46(4):947–59. https://doi.org/10.1007/s10508-016-0831-2.

Oksuzyan, Anna, Angela Carollo, Sven Drefahl, Carlo Giovanni Camarda, and Alyson van Raalte. 2017. *Does the Age Difference between Partners Influence the Career Achievements of Women?* Rostock, Germany: Max Planck Institute for Demographic Research. www.demogr.mpg.de.

Olson, Loren A. 2020. "Age Differences in Gay Couples." *Psychology Today*, March 23. www.psychologytoday.com/us/blog/finally-out/202003/age-differences-in-gay-couples.

Orenstein, Peggy. 2020. *Boys and Sex: Young Men on Hookups, Love, Porn, Consent, and Navigating the New Masculinity*. New York: HarperCollins.

Orne, Jason. 2017. *Boystown: Sex and Community in Chicago*. Chicago: University of Chicago Press.

Oswald, Flora, Shelby Hughes, Amanda Champion, and Cory L. Pedersen. 2022. "In Search of the Appeal of the 'DILF.'" *Psychology & Sexuality* 13(2):283–301. https://doi.org/10.1080/19419899.2020.1769164.

Parker, Kim. 2015. "Among LGBT Americans, Bisexuals Stand Out When It Comes to Identity, Acceptance." Washington, DC: Pew Research Center. www.pewresearch.org.

Parreñas, Rhacel Salazar. 2008. "Transnational Fathering: Gendered Conflicts, Distant Disciplining, and Emotional Gaps." *Journal of Ethnic and Migration Studies* 34(7):1057–72. https://doi.org/10.1080/13691830802230356.

Pascoe, C. J. 2011. *Dude, You're a Fag: Masculinity and Sexuality in High School*. New edition. Berkeley: University of California Press.

Pascoe, C. J., and Tristan Bridges, eds. 2015. *Exploring Masculinities: Identity, Inequality, Continuity, and Change*. Oxford, UK: Oxford University Press.

Perry, Nicholas S., David M. Huebner, Brian R. W. Baucom, and Colleen C. Hoff. 2016. "The Complex Contribution of Sociodemographics to Decision-Making Power in Gay Male Couples." *Journal of Family Psychology* 30(8):977–86. https://doi.org/10.1037/fam0000234.

Petsko, Christopher D., and Ashleigh Shelby Rosette. 2022. "Are Leaders Still Presumed White by Default? Racial Bias in Leader Categorization Revisited." *Journal of Applied Psychology*. Advance online publication. https://doi.org/10.1037/apl0001020.

Petts, Richard J., Kevin M. Shafer, and Lee Essig. 2018. "Does Adherence to Masculine Norms Shape Fathering Behavior? Masculinity and Father Involvement." *Journal of Marriage and Family* 80(3):704–20. https://doi.org/10.1111/jomf.12476.

Pietilä, Ilkka, and Hanna Ojala. 2011. "Acting Age in the Context of Health: Middle-Aged Working-Class Men Talking about Bodies and Aging." *Journal of Aging Studies* 25(4):380–89. https://doi.org/10.1016/j.jaging.2011.01.005.

Pini, Barbara, and Mary-Lou Conway. 2017. "Masculinity and Fathering in the Lives of Rural Men with a Disability." *Journal of Rural Studies* 51:267–74. https://doi.org/10.1016/j.jrurstud.2016.12.005.

Poppel, Frans Van, Aart C. Liefbroer, Jeroen K. Vermunt, and Wilma Smeenk. 2001. "Love, Necessity, and Opportunity: Changing Patterns of Marital Age Homogamy in the Netherlands, 1850–1993." *Population Studies* 55(1):1–13. https://doi.org/10.1080/00324720127681.

Powell, Brian, Catherine Blozendahl, Claudia Geist, and Lala Carr Steelman. 2010. *Counted Out: Same-Sex Relations and Americans' Definitions of Family*. New York: Russell Sage Foundation.

Prestage, Garrett, Graham Brown, John De Wit, Benjamin Bavinton, Christopher Fairley, Bruce Maycock, Colin Batrouney, Phillip Keen, Ian Down, Mohamed Hammoud, and Iryna Zablotska. 2015. "Understanding Gay Community Subcultures: Implications for HIV Prevention." *AIDS and Behavior* 19(12):2224–33. https://doi.org/10.1007/s10461-015-1027-9.

Pribilsky, Jason. 2012. "Consumption Dilemmas: Tracking Masculinity, Money, and Transnational Fatherhood between the Ecuadorian Andes and New York City." *Journal of Ethnic & Migration Studies* 38(2):323–43. https://doi.org/10.1080/1369183X.2012.646429.

Qian, Yue, and Zhenchao Qian. 2014. "The Gender Divide in Urban China: Singlehood and Assortative Mating by Age and Education." *Demographic Research* 31:45. https://doi.org/10.4054/DemRes.2014.31.45.

Qian, Yue, Yang Shen, and Manlin Cai. 2022. "Gendered Age Preferences for Potential Partners: A Mixed-Methods Study among Online Daters in Shanghai." *Chinese Sociological Review* 54(3):304–31. https://doi.org/10.1080/21620555.2022.2059459.

Quidley-Rodriguez, Narciso, and Joseph P. De Santis. 2019. "A Concept Analysis of Bear Identity." *Journal of Homosexuality* 66(1):60–76. https://doi.org/10.1080/00918369.2017.1392131.

Randall, Devin. 2019. "Should Gays Do Away with the Term 'Daddy'?" *Instinct Magazine*, June 18. https://instinctmagazine.com.

Rapoport, Eli, Christian E. Athanasian, and Andrew Adesman. 2021. "Prevalence of Nonheterosexual Identity and Same-Sex Sexual Contact among High School Students in the US from 2015 to 2019." *JAMA Pediatrics* 175(9):970. https://doi.org/10.1001/jamapediatrics.2021.1109.

Rios, Victor, and Rachel Sarabia. 2015. "Synthesized Masculinities: The Mechanics of Manhood among Delinquent Boys." Pp. 166–77 in *Exploring Masculinities: Identity, Inequality, Continuity, and Change*, edited by C. J. Pascoe and T. Bridges. Oxford, UK: Oxford University Press.

Robinson, Brandon Andrew. 2020. *Coming Out to the Streets: LGBTQ Youth Experiencing Homelessness*. Oakland: University of California Press.

Rosenfeld, Dana, Bernadette Bartlam, and Ruth D. Smith. 2012. "Out of the Closet and into the Trenches: Gay Male Baby Boomers, Aging, and HIV/AIDS." *Gerontologist* 52(2):255–64. https://doi.org/10.1093/geront/gnr138.

Rosenfeld, Michael J., and Byung-Soo Kim. 2005. "The Independence of Young Adults and the Rise of Interracial and Same-Sex Unions." *American Sociological Review* 70(4):541–62. https://doi.org/10.1177/000312240507000401.

Rosenfeld, Michael, Reuben J. Thomas, and Sonia Hausen. 2019. "Disintermediating Your Friends: How Online Dating in the United States Displaces Other Ways of Meeting." Preprint edition. Stanford University. https://web.standford.edu.

Rotundo, E. Anthony. 1989. "Romantic Friendship: Male Intimacy and Middle-Class Youth in the Northern United States, 1800–1900." *Journal of Social History* 23(1):1–25. https://doi.org/10.1353/jsh/23.1.1.

Rubin, Gayle. 2000. "Sites, Settlements, and Urban Sex: Archaeology and the Study of Gay Leathermen in San Francisco, 1955–1995." Pp. 62–88 in *Archaeologies of Sexuality*, edited by R. Schmidt and B. Voss. London: Routledge.

Ryan, Gery W., and H. Russell Bernard. 2003. "Techniques to Identify Themes." *Field Methods* 15(1):85–109. https://doi.org/10.1177/1525822X02239569.

Safdar, Khadeeja. 2017. "Who Pays on the First Date? No One Knows Anymore, and It's Really Awkward." *Wall Street Journal*, June 26. www.wsj.com.

Sandberg, Linn. 2013. "Just Feeling a Naked Body Close to You: Men, Sexuality, and Intimacy in Later Life." *Sexualities* 16(3–4):261–82. https://doi.org/10.1177/1363460713481726.

———. 2016. "In Lust We Trust? Masculinity and Sexual Desire in Later Life." *Men and Masculinities* 19(2):192–208. https://doi.org/10.1177/1097184X15606948.

Savin-Williams, Ritch C. 2017. "More Bisexual Women? Think Again." *Psychology Today*, January 30. https://www.psychologytoday.com/us/blog/sex-sexuality-and-romance/201701/more-bisexual-women-think-again.

———. 2021. *Bi: Bisexual, Pansexual, Fluid, and Nonbinary Youth*. New York: NYU Press.

———. 2022. "Sexual and Romantic Spectrums: Mostly Straights and Mostly Gays/Lesbians." *Current Opinion in Psychology*. Advance online publication. https://doi.org/10.1016/j.copsyc.2022.101503.

Savin-Williams, Ritch C., and Zhana Vrangalova. 2013. "Mostly Heterosexual as a Distinct Sexual Orientation Group: A Systematic Review of the Empirical Evidence." *Developmental Review* 33(1):58–88. https://doi.org/10.1016/j.dr.2013.01.001.

Schnarrs, Philip W., Stephen Scott Jones, Jeffrey T. Parsons, Aleta Baldwin, Joshua G. Rosenberger, Mitchell R. Lunn, and H. Jonathon Rendina. 2021. "Sexual Subcultures and HIV Prevention Methods: An Assessment of Condom Use, PrEP, and TasP among Gay, Bisexual, and Other Men Who Have Sex with Men Using a Social and Sexual Networking Smartphone Application." *Archives of Sexual Behavior* 50(4):1781–92. https://doi.org/10.1007/s10508-020-01784-x.

Schwartz, Christine R. 2013. "Trends and Variation in Assortative Mating: Causes and Consequences." *Annual Review of Sociology* 39(1):451–70. https://doi.org/10.1146/annurev-soc-071312-145544.

Schwartz, Christine, and Nikki Graf. 2009. "Assortative Matching among Same-Sex and Different-Sex Couples in the United States, 1990–2000." *Demographic Research* 21(28):843–78. https://doi.org/10.4054/DemRes.2009.21.28.

———. 2010. "Can Differences in Partner Availability Explain Differences in Interracial/Ethnic Matching between Same- and Different-Sex Couples?" Working paper 2010-07. Madison: University of Wisconsin, Center for Demography and Ecology. https://cde.wisc.edu.

Schwartz, Christine R., Zhen Zeng, and Yu Xie. 2016. "Marrying Up by Marrying Down: Status Exchange between Social Origin and Education in the United States." *Sociological Science* 3:1003–27. http://dx.doi.org/10.15195/v3.a44.

Scull, Maren T. 2020. "'It's Its Own Thing': A Typology of Interpersonal Sugar Relationship Scripts." *Sociological Perspectives* 63(1):135–58. https://doi.org/10.1177/0731121419875115.

———. 2022. "From Seeking Financialships to Satisfying Curiosity: Women's Motivations for Entering Sugar Relationships." *Sexuality & Culture* 26(1):222–48. https://doi.org/10.1007/s12119-021-09888-9.

Setinova, Marketa, and Renáta Topinková. 2021. "Partner Preference and Age: User's Mating Behavior in Online Dating." *Journal of Family Research* 33(3):566–91. https://doi.org/10.20377/jfr-540.

Seto, Michael C. 2017. "The Puzzle of Male Chronophilias." *Archives of Sexual Behavior* 46(1):3–22. https://doi.org/10.1007/s10508-016-0799-y.

Shafer, Kevin, Richard J. Petts, and Casey Scheibling. 2021. "Variation in Masculinities and Fathering Behaviors: A Cross-National Comparison of the United States and Canada." *Sex Roles* 84(7):439–53. https://doi.org/10.1007/s11199-020-01177-3.

Shahzad, Ramna. 2016. "Women Strip-Searched, Charged in Bathhouse Raids Reject Public Apology." *CBC*, June 23. https://www.cbc.ca.

Shuster, Stef M., and Laurel Westbrook. 2022. "Reducing the Joy Deficit in Sociology: A Study of Transgender Joy." *Social Problems*. Advance online publication. https://doi.org/10.1093/socpro/spac034.

Silva, Tony. 2019. "'Daddies,' 'Cougars,' and Their Partners Past Midlife: Gender Attitudes and Relationship and Sexual Well-Being among Older Adults in Age-Heterogenous Partnerships." *Socius* 5. https://doi.org/10.1177/2378023119869452.

———. 2021. *Still Straight: Sexual Flexibility among White Men in Rural America*. New York: NYU Press.

———. 2022a. "Subcultural Identification, Penetration Practices, Masculinity, and Gender Labels within a Nationally Representative Sample of Three Cohorts of American Black, White, and Latina/o LGBQ People." *Archives of Sexual Behavior* 51(7):3467–83. https://doi.org/10.1007/s10508-022-02285-9.

———. 2022b. "Masculinity Attitudes across Rural, Suburban, and Urban Areas in the United States." *Men and Masculinities* 25(3):377–99. https://doi.org/10.1177/1097184X211017186.

Silva, Tony, and Clare R. Evans. 2020. "Sexual Identification in the United States at the Intersections of Gender, Race/Ethnicity, Immigration, and Education." *Sex Roles* 83(11–12):722–38. https://doi.org/10.1007/s11199-020-01145-x.

Simpson, Paul. 2016. *Middle-Aged Gay Men, Ageing, and Ageism: Over the Rainbow?* London: Palgrave Macmillan.

Simula, Brandy L. 2019. "Pleasure, Power, and Pain: A Review of the Literature on the Experiences of BDSM Participants." *Sociology Compass* 13(3):e12668. https://doi.org/10.1111/soc4.12668.

Skentelbery, Sara G., and Darren M. Fowler. 2016. "Attachment Styles of Women-Younger Partners in Age-Gap Relationships." *Evolutionary Behavioral Sciences* 10(2):142–47. https://doi.org/10.1037/ebs0000064.

Slevin, Kathleen F., and Thomas J. Linneman. 2010. "Old Gay Men's Bodies and Masculinities." *Men and Masculinities* 12(4):483–507. https://doi.org/10.1177/1097184X08325225.

Smith-Rosenberg, Carroll. 1975. "The Female World of Love and Ritual: Relations between Women in Nineteenth-Century America." *Signs* 1(1):1–29. https://doi.org/10.1086/493203.

Spring, Amy, and Kayla Charleston. 2021. "Gentrification and the Shifting Geography of Male Same-Sex Couples." *Population Research and Policy Review* 40(6):1163–94. https://doi.org/10.1007/s11113-020-09625-4.

Springer, Kristen W., and Dawne M. Mouzon. 2019. "One Step toward More Research on Aging Masculinities: Operationalizing the Hegemonic Masculinity for Older Men Scale (HMOMS)." *Journal of Men's Studies* 27(2):183–203. https://doi.org/10.1177/1060826518806020.

Stacey, Judith. 2004. "Cruising to Familyland: Gay Hypergamy and Rainbow Kinship." *Current Sociology* 52(2):181–97. https://doi.org/10.1177/0011392104041807.

Statistics Canada. 2022. *State of the Union: Canada Leads the G7 with Nearly One-Quarter of Couples Living Common Law, Driven by Quebec*. Ottawa, Ontario. https://www150.statcan.gc.ca.

Sterrett, Emma M., Michelle Birkett, Lisa Kuhns, and Brian Mustanski. 2015. "Non-Parental Adults in the Social and Risk Behavior Networks of Sexual Minority Male

Youth." *Children and Youth Services Review* 55:62–70. https://doi.org/10.1016/j.childyouth.2015.05.007.

Stewart-Winter, Timothy. 2016. *Queer Clout: Chicago and the Rise of Gay Politics.* Philadelphia: University of Pennsylvania Press.

Stillwagon, Ryan, and Amin Ghaziani. 2019. "Queer Pop-Ups: A Cultural Innovation in Urban Life." *City & Community* 18(3):874–95. https://doi.org/10.1111/cico.12434.

Sueyoshi, Amy. 2018. *Discriminating Sex: White Leisure and the Making of the American "Oriental."* Champaign: University of Illinois Press.

Suzman, Richard. 2009. "The National Social Life, Health, and Aging Project: An Introduction." *Journals of Gerontology: Series B* 64B(suppl.1):i5–11. https://doi.org/10.1093/geronb/gbp078.

Swidler, Ann. 2001. *Talk of Love: How Culture Matters.* Chicago: University of Chicago Press.

Sy, Thomas, Lynn M. Shore, Judy Strauss, Ted H. Shore, Susanna Tram, Paul Whiteley, and Kristine Ikeda-Muromachi. 2010. "Leadership Perceptions as a Function of Race–Occupation Fit: The Case of Asian Americans." *Journal of Applied Psychology* 95(5):902–19. https://doi.org/10.1037/a0019501.

Syrett, Nicholas T. 2021. "Age Disparity, Marriage, and the Gendering of Heterosexuality." Pp. 96–119 in *Heterosexual Histories*, edited by R. L. Davis and M. Mitchell. New York: NYU Press.

Tannenbaum, Cara, and Blye Frank. 2011. "Masculinity and Health in Late Life Men." *American Journal of Men's Health* 5(3):243–54. https://doi.org/10.1177/1557988310384609.

Thompson, Edward H., Jr. 2018. *Men, Masculinities, and Aging: The Gendered Lives of Older Men.* Lanham, MD: Rowman & Littlefield.

Thompson, Edward H., and Kaitlyn Barnes Langendoerfer. 2016. "Older Men's Blueprint for 'Being a Man.'" *Men and Masculinities* 19(2):119–47. https://doi.org/10.1177/1097184X15606949.

Torche, Florencia, and Peter Rich. 2017. "Declining Racial Stratification in Marriage Choices? Trends in Black/White Status Exchange in the United States, 1980 to 2010." *Sociology of Race and Ethnicity* 3(1):31–49. https://doi.org/10.1177/2332649216648464.

Tsai, Ming-Chang. 2011. "'Foreign Brides' Meet Ethnic Politics in Taiwan." *International Migration Review* 45(2):243–68. https://doi.org/10.1111%2Fj.1747-7379.2011.00847.x.

Uggla, Caroline, and Ben Wilson. 2021. "Parental Age Gaps among Immigrants and Their Descendants: Adaptation across Time and Generations?" *Population Studies.* Advance online publication. https://doi.org/10.1080/00324728.2021.1998583.

Unnever, James D., and Cecilia Chouhy. 2021. "Race, Racism, and the Cool Pose: Exploring Black and White Male Masculinity." *Social Problems* 68(2):490–512. https://doi.org/10.1093/socpro/spaa010.

Upadhyay, Srushti. 2021. "Sugaring: Understanding the World of Sugar Daddies and Sugar Babies." *Journal of Sex Research* 58(6):775–84. https://doi.org/10.1080/00224499.2020.1867700.

Van Doorn, Niels. 2016. "The Fabric of Our Memories: Leather, Kinship, and Queer Material History." *Memory Studies* 9(1):85–98. https://doi.org/10.1177/1750698015613975.

Vasilenko, Sara A., Cara Exten, and Joshua G. Rosenberger. 2021. "Physical and Emotional Satisfaction at First Same-Sex Anal Sex in Young Gay and Bisexual Men." *Archives of Sexual Behavior* 50(3):1047–55. https://doi.org/10.1007/s10508-020-01738-3.

Verbakel, Ellen, and Matthijs Kalmijn. 2014. "Assortative Mating among Dutch Married and Cohabiting Same-Sex and Different-Sex Couples." *Journal of Marriage and Family* 76(1):1–12. https://doi.org/10.1111/jomf.1208.

Villar, Feliciano, Rodrigo Serrat, José Manuel de Sao José, María Montero, Claudia Josefina Arias, Ruth Nina-Estrella, Camen-Lucía Curcio, Maria Carbajal, Rita da Cassia Oliveira, Victoria Tirro, and Alina Alfonso. 2019. "Age-Discrepant Couples Involving an Older Adult: The Final Frontier of Ageism? Attitudes in Eight Latin American Countries." *Journal of Intergenerational Relationships* 17(4):430–48. https://doi.org/10.1080/15350770.2019.1579153.

Vogels, Emily A. 2020. *10 Facts about Americans and Online Dating*. Washington, DC: Pew Research Center. www.pewresearch.org.

Warren, Carol A. B. 1996. "Older Women, Younger Men: Self and Stigma in Age-Discrepant Relationships." *Clinical Sociology Review* 14(1):62–86. https://digitalcommons.wayne.edu.

Wentzell, Emily A. 2013. *Maturing Masculinities: Aging, Chronic Illness, and Viagra in Mexico*. Durham NC: Duke University Press.

———. 2017. "How Did Erectile Dysfunction Become 'Natural'? A Review of the Critical Social Scientific Literature on Medical Treatment for Male Sexual Dysfunction." *Journal of Sex Research* 54(4–5):486–506. https://doi.org/10.1080/00224499.2016.1259386.

Weston, Kath. 1991. *Families We Choose: Lesbians, Gays, Kinship*. New York: Columbia University Press.

Wignall, Liam, and Helen Driscoll. 2020. "Women's Rationales and Perspectives on 'Mostly' as a Nonexclusive Sexual Identity Label." *Psychology of Sexual Orientation and Gender Diversity* 7(3):366–74. https://doi.org/10.1037/sgd0000385.

Wignall, Liam, and Mark McCormack. 2017. "An Exploratory Study of a New Kink Activity: 'Pup Play.'" *Archives of Sexual Behavior* 46(3):801–11. https://doi.org/10.1007/s10508-015-0636-8.

Winer, Canton. 2022. "'The Queers Hate Me Because I'm Too Butch': Goldilocks Masculinity among Non-Heterosexual Men." *Sexualities*. Advance online publication. https://doi.org/10.1177/13634607221097332.

Winkler, Richelle. 2013. "Segregated by Age: Are We Becoming More Divided?" *Population Research and Policy Review* 32(5):717–27. https://doi.org/10.1007/s11113-013-9291-8.

Wright, Les. 1997. *The Bear Book: Readings in the History and Evolution of a Gay Male Subculture*. New York: Routledge.

———. 2001. *The Bear Book II: Further Readings in the History and Evolution of a Gay Male Subculture*. New York: Routledge.

Xie, Yu, and Hao Dong. 2021. "A New Methodological Framework for Studying Status Exchange in Marriage." *American Journal of Sociology* 126(5):1179–1219. https://doi.org/10.1086/713927.

Yang, Yuchen. 2020. "What's Hegemonic about Hegemonic Masculinity? Legitimation and Beyond." *Sociological Theory* 38(4):318–33. https://doi./org/10.1177/0735275120960792.

Zhang, De-Chuan, Zun-You Wu, and Sarah Robbins Scott. 2019. "Factors Associated with Unprotected Anal Intercourse among Male Students Who Have Sex with Men in Three Northern Regions of China." *Chinese Medical Journal* 132(14):1639–44. https://doi.org/10.1097/CM9.0000000000000311.

Zhang, Huiping, Petula S. Y. Ho, and Paul S. F. Yip. 2012. "Does Similarity Breed Marital and Sexual Satisfaction?" *Journal of Sex Research* 49(6):583–93. https://doi.org/10.1080/00224499.2011.574240.

INDEX

Page numbers in italics indicate Figures and Tables.

BDSM, 42–43, 65–66, 178. *See also*
 dominance; leather communities;
 submissive-dominant power dynamics; submissiveness
bears, 133–34; on daddies, 8; terminology
 of, 8
behavioral traits, of daddies, 80–81
biological fathers. *See* fathers, biological
bisexuality, 6–7, 125; identification with,
 205n61; mentorship and, 72–77;
 relationship status and, 204n22; of
 women, 187
Black men: ageism faced by, 201n17; on
 boy as term, 62; masculinity associated
 with, 56
bondage. *See* BDSM
bottoms and bottoming: in age-gap
 partnerships, 46–47; daddies as, 43–
 44; daddyness enhanced by, 45–46;
 dominance and, 45–46; younger men
 on, 47–48
boundaries, older men respecting, 110
boys (term), 8–9, 34; aging out of, 67;
 autonomy infringed upon by, 63–64;
 Black men on, 62; daddy identity
 contrasted with, 66–67; formal training as, 65; identification as, 64–67;
 in leather communities, 61, 65–66;
 masculinity of, 135; meaning of, 60–64;
 as objectifying, 63; power dynamics
 associated with, 66; submissiveness
 associated with, 62, 64–65, 117–18;
 trophy, 158; younger men on, 61–62.
 See also younger men

caretaking, 141; in age-gap partnerships,
 168–69; fear about, 156
caring: in emotional intimacy, 86; from
 older men, 103–4; for younger men,
 84–86
caring masculinity, 181
chemistry, 98
Chicago, 11–12

child-rearing, 179
chosen family, 150, 175
codependency, 158
cohorts, connections between, 86–91
comfort: emotional intimacy linked to,
 102; from older men, 101–3
coming out, 153–54; housing instability
 following, 73; mentorship on, 73–74
commitment, of younger partners, 144–45
communication: difficulties, 153; with
 older men, 110–11
community building, 86–87; in gay history, 203n9
compatibility: in age-gap partnerships,
 159; with older men, 98–111
condomless sex, 204n43
confidence: of daddies, 37–38; dominance
 linked to, 41–42; masculinity and, 41;
 older partners on, 37–38; sexual experience and, 37, 38
consciousness, daddy, 23–25
consensual dynamic, dominance and,
 40–41
control: daddyness and, 40; older men
 and, 117–19; power dynamics and, 148.
 See also dominance
credit scores, 52
cruising, 204n18
cubs, 8
cuddling, 104, 149–50
culture, age-gap partnerships impacted
 by, 173–74

dad bods, 1; masculinity and, 133–34
daddies: age-related traits of, 34–39; aging into, 19; archetypes of, 132–33; in
 bear culture, 8; becoming, 21–22; behavioral traits of, 80–81; as bottoms,
 43–44; boy identity contrasted with,
 66–67; confidence of, 37–38; defining, 1, 39; desirable characteristics of,
 92; dominance of, 40–42; emotional
 stability of, 35; experience of, 34–38;

ABOUT THE AUTHOR

TONY SILVA is Assistant Professor in the Department of Sociology at the University of British Columbia. His areas of expertise include gender, sexuality, rural sociology, and qualitative and quantitative methods. He is the author of *Still Straight: Sexual Flexibility among White Men in Rural America.*

www.ingramcontent.com/pod-product-compliance
Lightning Source LLC
Chambersburg PA
CBHW020537030426
42337CB00013B/880

* 9 7 8 1 4 7 9 8 1 7 0 3 0 *